GC
FAST BOWLER

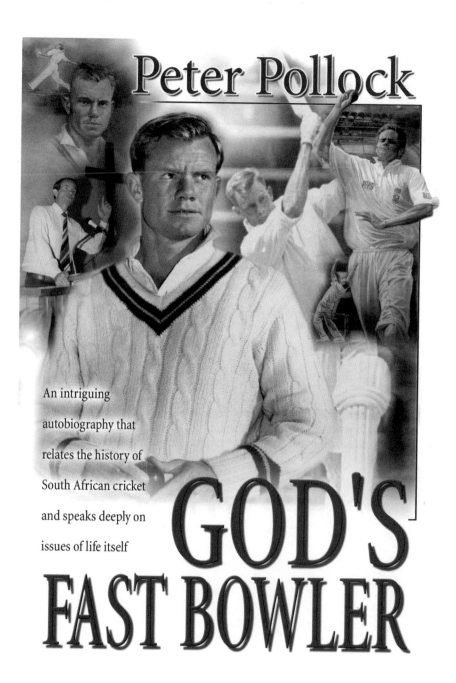

Peter Pollock

An intriguing
autobiography that
relates the history of
South African cricket
and speaks deeply on
issues of life itself

GOD'S FAST BOWLER

**CHRISTIAN ART
PUBLISHERS**

Published in South Africa by CHRISTIAN ART PUBLISHERS
PO Box 1599, Vereeniging, 1930

© 2001
First edition 2001

Cover designed by Christian Art Publishers

Photographs reproduced in this book are used with permission
of Independent Newspapers Kwa-Zulu Natal

Scripture taken from the Holy Bible, New International Version®,
Copyright © 1973, 1978, 1984 by the International Bible Society.
Used by permission of Zondervan Publishing house. The "NIV" and
"New International Version" trademarks are registered in the United
States Patent and Trademark Office by the International Bible Society.

Set in 11 on 13 pt WeidemannBook by Christian Art Publishers

Printed in China

ISBN-10: 1-86852-814-6
ISBN-13: 978-1-86852-814-1

06 07 08 09 10 11 12 13 14 15 – 12 11 10 9 8 7 6 5 4 3

CONTENTS

FOREWORD

INTRODUCTION   9

CHAPTER   1: Beginnings   15

CHAPTER   2: The climb   30

CHAPTER   3: Hitches   48

CHAPTER   4: Summit   57

CHAPTER   5: Clouds   75

CHAPTER   6: Glory   84

CHAPTER   7: Isolation   93

CHAPTER   8: Regeneration   110

CHAPTER   9: Renewal   126

CHAPTER 10: Revelation   138

CHAPTER 11: Return   150

CHAPTER 12: Reinstatement   172

CHAPTER 13: Farewell   193

ADDENDUM   223

FOREWORD

By Shaun Pollock

I have often been asked if there were times when the Pollock name was a burden and I suppose, as I was growing up, I could have felt the weight of expectation to perform, or there may have been times when others expected an explanation as to why my father had selected me to play for the national side! But, thankfully, the way my father looks at life has had an enormous influence on me and by adopting his approach, I've learnt to deal with most pressures in life positively.

What's so special about his outlook, you may ask. Well, by reading his life story I'm sure you'll come to know Peter Pollock more intimately. But to sum it up as well as I can; he has had an incredible life and yet has always been humble, believing that you should never take anything for granted. He values hard work, a balanced lifestyle and is committed to Christ.

His passion for and enjoyment of cricket, experienced from so many different perspectives over the years, have always been characterised by integrity and humility. His resourceful cricketing mind is well respected worldwide and this is not surprising when one considers his unique position of having been involved in the game in almost every possible way.

Not only was he an internationally renowned fast bowler in the 60s and early 70s, he is also the brother of Graeme, one of South Africa's greatest cricket legends. He was convenor of selectors for the South African team, a cricket administrator, journalist, supportive father and a successful businessman.

During his involvement as convenor, I was proud to recognize the respect my team-mates had for him and I must admit that one of our disappointments of not having come closer to victory in the 1999 World Cup, was that it would have been the perfect tribute to his contribution to South African cricket.

Believe it or not, my father had always been very much a "behind-the-scenes" dad! When it came to watching me play as a kid, he would usually be found sitting under a tree on the other side of the field or at a distance in his parked car. It wasn't because he was anti-social, it was just his way of making sure that whatever I achieved was through my own ability. It is ironic that he should have been the convenor when my time came for national call-up!

Another characteristic of Peter Pollock is his straight-forwardness. I think people seek his advice because they know he'll "tell it like it is." In our family we trust his opinion because we know what a deep thinker he is; he's consistent, realistic and there's never a hidden agenda.

With all the worldly success my father has achieved on the sports field and elsewhere, he sees himself as a servant, using his achievements as a catalyst to bring the Word of God to all people. As a devoted evangelist, he displays the same tenacity that had made him such an accomplished fast bowler.

There are few better qualified to reflect the story of South African cricket over the past 40 years and I am sure you will find his life story fascinating reading.

INTRODUCTION

Crash-landing

August 4, 1970: LONDON – Springbok fast bowler Peter Pollock was a passenger in a light plane piloted by former England cricket captain Ted Dexter, when it hedgehopped high tension wires and brick fences before it crashed in a Yorkshire field. Also aboard was West Indies wicket-keeper Deryck Murray. They were flying from the Headingly Test at Leeds to Southport.

"We owe our lives to Ted. It was a marvellous piece of flying. After the propeller of the Comanche PA-24 had begun to vibrate and the aircraft stalled, he succeeded in bringing us down to a belly flop landing. I have never been so scared in my life. I thought we were finished, but Ted was magnificently cool," Pollock said.

That's how the *Daily Dispatch* in East London, South Africa, recorded it. Dennis Done, their reporter in Fleet Street, had filed the story. When I first phoned to tell him what had happened to us, he didn't believe me. I often pulled his leg and he thought this was yet another of those cry-wolf pranks. When the journalists were finally convinced of its veracity, the story hit the wires. It made the headlines in some of the tabloids, the television news and even appealed to some cartoonists!

A day to remember. A turning-point in my life. Absolutely no doubt about it. That's the advantage of hindsight ...

I had had some sort of premonition about the flight. Though I had flown with Ted a couple of times before, on that particular day there was a distinct feeling of foreboding about the trip from Leeds to Southport. We were to play in a Freddie Trueman benefit match. There was no room for me in the sponsored car along with Eddie Barlow and brother Graeme. So it was a flight with Ted or else a train, a bus or hitchhiking! Heaven forbid!

I had come to England as a journalist to cover the Rest of the World Series, a set of five matches that was organized at the last minute because of the cancellation of the South African 1970 tour due to political pressure. I had not been an original choice like four other South Africans; Barlow, Graeme, Barry Richards and Mike Procter, but I had been co-opted for the third Test at Edgbaston. I should never have made myself available because I was out of condition. Sitting in the press box is no way to prepare for a Test, as I was to find out. I was summarily dismissed for the fourth encounter but still remained an appendage to the team, much to the envy of my co-reporters.

Anyway, unlike me, Ted was brimful of his usual, almost casual confidence. Deryck Murray was also tentative. That was his first flight in a light aircraft. "Are we gonna fly in this thing!" was his almost disbelieving comment as he stooped and crouched into his backseat. No options! Like it or lump it! Well, beggars can't be choosers.

The weather was good and everything was fine. Suddenly there were problems out front. You didn't have to be a genius to guess that something was wrong. A siren in the cockpit confirmed problems and Ted was suddenly radioing his may-day distress call. We were going down!

I looked at Deryck in the backseat, he had whitened with fear and as I looked out the window at the terrain below, I noted that it resembled a chessboard field surrounded by walls and hedges! Certainly not the ideal place to land! A crash-landing! My life was at stake.

I had not been much of a praying man, but silently though very fervently I cried out to God. I can't remember what I said, but I was panic-stricken. A pounding heart and some frightening thoughts dominated a veritable eternity as the ground got closer and closer. On the final glide-path in, some extra hurdles presented themselves – high-tension cables! Ted negotiated them and finally there was a crunch as earth met machine. A jumble of thoughts, noises and shouts followed the incredible relief when we realised, "We are alive!"

We had survived the crash. A wall stared us in the face, but no smoke, no fire and no broken bones! And we could open the door.

We stepped out of the wrecked plane. There was an element of bravado and intense relief. I had survived an air crash. Not too many people can say that. In a strange way it was like some notch on the belt of life's experiences.

The shock of it all would be delayed till later that night!

Ted became something of a hero after this incident. Deservedly so, I thought! But for me the nightmare was just starting. A few ales and some whiskey got me to sleep that night, but not for long. Over and over I relived the accident. A brush with death. How close can you get?

For the next twelve years I was to become a total neurotic on any aeroplane. The sweat formed in globules on my brow and my hands were always clammy when I flew. I often hung onto the armrests for dear life. It's downright embarrassing when the airhostess knows who you are and asks, "Is there anything wrong, Mr Pollock?" You can't tell her that you are petrified or neurotic! "Just check the air conditioning," I used to suggest. But I was scared to death. I avoided planes like the plague. My wife will tell anyone that 24 hours prior to any flight I was impossible to live with. Not that I wasn't under normal circumstances, but when I had to fly, I was like a caged lion.

Maybe I should have consulted a psychiatrist, but I felt that it was just the normal consequences to be expected after such a nightmarish experience. Not nice, but who promised that life would be easy!

At the crossroads

Questions and doubts abounded.

Why had 1970 turned so sour? Our second child, Anthea, had been born on 27 February with major complications. My wife, Inez, had to undergo a caesarean section and then the premature baby was found to have a hyaline membrane around the lungs. It was bad news, for in those days, eight out of ten babies born in this condition would not survive. Anthea went straight from birth into a respirator. But what agony we experienced as the weeks went by! Each phone call could be the death knell, but miraculously she survived.

I suppose that one could look at her survival and mine in the air crash as good news. After all, it was triumph after disaster, but at the time the whole issue was clouded by an endless supply of medical bills. A strapping South African fast bowler who would fearlessly dish out and receive bouncers in the heat of international cricket combat, had now also become fearful and frail in airplanes!

Out front we were heroes, cricketing stalwarts. But life is a lot more than that. My father had died in December 1969. He was editor of the *Eastern Province Herald* in Port Elizabeth. On the morning of 19 December, he had arrived at the office, pressed the lift button on the ground floor and then dropped down dead at the age of 55. What a shock. He had not even been sick, but suddenly he was gone. I was very close to him, for we shared the same interests, the most important of which was journalism. I had become a little despondent about the future as a sports writer, for the clouds of political isolation were building up. It was a poorly paid profession and I didn't know how I was going to approach Dad about these thoughts. He would certainly be disappointed. Journalism was his passion. I didn't share the vision.

My cricketing form was also drawing interest from the media. Bill Lawry's Australians arrived in South Africa in January 1970, but the months prior to their arrival had been most frustrating for me. My rhythm wasn't what it should have been and the critics were talking about me being "over the hill." Perhaps there was some justification in this.

My dad was so concerned about it that he didn't mind my taking time off from his newspaper to seek advice from my ex-school coach, Tommy Dean. Uncle Tom always appeared to have the knack and discernment to help me during tough times. And so we spent many fruitful hours getting the basics right in the nets.

Dad also had another complaint at that time. It was about brother Graeme and his inability to make really big totals. "Why is it that you can't make the really big scores?" he kept badgering. "You should be reeling off double and triple hundreds like Bradman." Certainly Graeme had the talent, but perhaps this genius of the batting crease had to be reminded of the tenacity, resolution and resilience needed if Bradman was going to be emulated.

In my efforts to prepare for the first Test at Newlands, I engaged the services of famous hypnotist, Max Collie, to cure me of the smoking habit. This he did quite easily, merely by convincing me under hypnosis, that cigarettes tasted like raw potatoes. What a terrible taste! It even affected me in a smoke-filled room.

But the triumph over smoking was short-lived. Dr Ali Bacher (note that he was a GP) heard about my giving up smoking. "Champion golfer Arnie Palmer did the same," said Ali, "and he couldn't sink a putt. Now that he is back on the weed he is knocking them in from all angles." Proper advice from a doctor? Surely not! Ali further suggested that he didn't need a neurotic fast bowler around and the sooner I started relaxing and smoking again, the better for the team and for me.

I didn't need my arm twisted that much. While I was puffing a cigarette and sipping a beer after our massive triumph in the first Test at Newlands, Ali came up and smiled, "Wasn't I right?" Who knows?

The Lawry visit of 1970 was a catastrophe for Australia, but a major triumph for South Africa. The 4-0 whitewash still causes major embarrassment to Australians, especially those who were involved. South Africa was unquestionably the best cricket side in the world and the country, and of course the players basked in the glory of it all. Mike Procter and I had established ourselves as number one and two in the world as fast bowlers – certainly the most feared combination – and my brother Graeme had answered his late father's wish by making a mammoth 274 in the second Test at Kingsmead. South African cricket had reached its all-time pinnacle – the best in the world. Not even the Aussies were going to argue.

It was a wonderful time for players and spectators and even though trouble loomed with anti-apartheid organizers making all kinds of threats, South Africans refused to take them too seriously. It's true, there are none so deaf as those who don't want to hear. You can't talk to an ostrich when his head is in the sand.

But it was foolish to believe anything except that the doors were closing. Finally they slammed shut. How could our English cricket friends do this to us? All sorts of dreadful things were said about "traitors" and "back-stabbers," but what South Africans failed to appreciate in their pent-up emotion and disappointment, was that quite simply our "friends" were still friends, but friendship doesn't mean condoning an iniquity like apartheid! In fact, it was unfair to expect them to side with us cricketers against the greater evil of a suspended tour. Of course to attempt to separate the issue into sport and politics was a naive tactic. But that didn't make it any easier for us. Ten Test matches had gone down the tube. Isolation threatened. What did the future hold?

It wasn't long before the tremendous triumph of those opening months of 1970 started to pale into insignificance compared to what was beckoning. Cinderella was at the ball in all her glory, but the stroke of midnight was imminent. The party was over!

All the positive talk in the world doesn't dismiss truth and fact. And so 1970 moved into a time of sad reflection. I was thirty years old, my cricket career didn't have much longer to go. Those tell-tale signs that suggested that fast bowlers don't have a limitless life-span were appearing. My daughter was in trouble and only time would tell if there were lasting side-effects. The newspaper game was bothering me profoundly and if my future was going to be tied up with travelling by air, it would be fair to say that the crossroads had been reached. A year earlier it all seemed so clearly defined. Now the waters had become murky. Just at the time when phase two should have been a mere formality, the goalposts were being moved. Cricket, writing and travelling seemed to face a dead end. Of course, I would be the last to admit this. To be honest, at that stage I didn't even begin to realize what was going on.

There is a sort of confidence and arrogance that declares you untouchable, especially if you have enjoyed any notable degree of fame or success. It's the type of curriculum vitae that becomes essential for enlistment at the greatest institution of all time – the school of hard knocks. Life is a learning process, but sadly the greatest lessons are learnt the hard way, not by theory or philosophy, but by experience. And it doesn't have to be a criminal act or public disgrace that edges you around the corner. It's just those very normal common fears such as wondering if there really is life after Test cricket or if the mid-life crisis is just another one of those thumb-suck topics in the Agony Annie columns.

But clearly, as a South African cricketer, one with ambitions to make cricket-writing a career, the year 1970 was not providing positive feedback. Many hours were spent in discussion with the likes of Freddie Brown, Ted Dexter, Trevor Bailey and Richie Benaud and in various different ways they were saying the same thing. The countdown had begun. The days of South African cricket were numbered. Justifiably so, was the consensus of world opinion.

Dad had warned that the consequences of apartheid and the ideology of the regime would have a devastating effect on a wonderful land and that all would suffer. He had passed on, but I will never forget his prophetic words, "Your life and destiny are inextricably linked to a land that will see much heartache and suffering." Cricket was to be the ears and eyes of that destiny.

But let's begin at the beginning.

1

BEGINNINGS

Reflecting the roots

Grey's Hospital in Pietermaritzburg, a then rather sleepy hollow Natal Midlands town, was where I yelled for the first time. I was a tax-baby, born on 30 June 1941, just in time to be included as a benefit with the Receiver of Revenue! My dad, Andrew Maclean, widely called Mac, was a journalist, columnist and author, but at that time was up North doing service in the war against Adolf Hitler. But mom Edith ensured that I was given the proper Presbyterian start. My pedigree as a Christian couldn't be faulted at the outset. My grandfather was, after all, the Rev. James Pollock, not just a minister, but also once the highly venerated moderator of the Presbyterian denomination in South Africa! Needless to say it was he who christened me.

I am reliably informed that there was a little controversy about my christian name. The middle name, Maclean, was fixed, while Peter was the most popular option for the first name. But there were some alternatives. What they were I don't know, but granddad was adamant. Peter it was to be. Biblically it was a good call and with Dad away, the moderator was going to have his way!

Grandfather was strong in personality, faith and conviction and sadly this background made my father very anti-religious. His parents were devoutly committed to God and as a youngster he found it very difficult to understand why he had to live in such poverty if "the Lord was providing." It probably annoyed him that his mom and dad were so faithful and trusting and he couldn't see any material gain from their faith. I recall Dad once telling me how embarrassed he had felt because his cricket trousers were cheap and that everything else he owned was inferior to the other boys' possessions at school. It left a marked impression on him. Maybe it even became an obsession. He was utterly determined that his children would never have to suffer the same humiliation that he experienced.

And not surprisingly he had had enough of church.

Apparently as a kid he used to get up to mischief in the church services, rolling marbles down the aisles. I know that later during his varsity days he had to use an alias to play league hockey on Sundays. Obviously it would not have been right for the pastor's son to be playing sport on the Sabbath. Needless to say, he was caught out, further affecting his opinions of God and the church.

Anyway, on christening day, Grandpa got his way and who knows what he prayed as he blessed the young grandchild that was me. I was the firstborn in the family and some biblical tradition suggests that that means dedication to God's service!

My earliest recollections involve life in Durban, attending a kindergarten called Manley, in Berea Road and being so embarrassed when I had to act like a Christmas tree at the festive prize-giving. I remember lining the road with thousands of others to wave to King George and his two daughters, Elizabeth and Margaret and that a polio scare really frightened me out of my wits. My brother Graeme was born in February 1944, but by the time we left Durban in the late 1940s, he had not even really qualified as a playmate! Certainly he hadn't made any significant runs in the backyard, contrary to some of the legends and exaggerations that do the rounds.

Our move to Port Elizabeth had to do with Dad, once a columnist of the *Natal Mercury*, being offered an appointment as assistant editor of the *Evening Post*. It was a career move he could not pass up. We were all agog, especially Graeme and I on our first Union Castle boat trip.

The first hotel we stayed in carried our surname, as did the beach out front, but it was spelt differently. Subsequently it changed to our spelling, but it had absolutely nothing to do with the Pollock family, except, as stated, it was our first accommodation. What a coincidence! But who would argue that it was a very good start! We loved Port Elizabeth from the very beginning. And dare I say PE was good to us.

Budding players in the backyard

Junior schooldays were spent at Grey, where Stan Edwards was the headmaster, but more significantly, where Henry Martin, one of the teachers, strode into our lives.

The 1949 tour of South Africa by Lindsay Hassett's Australians must have been about the first time that Graeme and I became aware of the full implications of international cricket. The Aussies were treating South Africa very harshly and the man who was flaying the Springbok bowlers was Neil Harvey.

"One day, when I am old enough to play for South Africa, I am going to show those Aussies what it's like to play against Neil Harvey" – those were the words, almost prophetic, of my fair-haired pint-sized little brother of no more than five years of age.

A mad dog in a chicken run would hardly have been more savage and brutal as Harvey was in dealing with our bowlers. Nevertheless, Graeme hero-worshipped this Australian and although his adulation was tempered by a good sprinkling of patriotism, he loved every moment of the slaughter. To him Harvey epitomised the very essence of cricket – attacking, exciting batsmanship. My heart-felt sympathies lay with the bowlers. I felt that it was not fair that someone should have been so blessed with talent as Harvey. It seemed so easy, almost too easy. Maybe he even took on the image of an ogre in my fast bowler's heart and mind.

The image was further enhanced by the fact that once we unglued our ears from the crackling radio and adjourned to the backyard, I was again faced by the nightmare of a Harvey – my little brother! Graeme always assumed the Harvey nom de plume in our tree-stump tussles and I found it just as difficult to dismiss this impersonator as the Springbok bowlers must have found it with the real live Aussie.

Be that as it may, the most intriguing aspect of Graeme's rather forthright threat to Australia was the confidence and conviction of his "when I am old enough." No mention of ifs and buts, just a case of when. The cheek of it, I thought. Yet, Pikkie (the nickname that the diminutive youngster had acquired) remained undaunted. In a quaintly modest and inoffensive way, he almost took Springbok colours and the glory of wearing them for granted.

Almost like King Arthur, who drew the sword Excalibur from its stone sheath, there was a certain inevitability about Graeme's future as a cricketer and this, no doubt, made me even more determined not to be left behind. In those early days I was not in a position to realize that I had set myself a rather high standard. Although Graeme was extremely talented and promising, the thought that I might be competing against a cricketing genius never entered my head. In retrospect I am glad, for had I been aware of this, I might have conceded this personal battle long before it had really started. But it was this spirit of competitiveness which laid the foundation for what was ahead.

No holds were barred and no quarter was given or asked. We both really hated to lose – all the right ingredients for winning and success.

Though all forms of sport intrigued us in our early days, somehow cricket always took pride of place. Selling a dummy at rugby, smashing a lob at tennis – even with school chum Cliff Drysdale, out of position – or booting a soccer ball past a goalkeeper, never quite provided the same thrill as a few hefty clouts with the willow.

Of course, interest was nurtured by the fact that Dad had been a pretty useful wicket-keeper for Free State. That was in his day; the era of Cameron, Mitchell, Nourse and Rowan.

It was safe to say that cricket was in our blood. We loved the game, ate, drank and slept it. Nobody had to motivate us. From reveille to sundown cricket called the tune. Besides playing Currie Cup cricket, Dad was also a provincial hockey exponent. Mother was a tennis player of no mean calibre and her brother, Bob Howden, played rugby and cricket for Natal while still at school and later achieved Springbok colours for hockey. Further back in the family tree are more sporting credentials.

But perhaps, as some wag once pointed out during a match in Durban, the most significant aspect was that both Graeme and I were born in Natal, a province that over the years has produced prolifically in terms of cricketing heroes. Parochial? For sure!

Our early backyard tussles were contested in rather crude conditions and the bumpy pitches did favour the faster deliveries, which suited me. Graeme still wasn't easy to dismiss. Worse, to get him to play I had to let him bat first. Flowers, pots and chairs acted as fielders, but inevitably there were arguments. Mother would be called in to arbitrate and usually suggested, "Shame he's just small. Give him another chance." She certainly didn't understand. He was absolute hell to remove, whatever way you looked at it! As the elder and bigger brother, I often decided to take the law into my own hands. This also didn't help, because again Mother would arrive and send us off to our rooms to cool down. The bottom line was that I just wasn't getting a turn at the bat. Maybe that's why he became the batsman and I the bowler.

Our most prized possession in cricketing equipment was a moth-eaten old Rhodesian cap which my dad had obviously swopped. Being green, the cap represented to us Springbok colours and even though the badge was a lion, not the genuine bokkie, we wore it with pride. Our friends from the neighbourhood also regarded it with awe and I have a sneaking suspicion that one of them had a hand in its apparent misplacement.

The first year or two in the Friendly City saw us move houses a few times and as Graeme said, "Mom, we hardly get time to prepare one wicket when you move to the next house and we have to start all over again." That's getting priorities right!

Eventually we lived very close to the Josephs in Burton Road, Mill Park and they had a big garden in which a concrete pitch had been laid. Most days we batted and bowled there and the true surface allowed the luxury of fast bowling. I was allowed to go for it and I became the terror of the neighbourhood. Even at this stage I had developed a pretty long run and I clearly remember having to make a detour around a couple of hedges to fit in the full approach. Mr Joseph was good enough to arrange the odd test against the fathers and mothers. The little Harveys, Lindwalls, Bradmans and Millers were in their element. We did not enjoy much success against the older generation, partly because they were also the umpires, but this did not stop us from coming back for more and more. It was our lifeblood.

Cricket meant everything and minor frustrations tended to be exaggerated out of all proportions. My parents could not console me as I howled my heart out the evening following the fifth Test between Australia and South Africa in Port Elizabeth in 1950. As the final wicket fell, Keith Miller, one of my heroes, picked up a bail and threw it into the crowd. It landed right in front of me and I scrambled to get the souvenir. I had it firmly in my hands, but in the ensuing mêlée, some adult neatly wrenched the bail from my clenched fist and despite my desperate pleas, kept it for himself. I sobbed bitterly all the way home on my bicycle. Once in the solitude of my room, I let it all go.

That was my first day at a Test match. South Africa had been thrashed. But Keith Miller's bail had landed at my feet. I had lost the scramble this time, but would never give up that easily again.

Our early days as young cricketers were spent very happily thanks to Henry Martin, a schoolteacher in a million. He did everything humanly possible to help us along. He even 'adjusted' Graeme's age so that he could attend special nets with George Cox, the former Sussex player who was coaching at the Grey High School. He was like a second father to us and was often accused of showering liberties upon us later in our careers when he became a first league umpire.

It wasn't easy to get Graeme out at the best of times, but with Henry standing, it was well nigh impossible. Similarly, I was often the beneficiary when batsmen got their pads in front, or close enough for Henry's finger! Of course these accusations were made jocularly, but Henry Martin and the two Pollocks were synonymous. Henry was proud of the association. We were his boys. We would always be his boys – the Pollocks. He didn't mind the ribbing!

When Graeme was a mere nine years old, a Grey Junior under eleven side was invited to Graaff-Reinet to play against Union High School. Mom and Dad were not very keen to let Graeme go, but assurances from Henry that he would "look after him as if he were my own son" eventually broke the deadlock. So, off went an excited youngster on his first tour, wide-eyed and expectant.

What an impact he made. First he took all ten wickets as a fast bowler in the Union High innings and then proceeded to notch his first century. The match was played on a concrete wicket and the onside boundary was rather short, being separated from an adjoining cemetery by a six-foot fence. Almost monotonously Graeme lifted the ball over the hedge and in his eagerness to get on with the game, was the first player into the cemetery to recover the ball.

This rather cute story made national headlines and this represented the first public notice that there was a young superstar on the way. And Henry returned him safely to his proud parents!

Those were wonderful days, those junior schooldays. If Henry was the fairy godfather, his aide in our cricket nurturing was George Cox, a Sussex professional who spent much time coaching at Grey during the English winter. Early on George spotted Graeme's natural flair for stroke play. He spared the young lad the formalities of routine coaching, rather encouraging him to strike the ball and attack, while gently correcting any minor flaws in technique. To George Cox the thrill of unearthing my brother must have rivalled Cullinan's delight in finding that famous diamond. "There is nothing I can teach him," he was once overheard to say and he confidently predicted a Test player – labelled, packaged and delivered. No arguments. There was an inevitability about it all.

Growing pains

George had to work a bit harder with me, but I spent many happy hours under his tutelage and soon learnt that discipline and application are the key prerequisites for my chosen trade – that of a fast bowler. I fancied my batting, but George was adamant that finally it was bowling that would pay for the meals. "You will always be good for a few runs," he said, "but stick to the bowling, the long runs and keep that arm up."

At Grey we were very fortunate because the school's first team played in the men's first division and consequently at the tender age of 15 years, I was trading blows with the province's best cricketers. Brother Graeme was even younger, but I must recall that in those early days I actually batted higher than he did. My role was opening batsman while Graeme's initial matches saw him batting as low down as number nine, with his leg-spin bowling contributing more than his precocious batting talent.

In my formative years as a cricketer, I had always been something of a speed merchant, coming off a long run and obstinately refusing to shorten it. Experts persistently nagged me about my marathon run-in, but I scorned their advice because I felt that my bowling rhythm stemmed from my long prancing approach to the wicket. At junior school I developed a rather pudgy frame and there was much panting, puffing and blowing. Hence the advice to cut it short.

The turning-point came in 1956 when jaundice laid me low and kept me from sport for some five months. While being confined to bed for three of those months, my height increased an almost unbelievable six inches and the puppy fat vanished. I was suddenly a rejuvenated six-footer, full of energy and loving every moment of fast bowling. Quite frankly, I was happy to give up my dreams about becoming a batsman.

A new hero now presented himself in the form of Neil Adcock, perhaps one of South Africa's greatest pacemen. All I wanted to do was knock batsmen's heads off, strike fear into them and send the stumps cart-wheeling. Naturally I didn't lose my affection for batting – what fast bowler does? – but to me it couldn't equal the satisfaction of hurling them down at pace, splattering those wickets or seeing timid batsmen taking off in the direction of square-leg to avoid injury. This, I decided, was my game.

I wanted to be a fast bowler: the fastest bowler in the world. Nothing small about that ambition! With this goal came a disappointment. It arrived in the form of my dad telling me that he had been involved in a long discussion with the cricket master and they had decided that, in the best interests of my cricket career, I should not be made the first team's cricket captain. "Fast bowlers shouldn't be captains," said Dad. I had wondered when this would be coming, for I had long felt that the cricket master was angling elsewhere for a captain. We hadn't always seen eye to eye and I had never been afraid to express my disagreements. Now my dad was being used as a lever. He couldn't exactly disagree. It was all being paraded as being in my best interests.

Well, I just had to grin and bear it. It wasn't just the honour that was the issue with me. Every kid likes to captain his school's first eleven. I enjoyed leadership and the tactical challenges involved. I was to be denied it and that would set the pattern for the rest of my career. Fast bowlers traditionally shouldn't be captains – that was the voice of the old school blaring down the icy corridor! A lot of nonsense, I thought, but there was nothing I could do about it. However, I was annoyed with Dad, something I told him many years later. Spilt milk, nonetheless!

As a youngster I never dared to cheek my father. This was part of my strict Presbyterian upbringing. His background – that of a pastor's son – was one of the factors that influenced my mom in her initial choice of a mate, but she was soon disillusioned. On their honeymoon the car broke down and Dad used some language that would make a sailor blush. She was utterly dismayed.

My parents were both strong-willed and needless to say there were times when their wills clashed. But on the issue of religion there were no strong feelings. Dad's philosophy was that we should attend Sunday school until we were old enough to make up our own minds on "delicate and personal" issues! Certainly we never discussed the Bible or Christianity. Dad once or twice suggested that you did not have to go to church to prove your belief in God.

Very occasionally we did attend a church service and our pastor was obviously very learned, intellectual and educated. He also had a broad Scots accent and loved uttering direct quotations from the archaic King James Version. His sermons were laced with highfalutin language and I seldom understood a word he was saying. As I looked around the congregation it seemed that others were experiencing the same difficulties! Nobody ever smiled. It might have been very reverent, but if left me stone cold. Anyway, my passive association with the church in those schooldays was broken when my father had a major disagreement with the pastor. It had something to do with local politics. My dad was editor of the morning newspaper, the *EP Herald*, and he didn't believe that the clergy should be involved in preaching politics or interfering and meddling in such things. My father very bluntly gave him an editorial roasting and that was that – no more church for the Pollocks! It was, quite frankly, neither here nor there. It simply was not an issue in our lives.

In December 1957 I received the first big selection honour, gaining a nod in the Eastern Province team to take part in the Nuffield tournament in East London. But Pietermaritzburg, my birthplace, saw my first real step into big cricket – inclusion in the South African Schools XI in January 1959. To make an SA schools side you need a healthy dose of good fortune. You need to strike a rich patch to catch the selectors' eyes.

But my fairy godfather was there. Henry Martin was manager of the Eastern Province team and he was going to leave no stone unturned to get me in the national team. First he told everyone that I was by far the fastest bowler at the tournament, then in the match between Eastern Province and Transvaal he challenged all the selectors to be there to see me give them carrots! Henry arranged that I could bat at number three and I duly performed with a half-century. When the Transvalers went in to bat, boasting a line-up that included Ali Bacher, the media's future superstar, the stage was set. Bacher made a duck, as did others, as I literally tore into them.

A moment of destiny had arrived and I grasped it with both hands. My place in the SA schools side was sealed. Life is about those moments and whether you respond or not. In the final match of the tournament the SA schools side played Natal, the Currie Cup champions, a team which included Jackie McGlew and a whole heap of Springboks. I faced Geoff Griffin for the first time. He was later to make world headlines as a chucker. My contribution to the match was a face-saving 33 not out as Neville Holmes and I held out for a draw.

My schooldays were now over and my first-class career was about to start. In one week I had somersaulted into the limelight. My birthplace had also become the start of my cricket career. Grey's Hospital had brought me into the world, the Jan Smuts stadium heralded my cricket career. Coincidence?

While Richie Benaud's Australians and Peter May's Englishmen were doing battle during the English summer of 1961, a team of young South African cricketers headed by veteran gladiator Roy McLean, arrived at Heathrow Airport in London. They were called the Fezelas – meaning the sting in the tail of the scorpion – and they were to make something of an impact during their short tour. The manager of the team was C.O. Medworth, then sports editor of the

Natal Mercury. The late Stanley Murphy, who was a generous benefactor of cricket, had sponsored the sojourn.

The 1960 Springbok tour of England had been a disaster with political demonstrations and the Griffin throwing episode. South African cricket, according to the pundits and the pessimists, was at the crossroads. Stan Murphy wanted to make his contribution and he gathered his team. I do believe that this tour had a lot to do with a decade of South African cricket that will probably go down in the annals as the greatest ever. The Fezelas trip produced eight Springboks, but it was the positive and pugnacious attitude that the tour engendered that saw a new type of cricketer emerge.

Graeme was so nearly invited but was just a bit young at that stage. He had only just completed two successful Nuffield tournaments, both with a prized SA cap, plus the captaincy in his final tournament.

The Fezelas came, saw and conquered. They went to England to learn, but ended up giving lessons all round. Back home the critics were a little cynical. They questioned the standard of the opposition and while appreciating that there was much potential in the Fezelas line-up, they felt a sterner Test was needed.

But the storm clouds were brewing on the political horizon. I didn't particularly enjoy military training. We got an overdose thanks to an attempt on Dr Verwoerd's life and the ensuing state of emergencies. In fact, we had to pull a few strings to get out of the barracks and onto a plane for the Fezelas tour. Army uniforms, camps and armoured cars were now becoming a part of the South African scenery and way of life. I cursed my luck for being drawn in the ballot for compulsory military training. Graeme similarly served his country.

Cricketwise Graeme had been doing very well. Even at the tender age of seventeen they were talking of a Test career. I suppose secretly I wanted to become a Springbok first. Our progress in quest of the green and gold had followed much the same pattern except that Graeme was always younger at each rung in the ladder. I was 17 when I made the SA Schools side, but Graeme got in at 15 years. At 16 he became the youngest in first-class combat to score a Currie Cup century.

The critics were running out of superlatives and adjectives in acknowledging and describing his genius and I was apparently losing ground in the sibling rivalry. Though it wasn't obsessive, I would be dishonest to deny it as a strong motivating factor. Perhaps the secret for me was that I realised that he was no ordinary batsman. When someone is so vastly superior, it is hard to begrudge him and I am sure that this was the case in my enjoying his achievements and not being unduly threatened by his talent and success. Besides, we were always on the same side!

Amazing, isn't it, that Graeme never scored a first-class century against me nor did I ever get him out. We were destined never to face each other in anger.

I never complained! Perhaps I had done my stint serving my apprenticeship in the backyard! That he was heading for stardom also didn't require too much discernment. He was literally breathing down my neck.

From tree stump to Test cricket

I still remember that Saturday evening, 2 December 1961 vividly – the night that saw my boyhood dream and fantasy become reality. A roar so tremendous that it seemed to stir the very foundations of the main pavilion at St George's Park, greeted the announcement of my name in the Springbok line-up for the first Test against New Zealand at Durban. The prized Springbok cap. Yet in that moment of triumph I found myself disbelieving. Had this really happened to me?

Certainly the handshakes, backslaps and congratulations were very real, but it was not until I heard three simple little words, "Well done, Pete," from a man slightly greying and with tears in his eyes, that the truth of the moment struck home. Those three words meant more to me than all the others, for that joyously tearful man was Dad. All the sincerity and pride of a father who has watched his son, helped him and consoled him, were packed into that short utterance.

The previous summer had been a season of injury and frustration. Would I ever get amongst the wickets? Dad was a pillar of encouragement. He was, in fact, convenor of the selection committee for Eastern Province when I was first selected, fresh out of school. He later resigned to avoid any accusations of nepotism. He had lived through three seasons of provincial combat. It was a moment to be sipped and savoured.

Dad never showered much praise and was continually on the lookout for any tendencies towards a swollen head. This is something he never stood for and even the slightest hint of bigheadedness was met with drastic disapproval. We respected him for this, perhaps understanding that it was for our own good. It did not mean, however, that we were not encouraged. Nobody was keener for us to do well than Mom and Dad and they were always there to watch, no matter what the sport. But praise was strictly limited and the very best individual performance received no more than a sincere "Well done."

The life of a sportsman's parents is not one long glorious bask in reflected glory. When things go wrong, and they often do, there are anonymous phone calls, poison-pen letters and other forms of cowardly retribution from obsessed fans. A close family is a vital foundation, and that certainly doesn't mean doting parents.

Dad was once invited to write a guest piece for the *Daily Telegraph* of London. This is how he described his sons:

Temperamentally Peter and Graeme differ considerably. Graeme is phlegmatic and gives the impression of being impervious to distraction. Deep down he is a little more sensitive than he appears, but his moods are not readily discernible behind an infectious smile.

Peter is a man of somewhat conflicting moods. Mentally alert to a high degree, he has remarkable powers of concentration when his sense of almost devout determination dictates the tone. He works incessantly hard at his cricket and is arduous in any task he might undertake.

There it was in a nutshell from the man who knew us better than anyone. He added though, "I don't think that either of the lads has been spoiled by the feast of publicity they have enjoyed. Having grown up against a background of newspapers, they have learned to become somewhat cynical about the fickleness of public acclaim."

So to the first Test at Kingsmead. It was butterflies and wide-eyed expectancy. I felt a little like a naughty schoolboy who had cheated on his homework and wasn't quite sure whether he was going to be caught out. Would I be snookered by fate before it even began?

Indeed, I had no right to be playing in the Test. Statistically, and on current form, the faith shown in me by chief selector Jack Cheetham and his panel was probably justified, but they didn't know, nor was I going to tell them that my left ankle was swollen and extremely sore. The injury was sustained the previous weekend in the tour match against the New Zealanders. I had scuppered six wickets in virtually clinching my place in the national team, but in the process I went over on my ankle. Fortunately a day of rest came in between and I went to see my friend Hugh van der Post, an orthopaedic expert. He gave me some emergency treatment and promised not to say a word. I deserved an Oscar for managing to keep the injury a secret.

Deep down in my heart I knew that this could be one of the most foolish things I had ever done. But when you are young, you live for today and you are prepared to take on the odds. I wasn't going to let this opportunity slip, not for anything. I knew that even the faintest hint of an injury would see me replaced.

Standing trial that Friday morning, 8 December 1961, were seven new Springboks. It was as hot and sultry as a midsummer's day can get in Durban and I perspired profusely. It was sweat, heat and nervousness, but what intense excitement. Jackie McGlew, striped Springbok blazer and all, went out to the middle to toss the coin with John Reid, captain and burly batting cavalier of New Zealand.

It was the debut of Eddie Barlow, Colin Bland, Kim Elgie, Goofy Lawrence, Kenny Walter, Harry Bromfield and me. One of us three fast bowlers was in the team only because Neil Adcock had been sidelined through injury. Anyway, there we were – thrown into the hurly-burly of Test cricket with only four veterans to guide us. The skipper, Jackie, a man whose tactical genius, grit, determination and utter dedication could never be questioned, was a tower of strength and inspiration. There was Roy McLean who stroked the ball with such grace and ease that it suggested he was a cut above the mere mortals who were playing with him. Also in the team were Johnny Waite, the wicket-keeper who had no peer and Sid O'Linn, though not in the same class as the other three, but a man renowned for his fighting spirit and doggedness. It was such a mixed bag that one couldn't blame McGlew for feeling like a Christian martyr on the way to a feeding session with the lions!

But our captain was equal to the task, even enjoying it with the tenacity and enthusiasm of a mother hen with her chickens. Jackie had no option, I guess. But he was going to make the best of what was available and he got the ball rolling by winning the toss.

Veterans McGlew and Mclean who put on 103 runs for a third wicket partnership, drew first blood. McGlew who finished with a typically responsible century and Mclean who breezed in with 63 scintillating runs, helped us shoo away the butterflies. The shot of the innings came from John Waite. Not often did Johnny hit sixes, but he actually opened his score with a maximum! The Kiwi speedster Gary Bartlett whose action was somewhat jerky and dubious, was certainly extremely fast. He sprayed them all over the place, but this made him dangerous because if he didn't know where the ball was going there was always the risk of uncalculated rashness on the part of the batter.

From Bartlett you got the lot: bumpers, beamers, yorkers and wides! And in any order! Anyway, Johnny let the first ball to him go a little wide down the leg side. Johnny merely waved his bat, one-handed, more as a gesture than anything else. But he connected perfectly and helped the ball soar over fine-legs head. Dare I say it was a fluke! Certainly it was the most spectacular start ever to a Waite Test innings.

At one stage the Springboks were sitting rather handily at 185/2, but the next eight wickets fell for the addition of only just over 100 runs. With about 40 minutes to spare on the opening day, we were all out for 292. The babes had made little contribution. They had all failed and none as miserably as I with a duck. What an inauspicious start, though I might add that noughts on a debut are reasonably commonplace in Test history. Statistically, I was in eloquent company, but that was of little solace.

There was soon some consolation late that first afternoon. With the clammy humidity and the nerves, it was small wonder I could even hold the greasy new ball. My heart was thumping as I launched in from the Umgeni River end. But the butterflies were operating in formation and there was pace and rhythm. The adrenalin pumped, the crowd supported us and soon I had my first Test scalp – left-hander John Guy. No thoughts about the swollen ankle!

It was such an overpowering occasion that there was no time to feel pain. So the first day moved on to the second and third and South Africa managed a first innings lead of some 47 runs, though Paul Barton and Zin Harris did at one stage threaten to take the Kiwis past our first innings tally.

My lasting memory of that NZ innings revolved around the dismissal of their prolific run-getting skipper, John Reid. On that tour, Reid single-handedly kept the tourists in the picture. Like the little Dutch boy who kept his finger in the dyke, Reid was their saviour. Consequently his wicket was the ultimate prize and seeing the back of his burly figure heading to the pavilion was a key moment. I was fielding at mid-on and Goofy Lawrence was the bowler. With Reid on unlucky 13, Goofy varied his pace and enticed Reid into an on-drive, which unfortunately for him, he played just a fraction too early.

The ball took the outside edge and skied in my direction. I didn't pick it up till rather late and then, adjusting myself under its flight happened to utter, "Help me God, it's mine." "He won't help you," came a retort from the direction of mid-off. After what seemed like an eternity, the ball eventually nestled into my hands. Much relieved I tossed it heavenwards. There were backslaps and happiness, but I only appreciated the full significance the next day, and naturally, at the conclusion of the match.

The morning newspaper published a picture of me taking the catch. There was Goofy with his head in his hands, not daring to look. It was the easiest of catches, but I still wonder what would have happened if I had grassed my very first catch in Test cricket. Test matches are won and lost on ridiculous errors and a Test debut is as good a time as any to succumb to the pressures. Considering that we finally sneaked home by a mere 30 runs, a second chance for John Reid that day might have altered the course of cricket history. These are the sort of thoughts that nightmares are made of!

Our second innings was a disaster, to say the least. Only Waite (63), Bland (30) and I scored double figures and we were all out for a meagre 149. Dick Motz, Frank Cameron and Jack Alabaster shared the spoils and the Kiwis were set for a well-earned triumph. Some of the critics were patronising in suggesting that a win for New Zealand would do the series good. But it would have been a death-knell for us youngsters.

Nothing motivated me more than a comment made by Roy McLean. Perhaps he was just being nice and sporting. Perhaps he was preparing the fans for a Springbok defeat and lightening the load.

I know he hated losing as much as any one us but he said, "A win for the Kiwis will give cricket in their country a much needed boost. It will be good for the game."

That wasn't music to our ears, but it got me going. Maybe it was reversed psychology, but the survival of us youngsters was at stake.

The Springboks won with 30 runs to spare, my contribution being six wickets for 38. The press were very generous in their praise, but the classic to me was the cartoon by Jock Leyden. His sketch depicted the last day's play in our memorable triumph and this comment:

Not since Dick King set off from this historic spot has anybody been on such a hazardous mission as the one that Jackie McGlew had entrusted to his faithful Pooch Pollock.

With the Kiwis needing only 118 more runs to win the Test, young Pollock set about his errand of no mercy. The tension among the spectators was unbearable. Kingsmead's barmen can't recall when so little has been drunk by so many.

And so the curtain came down on the Kingsmead Test with Pollock taking the curtain call with the finest bouquet we've seen in years.

There was a drawing of me holding a bouquet of nine stumps, each with a name of a Kiwi batsman. At my feet were two Indian Mynahs staring at the bouquet. The one turns to the other and says, "He's not a pooch – he's a genuine retriever."

Athol McKinnon, burly spin bowler of the Eastern Province had once called me "Pooch," following an appeal for lbw. My young voice had hardly broken in those early days of playing for Eastern Province and Athol felt the appeal sounded rather like a little pooch barking or yelping. The name stuck and the two Pollocks were later to become Big Dog and Little Dog – a question still sometimes posed in trivial pursuit games.

Anyway, the game was won. That's what counts. I took nine wickets for 99 in a dream debut, but whatever the personal glory, it would all have been in vain had the Springboks not triumphed. There would have been recriminations and changes. What's scary is that the margin was so narrow.

Those four sultry humid days at Kingsmead set in motion a mighty wheel. The Test was the starting point for a cricketing era that was going to take South Africa into a new dimension. It was a game that just had to be won. It was essential to taste victory the first time out. Analyse as you will, but the nature, timing and circumstances of that Kingsmead triumph set a definite course.

After the match I was required to plant a tree at the ground, an honour and tradition accorded to anyone who had either taken five wickets or made a century at this famous venue. As I plunged the spade into the sanctity of Kingsmead I couldn't help but feel that I was symbolically burying the decaying old tree stump which had once served as a set of backyard stumps and replacing it with an inexperienced young sapling so ill-equipped to meet the demands that lay ahead. The one day I was just a young provincial cricketer dreaming his dreams, the next day I was a Test hero. It happened with frightening speed.

I've made it. Such glory makes one's head spin. Of course you can't admit that you are a little frightened. Heroes don't do that. They learn to take these things in their stride. Peter Pollock had arrived on the Test arena.

Single-handedly I had snatched a Test out of the jaws of defeat. It's the type of script that dreams are made of. Fourteen days ago I was a complete outsider for a Test place – a long shot at best.

Now it was interviews and a whole new status in my hometown, Port Elizabeth. Once you taste the sweet champagne of success, adulation and hero-worship, it's too heady to want to give it up. I was into the mainstream. It's now the end of the beginnings. The sport's Bronco. I have bought it. Now I had to ride it bareback!

2

THE CLIMB

The Kiwis – "bumper warfare":

1961 – 1962

I wanted the green and gold Springbok cap. Moreover, I wanted to be part of a team that would beat the world. To be the best! Nothing small about that goal! If my entrance into the Test arena was spectacular, it didn't take long to be brought down to earth.

The second Test at the Wanderers was a pawky affair. It never quite got off the ground and this often happens when rain reduces the first day of a four-day Test to a mere 80 minutes of action. It shouldn't really be possible to get a result in just over three days and the game simply dragged to an inevitable conclusion.

There was a century from John Waite in our first innings of 322. He was made to look all the more stylish and professional in contrast to his young partner, Eddie Barlow who introduced to the game an approach that was completely divorced from the normal post-war pattern. He showed such a refreshing attitude to the subject of hitting the ball and taking the odd chance against the new ball, that some critics literally shook their heads in sheer wonder and dismay. "Just lie back and cut," was his motto!

Eddie's later record speaks for itself, but at that stage I think that even some of us were disturbed and concerned about the calibre of Eddie's shots and the response of media and public. "It is a bit of a circus," suggested some of our more experienced team-mates. "It can't last," was the verdict.

The New Zealanders even found a new fielding position necessary. They placed a man halfway between slips and third man and he was there obviously to take the fly-catch that they were constantly expecting from Barlow's bat. If my memory serves me correctly, they didn't once snare him in this trap and I am sure his career records would vouch for the fact that he was a winner by miles in this trademark overhead cut!

Brilliant swing and seam bowling by Goofy Lawrence saw New Zealand finish about 100 back and his eight wickets cost him 53 runs. South Africa declared at 178/6 in the second innings, pushing for a victory. I got a couple of early wickets, but it would have required a miracle on the tame Wanderers strip, so the game petered out to a tame but controversial finish.

I had to bowl the last over of the final day. Everything had been so pointless that – at the instigation of my skipper – I decided to let go a barrage of rather venomous bouncers. With the very last ball I bowled one of the best bouncers of my life. To put it bluntly, it nearly skinned poor Zin Harris! I didn't hit him, but it had been a close shave. The Kiwi took it in good smiling spirit. Or so I thought! But at the other end was the New Zealand skipper, John Reid, undefeated with 75. He felt it was unnecessary to introduce needle at this late stage of the encounter and he obviously whispered his thoughts to one of the pressmen, Dick Whitington, who was known for his controversial writing. There was nothing much to write about that final day so Dick decided to stir the pot.

He interviewed some former Springboks, all batsmen incidentally, who agreed that I had introduced a nasty element of "bumper warfare" into the series. I was shattered when I read the morning newspaper, but there it was for all to see. Reid added to the controversy by suggesting that there would be "repayments." It carried on for a couple of days and nobody came to my support. I was learning fast! Jackie told me just to lie low and convinced me that the best policy was silence. He obviously had no intention of telling anyone that the bumper barrage was his idea. I have to admit that I did enjoy getting his instructions! But I was beginning to see that as executioner, you are always on your own!

'Horses for courses'

Three days later we were back in action, this time at Cape Town with the New Year spirit very much in the air. The Coon Carnival had started down Sea Point way while New Zealand and South Africa were squaring up to each other at Newlands, that most picturesque of cricket grounds.

Will I ever forget the first morning of the match! I was nominated among the twelve, but with just 45 minutes to starting time, Jack Cheetham, convenor of the selectors came up to me. At first I thought he was going to wish me luck. I was wrong. "Peter," he said, "it's a case of horses for courses. We don't think the pitch will suit your bowling, so you will stand down and be twelfth man. Sid Burke will be playing."

What a shock. Omission had not even entered my mind. It came as a mortal blow to a youngster who had taken 11 wickets in his first two Tests and had also notched up a batting contribution of 37 at the Wanderers. But there are no options. You have to accept these setbacks.

As it turned out, I spent most of the match on the field because Lawrence broke down early on. I was later to surmise – with justification – that my omission had had something to do with those controversial bumpers. It was a sort of underhanded disciplinary action, though nobody owned up to it!

The Test was a disaster for South Africa. The pitch turned out to be ideal for the faster bowlers – which made a mockery of the convenor's prematch apprai-sal – and the bumper warfare in the Test saw the Springboks collapse. The SA attack was in the hands of "military medium" paced Lawrence, until he was injured, Burke and Barlow.

Speedster Gary Bartlett and burly Dick Motz had Jackie and company ducking and diving all over the place. Bartlett actually went overboard in highly conducive conditions. Some suggested that it was just lack of control, but he bowled enough bouncers to get tempers between the two sides to a boiling point.

I had never seen McGlew so furious. We were losing, but he was more concerned about the bumpers. "I am going to insist on the recall of Peter Heine and Neil Adcock," he fumed. "We'll show these New Zealanders what intimidation is all about." Jackie was seething. He was like a man possessed and all he wanted was retaliation and revenge. He told me, "Neil, Peter Heine and you. You're the fastest we have and I am going to have all three of you in the fourth Test at the Wanderers."

The triumphant New Zealanders, while celebrating their victory at Newlands, had little idea of the hornet's nest they had stirred. John Reid had promised reprisals. Make no mistake, Gary Bartlett was quick, really fast! He was also a chucker, but none of the umpires would have anything to do with calling him. Ironically, he was probably not throwing well enough! It's only when you start winning matches and bowling out top players that the complaints start coming! McGlew was sensitive on this issue as well. After all his experiences in England in 1960 with Geoff Griffin, he had been exposed to the hypocrisy and expedience that govern this highly controversial issue.

Sid Burke, the "ghost" Springbok as he is often described, finished with an aggregate of 11 wickets at a cost of 196 runs after a marathon 71 overs. The horse was certainly given a full run on his course, but was promptly dropped for the next Test! If I had been baffled about the selectors' thinking, imagine what Sid thought! Anyway, next stop was the Wanderers and I had little doubt that I would be back in the side after the captain's assurances. The thought of lining up alongside Neil Adcock and Peter Heine was awesome.

But I never even came close. Neil Adcock and Peter Heine were named in the original squad, but because there was some doubt about fitness, the squad for the match read more like a touring party! There were stand-bys and stand-bys for stand-bys! But I wasn't even mentioned. What had I done? Who could have blamed me for smelling some sort of conspiracy! I really was most confused. There were no phone calls or explanations! I had been unceremoniously and ignominiously sidelined.

The Wanderers saw an innings victory for the Springboks. Revenge came, and it was sweet, but caused further controversy. Adcock and Heine were back in tandem, as McGlew had vowed. The bouncers and the verbal abuse flew! John Reid decided to bat first on winning the toss and that's not always wise at the Wanderers. On the first morning the quickies can always expect a little help from the pitch and indeed the Springbok pacers climbed in, bundling the tourists out for a paltry 164, with John Reid's contribution being 60. He was at the crease long enough to feel the lash of Peter Heine's sharp tongue.

Reid himself wasn't averse to caustic comment. He was certainly no angel, but newcomers like us did not have the experience or audacity to deal with him verbally. Heine, however, a past master at the art of psyching or plainly abusing batsmen, regarded Reid as a tremendous challenge. And his captain would have egged him on. Certainly he would not have been discouraged. All is fair in love and war, and Heine would have regarded cricket in the latter category. He was not prepared to take Reid's verbal handouts and he answered with interest. The cauldron was stirred, animosities came to the fore and the tension could be cut with the proverbial knife. It's a man's game and if you can't take it, you shouldn't be there.

The Springboks amassed 464 when they batted and McGlew produced another century as he glowed in the intensity of that particular battle. He was always at his best when the chips were down or the fur was flying! The Kiwis needed 300 to avoid the innings defeat and missed their target by 51 runs. All but 105 of their reply came from John Reid's bat and while he was at the crease he was subjected to everything imaginable in the way of bumpers both physically and verbally.

Whether Reid got what he deserved, I am not debating, but again the media took up arms on his behalf. Peter Heine became the villain and was again left to carry the can on his own. The administrators opted for expedience as they once again whitewashed Reid.

Reid's confidence trick carried him through the tour and it was only eventually revealed to me over some drinks three years or so later with Jack Alabaster, the Kiwi leg-spinner. Reid was without question the team's number one trump card, but his dislike of spin bowling was his Achilles heel. Speedsters he didn't mind, and medium-pacers he murdered, but spinners were always a severe test of his pugnacious temperament.

When the Kiwis arrived, Hugh Tayfield, one of the world's finest off-spinners, was still around, albeit less effectively than in his prime. So the plan was put into motion. Tayfield had to be blown out of the Test picture. Something had to be done to show that he was over the hill.

Transvaal came up against the tourists early in November 1961 and the massacre of Tayfield was the number one item on the Kiwi menu. They took every possible risk and the boldness paid off. Tayfield was hit out of the Transvaal attack and almost automatically out of Test consideration as the critics hailed Reid as the supreme plunderer of spin bowling. Each time a spinner was brought on against Reid in the series, he took his life in his hands and lofted the ball to all corners of the field. We should have clicked, but the Kiwis were sniggering up their sleeves. Had we only known that behind that bravado was actually weakness, Reid could so easily have got out, but when you are enjoying a golden summer, everything runs for you.

However, the fact that the Kiwis had actually planned the destruction of Tayfield, deserves recognition as tactical one-up-manship and it probably gave them the series. If we had just done a little homework, Reid's record against spinners would have come to light. In the whole series, the Springbok bowlers delivered 918 overs of which spinners bowled only 185. What makes it even more ridiculous, is that of the 185 overs bowled by spinners, 106 of them were delivered at Newlands – the "horses for courses" pitch that caused the South Africans such grief.

Anyway, on that tour all that John Reid said or did, seemed to be regarded as gospel by the local writers and Peter Heine's efforts at the Wanderers were destined to earn him a disciplinarian omission for the fifth Test at Port Elizabeth. It was his turn to be the twelfth man. It would be remiss of me not to mention one of the real highlights of the fourth Test, a highlight that heralded the emergence of a new facet to cricket.

Fielding, in most circles, had been regarded as extreme drudgery, but Colin Bland brought a whole new meaning to this department of the game. A superb athlete and fitness fanatic, Bland's dedication to the art of fielding proved to be one of the most important developments in the emerging era. In fielding alone, Bland was worth 20-30 runs an innings and that's meaningful in any circumstances.

In the NZ first innings, Bogo, as Reid was nicknamed, was dismissed by one of the greatest catches of all time. Lawrence bowled, what appeared to be, a half volley. Reid launched into his drive, but was just not there. He hit it beautifully, with all the power and timing at his disposal, but the ball carried inches off the ground into the covers. Four runs were written all over the shot, but Bland, diving forward full length, scooped the ball up literally fractions off the ground for a sensational catch.

So brilliant was the effort that even Reid stood his ground for several seconds to applaud and acknowledge the supreme effort. Bowler Lawrence shook his head in disbelief. The crowd erupted, superlatives flowed from the media and players and so a star was born. The "Golden Eagle" had landed and fielding was never to be the same again.

And so to the final Test at Port Elizabeth, a game studded with records, injuries and pre-match controversies. Bowlers opened the innings and Jackie McGlew came in at number eight with his thumb in splints and his shoulder encased in what was virtually a straitjacket of plaster. The pre-test atmosphere in the Springbok camp was hardly conducive to a top-rate performance. Peter Heine was in the twelve, but rumours were rife that he was going to be disciplined. The selectors, again unwisely, decided not to make their decision until the morning of the match.

Jack Cheetham, it appeared, liked last-minute drama, just to keep everyone on tenterhooks. Heine got the message and I was to replace him. How is that for a start?

I was the reluctant scapegoat – "horses for courses" again – on my home ground! Heine was a thorough gentleman about the whole issue. In fact, the way he took it earned him my enduring respect. The captain battled hard to hide his resentment and we all felt that Heine got a raw deal.

For me it was a great occasion. I was going to open the bowling with the man I had worshipped and admired from schoolboy days, on my home ground and before my home crowd.

Soon after the toss we were out there in tandem, bowling together and we each took an early wicket. But this was not to be the Springboks' Test. Paul Barton notched a century for the Kiwis, but one of his drives saw McGlew dive in the covers and mess up his shoulder. He was a passenger for the rest of the match and when the Springboks batted, facing the Kiwis' first innings of 275, Godfrey Lawrence had to open the batting with Barlow. He did an admirable makeshift job scoring 43. It turned out to be the highest score in our paltry innings of 190.

The New Zealanders had a great chance. McGlew was injured, the SA camp was unhappy and unmotivated and some of the Old Guard were fed up with a season of selections that were puzzling, to say the least. Maybe they felt there were too many youngsters, but most certainly the spirit was anything but conducive to winning cricket.

Slowly but systematically, the Kiwis drove home their advantage as they set a winning target of 314. At 199/8, with plenty of time to spare, it was all over. Adcock, whose batting had never been accorded any rave notices, joined me at the crease. The odds on success were not even worth contemplating, 114 more runs were needed – an impossible task!

But a ninth wicket record between Neil and me, brought some smiles from the changing room. We had passed 250 and with less than an hour remaining, the New Zealanders, for the first time in the match, were showing signs of frustration. With each shot Adcock was becoming more and more confident and defiant. We had our chats in the middle of the pitch and talk was about saving the game.

Then tragedy struck. It struck in the form of a bumper bowled by Dick Motz. There was apparently an unwritten law that fast bowlers shouldn't bowl bumpers to other members of their fraternity, but Motz, in desperation, let one go at Neil. I must admit it was a beauty. It nearly decapitated the lanky Springbok!

That the Kiwi dared to do such an unethical thing to a fellow pace bowler, infuriated Neil so much that he took a wild swing at the next ball and was clean bowled. A tragedy for South Africa – the 60 run record partnership was over. On his way back to the pavilion Neil kept looking back, cursing Motz and threatening revenge and retribution.

At the conclusion of the match Neil told me that after the bumper I should have walked down the pitch and calmed him. Perhaps so, but I didn't feel that at that stage of my career that I could go down the pitch and give Neil Adcock some fatherly advice! Had I done so, however, we might have saved the series.

Harry Bromfield, the last man, pottered around for a while, long enough for us to finish 40 runs short and for me to make my maiden Test half-century.

It was a match of records. McGlew, bandages, splints and all, battled in our first innings to add 47 runs for the last wicket with Harry Bromfield – a record. Artie Dick, the NZ wicket-keeper, equalled the world record of 23 victims, only to have it beaten by Johnny Waite with 26 dismissals in the series.

Neil and I set the batting record and Lawrence, with 28 wickets, set a new mark for a fast bowler in a five-match rubber. It was all very exciting, yet in the final analysis, all so disappointing. To us, sharing a series with the lowly New Zealanders was a failure. Granted, there were extenuating circumstances, but we were not looking for excuses. It is nice to have a striped blazer in the cupboard, nice to have a green and gold cap and it's nice to know that you are a Springbok. But we had shared the series – and that was a loss in our books. We had been exposed to what Test cricket is all about.

Jackie McGlew

Jackie McGlew bade farewell to Test cricket with a display of guts and determination that I will never forget. As good a captain as this country has ever produced, Jackie was the best I had played with, even though it wasn't the happiest of series. He was a vital participant, intense and beaver-like. Every match, day, hour and minute was a challenge to him. His batting was based on playing the percentages and minimizing mistakes. His captaincy was always shrewd and aggressive when the situation demanded it. He just never gave anything away. Jackie was a role model for me in many aspects of the game and I was sorry that we didn't have more years with him at the helm.

As a post-script to the series I was most amused at what finally happened in the Adcock-Motz duel. As he left the field, Neil vowed to avenge that bouncer at St George's Park.

Well, Neil had his chance later that year while touring New Zealand with a Cavaliers side captained by Richie Benaud. Richie had heard about the incident at Port Elizabeth and the ensuing threats, so when Dick came to bat, Benaud beckoned Adcock to bowl, but stipulated that there was to be "nothing short" at the burly Kiwi. Neil disregarded Richie and let him have a few. "Sorry, they slipped," he smilingly apologized.

Benaud said nothing, but eventually had the last word. As fate would have it, the Cavaliers were set to make 20 runs in their second innings to win the game. "Will you pad up, please Neil? You are opening," said Richie. In went the lanky Springbok to face the music. He had to duck under a few real scorchers before Motz dismissed him for a duck. So the vendetta ended. Don't mess with Mother Cricket! You learn that pretty early.

In my first Test I bagged a duck in the first innings, but fortunately got a couple of runs in the second. As I came to the crease, the incumbent batsman was veteran Sid O'Linn who was one of the very few successes of the 1960 tour to England. Jack Alabaster was the bowler. His tail was up and he was a pretty good exponent of leg-breaks and googlies. I tentatively parried the first few balls and at the end of the over went down the crease to see Sid, hoping that he would suggest that maybe he should shield me for a while. "Can you read Alabaster's googly?" he asked. Actually I couldn't, but didn't want to admit it. "That's great," came Sid's quick retort. "You can stay at that end and I will look after the seamers!"

How is that for being thrown in at the deep end!

Goddard's Cinderellas in Australia: 1963 –1964

History was to repeat itself when Trevor Goddard and his Cinderellas boarded a Qantas flight bound for Perth, Australia in October 1963. Almost a decade earlier, Jack Cheetham and a team of no-hopers had set off on a similar mission – to tackle the might of Australian cricket. As was the case with Goddard's side they returned having shattered all pre-tour predictions to share the rubber. Perhaps there had been a little pessimism from our side, because it was seriously considered at the highest levels that the tour should be cancelled. It was feared that it would be a waste of time, not to mention a huge financial loss.

For us a jolly good thrashing was predicted, but most thought it would be a worthwhile experience for the future: The school of hard knocks, there is no better learning institution! That was the awesome threat posed to us.

The McGlews, Adcocks, Tayfields and McLeans had retired and the only real experience that remained was Trevor, the skipper and Johnny Waite. The odds were against us, though I must admit we didn't feel any sense of hopelessness. Waiting for us were legends like Richie Benaud, Bobby Simpson, Peter Burge, Wally Grout, Bill Lawry, Brian Booth and the new golden boy, Norman O'Neill. At a farewell function Geoff Dakin quipped, "Pete, I will be feeling for you when you take that third new ball, the Australian total is in the 600's and the temperature is in the nineties." That was the type of send-off, though not intentionally meaning any ill will.

With us was a quietly confident manager, Ken Viljoen. He had heard all this mocking before because he had managed the Cheetham side as well. Ken was a strict disciplinarian. I didn't have a problem with that, but some of the other members did and at one stage of the tour the subject of curfews and other such restrictions came under heavy revue in a rather forthright meeting. There was a degree of relaxation thereafter, but with a team so young, I still believe that Ken's role was vital. We didn't always agree with him, but at all times there was utter respect for him and what he stood for. It would be fair to say that the Aussie public was also a little sceptical about us, but by the time we reached the first Test, this attitude had disappeared.

It happened in the match against New South Wales, then the might of Australian cricket. It was almost regarded as a sixth Test. We drubbed them unceremoniously by an innings and 101 runs and what made the feat even more astounding, is that one of the days of this four-day contest was actually washed out by rain. They were thrashed by an innings in three days. The Australian public took note of us for the first time. Even the Australian selectors, under the leadership of Sir Donald Bradman, appeared to panic.

The loss to retirement of famous left-arm speedster Alan Davidson, rattled them into including controversial Ian Meckiff. We were stunned by his inclusion. Our manager just smiled. "It's a great compliment to us," was his verdict. "They are worried." Bradman was known to oppose Meckiff's action and inclusion, so it was assumed that he was out-voted. Others suggested that Bradman, sick and tired of being continually pestered by the parochial Victorian fans, wanted him tested and put out of the game for once and for all. Maybe the real truth lay somewhere between these two theories. But certainly the Meckiff saga will always be indelible in our memories.

Brisbane's cricket ground – commonly referred to as the Gabba – though lacking the Test match atmosphere of such famous venues as Melbourne, Sydney and Lord's, has nevertheless seen its fair share of incidents. There was the famous tied Test between Australia and the West Indies. The Meckiff drama caused as many world headlines as that famous tie. The eve of the Test was tense. The teams assembled for the official mayoral function and there was an air of uneasiness. Everybody wondered if Meckiff would be called for throwing! The cocktail party provided the calm before the storm. I watched Meckiff, a delightful personality, as he joked and laughed with the aplomb of an academy award winner.

Deep down his fears must have been considerable. He was literally being thrown to the lions of cricketing justice – umpires Colin Egar and Lou Rowan. To make matters worse, Egar was a personal friend of the left-arm speedster. The Springboks fielded first, so the judgement of Meckiff was postponed for a day-and-a-half. The Aussies piled up 435 runs with a magnificent 169 from Brian Booth and 82 from O'Neill. I thought I had done an outstanding job finishing with six wickets for 95, but despite my weariness, it didn't take me long to swallow a few glasses of cool-drink, remove my boots and get out onto the balcony to watch what was going to happen to Meckiff.

The eyes of the cricket world were focused. The crowd tensed as Benaud handed Meckiff the ball and Egar took up his stand at square-leg. The first ball was passed, but with the second it was as if an atomic bomb had hit the place. "No-ball!" screamed Egar. He over produced five more calls and captain Benaud was forced to take the Victorian out of the attack. Benaud was later criticized for not trying him at the other end to test Lou Rowan's reaction, but somehow I think it would have been pointless. I have no doubt that a premeditated decision had been made.

Meckiff slouched around the field, an obviously despondent figure. He was accorded sympathetic applause each time he touched the ball. One could not help but feel sorry for him. He was a completely dejected and disillusioned man and what a tragedy that his final chapter in Test cricket was written in such fashion. Egar obviously became the villain and there were threats from some quarters. He was accorded police protection.

There was an amusing incident concerning this protection. When we arrived at the ground one morning, we were told that bullets had been found on the pitch. It turned out that the night watchman had dropped them in the course of his rounds! The classic quip involved Wally Grout, who was always full of fun. Egar was standing at square-leg when Grout put up his hand to stop play. He then shouted at the Aussie umpire, "Col, there is a chap in the crowd pointing a gun at you. Please move a bit to your right because I am scared that if he misses you he will hit me. I am in direct line at the moment."

Later that same day Bill Lawry continued with the same theme. He walked into the Aussie changing room with a raincoat draped over his shoulders and a hat neatly cocked on his head looking rather like a gangster. He had a newspaper over his right arm. He walked up to Richie and demanded to know why Meckiff had not been tried out with the other umpire at the other end. He then produced a toy gun, a very realistic one, and Richie fell out of his seat in sheer fright. The no-balling of Meckiff had spoiled the Test. All else paled into insignificance, even the brilliant century scored by Eddie Barlow.

The third day was totally washed out. Finally we were set to make 234 in four hours on the final afternoon and Eddie started by getting a duck. Consternation entered the camp, but at the same time some heavy clouds were building up. I was sitting next to Clive Halse, who hailed from Durban and I kept asking him what he thought about the clouds and the possibility of rain. Brisbane has a tropical climate, much the same as Durban. "There is absolutely no chance of rain," he declared. The words had hardly left his mouth when it started hailing and pouring.

It came so fast that the umpires and players were drenched in the short time it took to make the decision to abandon play and run for cover! In a matter of ten minutes the ground was under water in one of the most spectacular storms I have ever witnessed. It was awesome to watch, but it also was a major relief. There was no way the game would continue. On the one side of the field you could have paddled a canoe! Some of us actually went and splashed about afterwards.

The score line indicated a draw, but it was certainly a match to remember, although the statistical detail was totally overshadowed by the final over of Ian Meckiff's cricket career. All sorts of views and slants were presented by the media, not to mention some slanderous innuendos. Hypocrisy seems to be the word that crops up each time and I have to say that in some forty years since then, cricket and its administrators still have the issue of chucking as a major Achilles heel. Of course they will argue that it's been cleaned up, but only a hypocrite would believe that!

The finest cricket stadium in the world belongs to Melbourne. The MCG has a seating capacity of about 90 000 and it has a special and unique atmosphere. We started as favourites for the second Test, not because we had shown any great form, but because the Aussies were without three stars: Benaud, O'Neill and Booth, who were all injured. Simpson took over as skipper and the critics backed us.

But from start to finish the Test was a nightmare. Simpson won the toss and sent us in on a green-top and by the end of the first day we were already in the field. Graham McKenzie was a destroyer and Barlow was the only one who stood in his way. It wasn't Eddie at his best. This was guts, determination and tenacity, with a good slice of luck thrown in. Maybe I can make some sort of claim to the fact that he survived several onslaughts.

At the start of the tour Eddie failed three innings in a row. I decided to change his luck and before he went out to bat the fourth time I plucked a hair from his rather hairy chest. It worked – he notched a double century. For the rest of the tour I kept plucking and Eddie finished the Australian trip with an all-time South African record aggregate of 1523 runs!

Anyway, our total of 274 was not good by Australian standards and just to confirm this, Bill Lawry and Ian Redpath answered with a 219 run opening partnership. Early on, Lawry, in hooking a ball from Joe Partridge, knocked over his wicket – dislodging a bail. The TV replays showed him to be out, but the umpires saw nothing. Lou Rowan only became aware of any misdemeanour when we pointed to the broken wicket and the bail on the pitch. He apologized on seeing the replay, but the damage was done.

Lawry took advantage of his good fortune to the tune of 157 runs while Redpath made 97. We couldn't blame anyone but ourselves. We dropped catches galore. Even Colin Bland spilled an absolute sitter! At least six relatively easy chances went down and each time the massive crowd roared. I doubt if any of us will ever forget that day.

On the one side of the ground there is a caged tunnel which is used by the Australian Rules footballers. That caged tunnel, the roaring crowd and the huge amphitheatre that is the MCG, made me feel like the Christians of old, expecting at any moment to see a pride of hungry lions emerge from the tunnel. Certainly there were times when we had all wished for the ground to open up and swallow us. It was indeed a nightmare. After the massive opening partnership, I managed a three-wicket comeback with Simpson, Burge and Grout in quick succession. But then, my hamstring snapped.

I was in agony as I limped off the field, but getting out of this bad dream was some consolation. Defeat was inevitable and it came mercifully early on the fifth morning, by eight wickets.

We were to be on the receiving end from the Aussies only twice and this was the first. Wounded pride and a painful hamstring added to the woes. In fact, the only memorable aspect of the game was that it did present the first occasion in the history of Test cricket that two sets of brothers, Tony and David Pithey and the Pollocks, appeared in the same side. That of course was absolutely no consolation!

One week separated the second and third Tests and that was the week of a miracle. It was in fact more like ten days if you consider that I was injured on the second day of the Melbourne outing. But the experts' initial diagnosis confirmed that I would be out for at least three weeks. The outlook was gloomy and I was sent on ahead to Sydney while the rest of the team went off to Parkes to meet one of the many obligations that characterized that tour.

It was just routine ultra-sound treatment three times a day plus anti-inflammatory pills for me. Who recovers from a torn hamstring in one week?

Well, I didn't pray. I didn't have any expectations, but something miraculous did happen. When the team arrived from Parkes, manager Ken inquired about my injury. When I said, "I think I'll be fit," he thought I was joking! I attended nets the day before the Test and ambled in off a short run. There was no pain.

They wouldn't believe it. I was named in the twelve and I needed to undergo a full fitness test an hour before start of play. "It seems okay," was my verdict, "but how it will stand up to five days, I don't know." Ken consulted skipper Trevor. "We will take that chance. Go and get showered and ready to play." Initially I was thrilled, but in the shower came the dreadful thought – what if I break down?

The pitch was well grassed and Bobby Simpson looked long and hard before he decided to bat. In Melbourne he had sent us in, the right call. This time it backfired. Joe Partridge and I had a party. I enjoyed the pace and bounce and Joe thrived on the gentle breeze that came in from the main scoreboard. Between us we took nine wickets (five for me) to have Australia out for 260. The hamstring was just fine and Goddard's gamble had paid off. It was a miracle. As for our fielding, we grabbed every chance. You would not have believed this was the same butter-fingered mob that had been a disgrace at Melbourne!

The stage was now set for Robert Graeme Pollock. It was his third Test – the first two had not lived up to Sir Donald Bradman's rating of him after watching him demolish a Test-class attack at Perth in the opening weeks of the tour. A wag in Melbourne shouted at Graeme after he had been dismissed, "Pollock, you won't even make a half-century in this series, let alone a ton." Norm O'Neill on a Cavaliers trip to South Africa commented after his first innings failure, "We have promising youngsters like him by the dozen in Australia."

His view changed in the second innings when the blond PE youngster lambasted a double century. It's dangerous to scorn a genius, as O'Neill and that spectator were to find out.

Unfolding some of the grandest cover drives and hooks the Sydney Cricket Ground had ever seen, Graeme annihilated all who came to challenge his authority. His maiden Test century of 122 caused Lindsay Hassett to write, "I have never heard a sweeter note than the one young Graeme Pollock brought to Australia with his bat." A plaudit exemplar!

For the first time we had headed the Aussies on the first innings. The kangaroo's tail had been tweaked and we saw a vengeful response. Not a single century, but 450/9 is a massive reply in anybody's book. "Sonny, you are in Australia now," I could almost hear Geoff Dakin's prophecy! We had 433 minutes to score 409 to win. We couldn't afford to lose and go down 2-0. We were looking down the barrel. We were at the crossroads, the most crucial point of the tour. Skipper Goddard didn't have to say a word. We all knew what the next seven hours was going to mean. We didn't really contemplate winning. That would have been unrealistic. But an honourable draw we had to get. I doubt if seven hours have ever gone by slower, as we were hitting back with a truly magnificent team effort. Nobody got a century but nobody failed. Finally we were 83 runs short – 326/5, but it was a well-earned draw.

Our confidence had been boosted to the hilt. It was that moment of destiny. It's that defining fork in life's road, one way leads to success, the other to failure. And the route, the destiny, depends on your resilience and your will to succeed.

A memorable summer

The events in the next Test at Adelaide are what history raves about. Those seven hours at Sydney was the true delivery room. It was as good as a victory celebration as we cleared out of the Sydney changing room. For me the stress and tension had produced the grandmother of all migraine headaches. I had experienced a hamstring miracle, my brother's maiden Test century, seven hours of excruciating tension and a migraine. Statistically it was a match that is invariably glossed over, but to me it was one of the great contests – a Test in every respect.

Eddie, who had played such a vital role in convincing his team-mates that the positive approach was the only road to success, was quite fittingly the major figure in this triumph. It all started with a hassle. Johnny Waite wasn't fit and only minutes before the toss he decided to stand down. In came Denis Lindsay, a little angry and flustered, vowing that he would never get his wicket-keeping berth back. We lost the toss for the fourth time in a row but round one went to me. I had an altercation with Norman O'Neill at Sydney. Once the wicket had deadened in Sydney, Norman was full of back-chat describing my bouncers as "cream-puffs."

I struck early, getting Bill Lawry. In came O'Neill and six balls later he was back in the hut with a duck. In attempting to fend off a bouncer, he nudged the ball into Trevor Goddard's safe hands in the gully. "How is that for a cream-puff!" was the obvious retort as I followed through triumphantly down the pitch.

But again it was Simpson, Burge and Booth, the Aussie backbone who came to the rescue. Inexplicably, once again none of them got centuries. It was amazing how often in that series the home batters got out just short of the three-figure mark. The Australians are superstitious about 87 – representing 13 short of 100. That series saw many 87's, almost as if to confirm it as a dangerous mark!

The Australians totalled 345 and Goddard and Barlow began our innings. Trevor was nudging them here and there and Eddie whacked the odd boundary and the score mounted to 70. Then came the crisis and the turning-point. The bowler was Neil Hawke. His ungainly action was anything but textbook, but he had the ability to move the ball around quite disconcertingly. He started the over by clean bowling Goddard and then his next ball dismissed the luckless Tony Pithey.

In strode Graeme. The first two balls beat him all ends up. The next he met with the full face of the bat and sent it scurrying through the covers.

This was to be the pattern for the next four hours and forty minutes of play. Barlow and Pollock took complete control. They massacred the Australian bowling in a display of ruthless authority that was quite awesome. The duet that the two Springboks sang was so sweet that even the most ardent Aussie fan couldn't begrudge the sheer magnificence of it all. It was a double-barrelled assault. Like two matadors they accomplished the brutal and savage task with poise and grace. Barlow was cutting the Benaud flipper through the covers like Dad toying with his young son in the backyard while Graeme, as always, spoke with an eloquence that became his trademark.

Eddie finished with a brilliant double century and Graeme eventually succumbed to the wiles of Hawke for 175. But they had compiled 337 runs in one of the greatest partnerships of all time. Bill O'Reilly, Australia's doyen of cricket writers stood hatless in the press box to applaud Graeme as he left the crease. It's not customary for media men to get emotionally involved, but he stood to acknowledge greatness, not caring what anyone thought. Without wishing to detract from Eddie's contribution, there was little doubt that the role of Prince Charming belonged to Graeme. His innings was compiled with a laconic mastery almost incongruous and quite unbelievable in one so young and innocent of countenance!

An indelible chapter had been written in South African cricket history. Records tumbled and so did the reputations of the Australian bowlers. The Springboks finished with 595. A first innings lead of 250 was all the bowlers needed as inspiration and motivation.

The Aussies didn't give up easily. They never do. However, by late afternoon on the fourth day, a spirited sixth wicket partnership between Richie Benaud and Barry Shepherd was starting to raise a little consternation. Everything had been thrown at them but they were fighting back admirably.

At five o'clock, Eddie went up to the skipper. "Give me a go. I have a feeling I'll do them," demanded the burly Barlow. Eddie was hardly regarded as a genuine front-line bowler and Trevor ignored his initial pleas. But more badgering saw Eddie get his way, especially when he hinted, "If you don't give me the ball we will be in big trouble." There was such utter conviction. You ignore such determination only at your peril!

In his very first over Eddie sent down a long-hop and Shepherd, going for the hook, mistimed his shot and sent the ball skywards in the general direction of fine-leg. Denis Lindsay, pads and all, realizing that the ball wasn't going to carry to me at fine-leg, set off and a full-length dive climaxed a miraculous catch. But this was not to be the end. A couple of balls later Richie dragged one from outside the off-stump onto his wickets. In came Graham McKenzie. Eddie over-pitched a full toss which Graham hit in the meat, straight back at Eddie. Barlow relished the offering, snapped it up and in the space of a few minutes had changed the whole complexion of the match. It just goes to show what positive thinking can achieve.

The rest of the contest was a mere formality as we cantered home by ten wickets. Telegrams, long-distance phone calls and celebrations crowned it all. It was a moment to be sipped and savoured. Next was the decider at Sydney and the eyes of the cricket world would be focused on this new bunch of kids on the block! Certainly the Australian public had to take note.

There was, however, a rather interesting interlude, the match against the Prime Minister's XI at Canberra. Sir Robert Menzies was the Premier then and it was in this match that he had sacked Lindsay Hassett, the former Australian skipper. Sir Robert was a great friend to our team. He came to visit us in the dressing room at the Melbourne Test and we sensed not only his great love of the game, but also his wonderful way with people. Sir Robert's annual fixture against the touring team was an occasion to be treasured.

His team included two recently retired stalwarts in Alan Davidson and Neil Harvey. The most important men were, however, the two "technical advisers" appointed by the Prime Minister. Their duty was to ensure that the game finished in exciting fashion, a tie preferably! Who says match-fixing isn't as old as the hills! The two advisers were Hassett and Sam Loxton, with the former carrying the casting vote. One of the ground rules was that each batsman was entitled to a long-hop or full toss to get off the mark. Noughts were forbidden!

We amassed a total in the region of 280 and the home side, after a rather poor start, gradually got near 200. Then, horror of horrors, there was a collapse. With their last two batsmen at the crease the Prime Minister's team were 40 runs short.

The next few overs saw the South African bowlers giving away runs – full tosses down the leg-side with a packed offside field! The one tail-ender – Gallup by name – was rather inept with the bat, but our bowlers managed to keep him alive.

Eventually the scores were levelled and the crowd, ignorant of the "fixing" that was in progress, was getting very excited. Now Gallup had to get out. Brother Graeme was the bowler and as he delivered, he expected the dismissal to be a mere formality. But Gallup played the best shot of his innings. He cross-batted the ball to the boundary and the Springboks had been beaten. The fielders were dumbfounded. Graeme was a picture of bewildered amazement. "I was supposed to get a wicket with that ball," he declared. The umpires thought pretty quickly, but failed to find a solution.

In the grandstand, Sir Robert left his seat in disgust. He immediately fired his technical advisers but alas, too late! That evening at the banquet, Trevor Goddard jokingly ribbed Sir Robert about this great setback to our confidence! Gallup was called to explain himself. He pleaded guilty, told a joke and then was informed of his future non-availability for Menzies' teams! Hassett and Loxton were reinstated, but the record books will declare (forever) that South Africa were beaten by the Prime Minister's team at Canberra in 1964. It was all in fun, but we were reliably informed that Sir Robert was not only embarrassed, but also extremely annoyed about this "mistake."

The final Test at Sydney could be best described as "the one that got away." We were accused in many quarters of not knowing how to win. We were tagged "Goddard's Cinderellas." Many said that we lacked the self-belief and aggression to take the final step to victory. Goddard was accused of being negative or at least too tentative.

Trevor sent the Aussies in, hoping for a repeat of the third Test. It nearly worked, thanks to a magnificent spell by Joe Partridge, with seven wickets for 91. Australia made 311. Joe loved the Sydney ground. In the three matches he played there – two Tests and New South Wales – he claimed 27 wickets – nine on each outing.

This success inspired a wag to comment as the police circled the field at the close of play on day one, "Copper, you don't have to watch us. Watch Joe. He is going to steal that pitch and take it around the world with him." An apt summary of Joe's love affair with the Sydney ground! The Springboks replied with 411 and Colin Bland was the hero with 126. A first innings lead of 100 runs was a fair start.

With just over three hours remaining on the final day, the Aussies had 209/8 and it was South Africa all the way. But Tom Veivers and Neil Hawke came together and for nearly 80 minutes eked out an existence. They popped up catches, but in open spaces.

Finally, with only 85 minutes remaining, our victory target became 171 and the series ended with that empty feeling. We had lost because we were just a little too timid to take the initiative. Goddard's Cinderella's had run out on the Prince. Midnight, the destiny hour, had found them wanting.

Both Bill Lawry and Wally Grout in books titled *Run-digger* and *My Country's Keeper* echoed that sentiment. Grout called us the "bashful" Boks and suggested that we had beaten ourselves. In time we were to rectify that. Grout also acknowledged that I had truly got up their noses.

"Peter Pollock was a very fast bowler, but too prone to use the bouncer," he wrote. About the drawn final Test he acknowledged that the Aussies had escaped from jail but:

Our relief was offset by the fact that we could not get square with Peter Pollock. Peter probably doesn't know this, but there was a scheme cooking in the Aussie camp to cure him forever of his tendency to overdo the bumper, not against recognized batsmen who after all should be equipped to handle it. He was breaking the unwritten law by dealing it to tail-enders. In this match he got one up to Neil Hawke which cracked his fore-arm. We planned to give Peter what Heine and Adcock had given us in 1958, timed, as their attack had been to guarantee no retribution. But by not batting in SA's second innings, he escaped our wrath.

Lawry spoke in similar vein:

Pollock was a fiery speedster. Our batsmen came to dislike his bouncers. There were plans for retribution, but he never batted. Pollock had an outstanding foil in Joe Partridge. Pollock and Partridge were probably the best balanced new-ball attack in the world at that time, but the South African bowling standard fell away sharply once they had tired.

It had been a memorable summer. Australia had won my heart, not only as a country and a people, but also as a true kingdom of cricket. We had been, had seen, but had not quite been conquered!

3

HITCHES

New Zealand – 1964

New Zealand, especially after four and a half months of combat in Australia, was an anti-climax. From the magnificent grounds of Sydney and Melbourne to a showground shed at Dunedin, rugby changing rooms at Wellington and just a little sanity at Eden Park, Auckland, was a real come down. From a country that was vitally aware of the latest score or the form of Norman O'Neill, we moved to a nation that was more interested in how strong our Springbok rugby team was going to be for the tour of 1965!

Cricket appeared to be the last thing on any New Zealander's mind. Even the demonstrators at the airport appeared to enjoy more significance. Certainly they got more attention from the media and TV cameras. In Australia we had almost forgotten our status as skunks of apartheid as all eyes focused on cricket. Now they were back, hounding us like criminals.

In New Zealand life moved slower, the cars on the street were noticeably out of date and the weather and demonstrators were uncharitable. To get motivated under such circumstances was quite an achievement. We kept ourselves going simply by convincing ourselves that it had all been a thoroughly worthwhile trip so far, it should not be spoiled by any complacency on the final six-week leg! We had a reputation, albeit as "Cinderellas." We had shared a series with the mighty Aussies on their home turf and we were not going to allow any tarnishing from lowly New Zealand. For some of us there was also the matter of settling scores after the South African visit by John Reid's entourage. Elephants have good memories, so do cricketers!

We arrived a man short – Kelly Seymour had returned to South Africa for exams. To add to our problems, Graeme had broken a finger and Clive Halse was likely to restrict him to giving speeches and coaching sessions at schools!

That left us with only 12 fit players, so when Peter Carlstein had to leave the touring party during the first Test because of a family tragedy at home, we no longer even needed selectors. We all had to play! You couldn't just fly people in and out the way they do in these modern times.

Perhaps we are spoiled in South Africa with our fabulous facilities, but should anyone complain, just send him to New Zealand and he will soon stop beefing! The wicket was a veritable "cabbage patch" as we prepared for the first Test at the Basin Reserve ground in windy Wellington. Some demonstrators decided on the night before the game, to dig up the wicket. Fortunately they dug in the wrong place – so badly defined and prepared was the wicket. Even we, in broad daylight might have picked the wrong area! What chance did the demonstrators have under cover of darkness?

Coming from Port Elizabeth, I reckoned that I knew about wind, but Wellington was something else. It blew straight up and down the wicket and the icy blasts were even too much for me. One day it was so cold that I bowled with two long-sleeved sweaters. At the drinks break, we were served hot soup. How is that for congenial Test cricket atmosphere?

In the middle of the Test pitch was a deep trench caused by the rugby halfway line. Grass had grown in this trench and I had a wonderful time bowling there. If the ball pitched on the one side it was a bouncer, on the other it was a shooter. No wonder there was much ducking and weaving. John Sparling actually ducked to one of my deliveries, expecting a flier. It didn't get up and he was adjudged lbw! The pitch was also very slow and soft, so much so that the bowler's footmarks became a massive and highly dangerous hole. Without exaggeration, it really was a nightmare.

By the third day the foot-holes had become a hazard and could so easily have caused a broken ankle. I just couldn't bowl in these conditions and Trevor insisted that I came round the wicket. "But I can't," I replied, "otherwise I am going to run slap down the middle of the pitch." "Let me worry about that," he said and off I went on my mission of no mercy. Sure enough the umpire complained, but Trevor put him in his place. "Unless you have got a concrete mixer to fill that other hole, we don't have an option," was his terse comment. That was that. I carried on and finished with eight wickets in the match. The pace of the game matched the pace of the wicket and the uncharitable weather.

On the first day we managed 233 in six hours and on the second we added 69 before the Kiwis made 117/4 – a total of 186 in six hours. Maybe that's why New Zealanders prefer watching rugby! Finally we set the home side a target of 268 for victory and by close they were struggling at 138/6 in the most tiresome of draws. John Reid failed in both innings and he proved to be the real disappointment of the series – that is obviously to the home crowd! In three matches he only managed 88 runs and was completely bogged down by Trevor

Goddard and spinner David Pithey. It all just went to prove the validity of the "con" they had managed in South Africa, for Reid hated slow stuff. He couldn't stand being bogged down. The umpiring of Rowan and Egar in Australia had also spoilt the Springboks and their New Zealand counterparts were clearly not in the same bracket. In fact, they were downright poor and we soon got the message. We would definitely not benefit from any marginal decisions and lbw's would be hard to come by. Indeed we had our work cut out trying to persuade the officials that lbws were also part of the game!

Trevor wasn't one to complain about umpires. In fact he was usually pretty good at getting them on his side. But he often shook his head in disgust. Obviously the more you complain and show disagreement, the harder you make it for yourself. We were palpably aware of that, but the build-up of frustration was such that we just became our own enemies. Umpires are also only human with human emotions and responses. We had often talked about that and about how foolish it was to rub them up the wrong way. But we were not taking too much of our own advice!

The venue for the second Test was Dunedin, a good deal closer to the South Pole than Wellington. The first day was rained out completely, the second was cold and drizzly, but we played. On the third it was icier than the second and on the fourth and final day it was warm enough to survive with only a sleeveless pullover under your long-sleever! It was in Dunedin that we changed in "sheds" – for want of a better description. The floors were not even concrete, they were solid earth and outside the pitch looked rather strange. Set in a lush field of thick and heavy green grass, the wicket was almost as white as concrete, but as soft as chalk.

While the game was going on, construction work was proceeding in the main pavilion. We had hammers banging away all day working on what was to become a great rugby stadium. We felt like intruders. Most of the spectators were the workmen during their breaks. Had I not witnessed it for myself, I would never have believed that Test cricket could be played under such trying circumstances. Certainly it was a far, far cry from Lord's. New Zealand totalled 149 at snail's pace and at one stage, with Goddard and Barlow really motoring, we were 117/0. Joe Partridge and I were suffering from acute tonsillitis and with the openers going so well, manager Ken Viljoen suggested that the two fast bowlers should get back to bed at the hotel.

We were happy to go. Anything to get us out of the "shed" and the cold. We were both on antibiotics and happened to be sharing a room. We got back to the hotel. Each had a hot bath and settled down under the blankets. After a couple of hours we decided to switch on the radio – there was no TV – to get the latest score. Imagine the shock to hear that six wickets were down and that in fact I was next but one to pad up! We were scrambling into our gear as the telephone rang. It was manager Ken in a panic. Into a taxi and off we sped. I had just enough time to pad up before I was out in the middle. Needless to say that I didn't give the scorer much to do! Our first innings lead was a mere 74, but that could be enough on the clay-pit that was the pitch. David Pithey collected six wickets as he tumbled out the New Zealanders, but time was running out. Indeed it boiled down a target of 65 in 27 minutes. We managed only 42 with the New Zealanders ensuring a minimum of balls bowled. Eight hours had been lost, but we just so narrowly missed sneaking a win in two and a half days. But we couldn't get out of Dunedin fast enough!

The only really worthwhile encounter was the decider at Eden Park where the sun shone and you could even go without a jersey. The 'King of Swing,' Joe Partridge, took six wickets to help us lead by 108 runs on the first innings and a winning target of 309 in about five hours was set. The record books show that the Kiwis were eight wickets down and 118 in arrears when time was called. David Pithey shouted himself hoarse and Trevor Goddard did everything but suggest that the umpire was a cheat. But the series was drawn. Bad luck had followed us from the moment we had arrived in New Zealand. Many players sustained injuries, the weather was bad and tragedy struck the Carlstein family back home. Of interest is that not a single batsman notched a first-class century.

What I prefer to remember is that New Zealand is truly beautiful. The scenery is quite awesome. Those picturesque pastures, the sheep-covered hills, the snowy mountains, big fat trout and the amazing Rotorua where hot air bubbles even came out of the drains and the smell of sulphur kills even the most potent of deodorants. Maybe, as I wrote at the time, it is just as well that rugby rules supreme in the land of the long white cloud!

The time in New Zealand had been very successful for me personally. In the three Tests, I added another 15 wickets to the 25 I had taken in Australia to bring the Australasian haul to a massive 40 scalps, two more than Joe Partridge. In the process I had established some sort of record because in the first Test at Wellington I reached the 50 mark in Test wickets in only nine matches! Frightening however, was that 78 wickets belonged to the Pollock-Partridge combination.

While the Australasian tour could be described as a great success, it didn't stop the 'knockers' at home. Goddard's captaincy came under severe scrutiny and mixed with the plaudits showered on the players, were suggestions that the selectors had blundered by leaving a lot of better players at home. A fixture was arranged to test these opinions. Five months after we had returned, a Rest of South Africa side was selected to take on Goddard's tourists. There was some other reason given for organizing the match, but in real terms it was a trial. Trevor was absolutely livid as were many other members of the touring party. "I am dead against this sort of thing," he said most emphatically.

"We should learn to accept the success or failure of touring sides and not subject them to possible humility. Don't forget none of us has held a bat for five months," was the captain's view. There was great tension and determination on the first morning. It was an ill-advised exercise, to say the least.

Anyway, history records that it was the Rest who suffered the humiliation. Goddard's team notched an incredible 618/4 in the 360 minutes of the first day. Pithey, Pollock, Bland and Lindsay all smote centuries in an almost vengeful assault on Jackie McGlew's bowling attack. Bouncers flew as I took five wickets in bundling them out for 241. Trevor was not interested in what the media or public thought as he enforced the follow-on to complete the rout by an innings and 129 runs. To this day Trevor still regrets that match and particularly the motives that had conspired such a pointless duel.

England: 1964 – 1965

If ever a series was a long yawn, it was the 1964 – '65 tour to South Africa of Mike Smith's English side. "You can play the attacking cricket, we are more interested in the results," was a comment made at Port Elizabeth. This typified the general strategy of the English approach to Test cricket. Start out playing for a draw. If the opposition slips, then take full advantage. That's about it. Local fans and the media were crowing about the fluent attacking abilities of the South African side. In golf they say you "drive for show and putt for dough." That's all the English were saying. They were certainly not in the business of winning friends and entertaining the public. Their brief simply was to bring home the bacon and they were not going to apologize for, or be swayed from that philosophy.

The touring side had some natural stroke-makers of the calibre of Ted Dexter, Bob Barber and Jim Parks, but the lasting memories of that tour would revolve around the dogged survival of Geoff Boycott and Ken Barrington. These two deserve the highest accolades for their patience and endurance. Pitches that were as dead as the proverbial Dodo were a constant source of frustration. There was no help for pace and seam bowlers and it was a long, long summer. What really killed the series was the tourists' winning the first Test at Durban on a pitch that was nothing short of a cabbage patch.

Fred Titmus and Dave Allen, the two off-spinners, made merry and once the lead had been established, Smith was just happy to sit tight. Towards the end of the tour, injuries also came into the reckoning. Even Mike will admit to a somewhat fortuitous start, but he accepted his good fortune gratefully and left us to do the running.

The pitches were the big problem. When we first saw the Kingsmead pitch, we were shattered. The groundsman had been asked to prepare a hard, fast and bouncy pitch. Obviously to him that meant it had to be rolled hard as a rock and shaved clean! That's what he did, even going as far as especially hiring a heavy roller from the Durban municipality! His intentions were good. It was the application that went awry. You did not have to be an expert to see at first glance that it was going to be slow and might even crumble. Batting first was consequently a prerequisite. Smith called correctly and that was that! In my very first over I tried a bouncer at Geoff Boycott. I put everything I had into the delivery, but it just looped over his head – a "cream-puff."

It was ludicrous. I think I even managed one of those hopeless smiles as I shook my head in disgust. It was one of those extreme instances when you either laugh or cry. The new ball was worthless within six or seven overs, torn to shreds by the pitch. The humidity was high, the pitch was dead and the English couldn't believe their good fortune. An opportunity like this was not to be squandered.

By tea on the second afternoon only five wickets had fallen as England called it a day with 485. Then followed the Springbok procession and Titmus and Allen went through us like a dose of Epsom salts. The ball turned square and it was hard to avoid showing embarrassment as we trooped in and out with heads hanging low.

An interesting development came from the British media. Always on the lookout for fresh angles, it was suggested that the English spinners had discovered Graeme's Achilles heel – spinners! What a joke. All his life Graeme, like Barry Richards, had regarded spinners as runs for jam. In fact, he would talk about "milking" them. In other words, ensuring that you didn't blast them out of an attack! Maybe it was just an attempt at psychological warfare on the part of the pressmen. Graeme simply adored the slow bowlers. Had they already forgotten his mauling of Benaud in Australia? "Don't let the facts stand in the way of a good angle" – that's the adage of some tabloid media men.

The Kingsmead pitch was a travesty. I would only have rated the pitch at Duneden in the same category. There were the inevitable witch-hunts. The pitch got far more blame than the cricketers, but it didn't help us, for the shattering defeat clearly affected our morale and this was evident in the early stages of the second Test at the Wanderers. Largely as a legacy of the Durban shambles, Titmus and Allen had us in trouble again. Although the Wanderers was a good batting strip, once you lose confidence against bowlers of Test calibre, it becomes a long psychological haul to turn the tables.

The Wanderers game followed much the same pattern as Durban with England first up and amassing a huge 531. Barrington notched another century, but the colossus of the innings was Ted Dexter, with a magnificent 172. He showed himself to be governed by discernible moods. He was irresistibly brilliant at times and then for no rhyme or reason, he just seemed to lose interest merely tapping the ball back to the bowler. We had to follow on after 317 first innings runs, but then the tide turned.

Muddying the water for the English spinners was a brilliant Colin Bland whose undefeated 144 turned Titmus and Allen from ogres to pretty ordinary guys. For the first time in the series Mike Smith was forced to remove his spinners from the firing line as Bland heaved some soaring sixes. This innings was the injection we needed as we moved down to Cape Town for the traditional New Year's Test at Newlands. In those days winning the toss was essential. Trevor called right and we declared at 501/7. That took two days to which England replied with two days occupation, a first innings deficit of 59 and no earthly chance of a result. In three Tests England had lost only 25 wickets while amassing nearly 1500 runs. We were also starting to join in the run-glut. The ball was losing its unequal battle with the bat and the fans were fidgeting in the stands.

Fortunately for the media there was a little controversy. Eddie Barlow and Ken Barrington were the major role players and the encounter was finally tagged the "Tarnished Test."

Wisdens' comment was: "Long after the un-enterprising cricket of this Test is forgotten, people will talk of the two incidents which brought to a head whether a batsman should walk or not. With close in-fielders convinced both times that umpire Warner was wrong to turn down appeals for catches, the first at short leg and the second by the wicket-keeper, Barlow of South Africa stood his ground and Barrington of England made his way to the pavilion."

Whether by design or not, Barlow was made the villain and Barrington the hero! Barlow played forward to Titmus, got his legs in a tangle and the ball popped amiably into the eager hands of gully.

Barlow stood and the umpire signalled not out. Titmus accused the South African of being a cheat and Barlow retaliated with a few choice words of his own plus the threat of putting his bat across the bowler's head. Eddie had 40 at the time and proceeded to concentrate even harder to accumulate 138.

The Englishmen failed to applaud any of his milestones and their annoyance was made even more obvious by the exaggerated enthusiasm they showed in acknowledging the other South African achievements that day. Eddie was within his right to stand. It was by no means a clear open and shut case. Titmus erred in his verbal onslaught. Later in the match Fred ventured into our changing room to tender an apology, "My captain has ordered me to apologize," he said, clearly under protest! Eddie's stance was more jocular, "I couldn't walk because my toe was too sore," He steadfastly maintained that he didn't edge the ball. He stuck to his story. The jury is still out on that one!

Then came Barrington. He was nearing his half-century when I was brought on just before tea. One delivery rose sharply just outside the off-stump and

Barrington tickled it neatly into the hands of Lindsay. The whole team joined in the appeal and I didn't even look back as I triumphantly marched down the pitch, hands held aloft. But then I stopped. Barrington had not moved. I swung round and looked at the motionless umpire. He was not going to give him out.

Seconds ticked by like an eternity and it was clear that umpire Warner didn't feel that Barrington had got a nick. He was not going to put his finger up. Finally, after waiting long enough to make a mockery of the umpire, Barrington put his bat under his arm and walked. I was most relieved and applauded his gesture of sportsmanship. I believe Ken's gesture was sincere, but it certainly stirred up a hornet's nest in the press box.

The hours preceding the fourth Test at the Wanderers were full of high drama. I was sharing a room with my comrade-in-arms, Joe Partridge, and after our team talk on the eve of the Test we had a team dinner. Joe and I unwisely decided on prawn cocktails as starters. These turned out to be anything but amorous prawns and in the middle of the night both of us got very sick. Poor old Joe just could not stop vomiting.

The selectors were informed early the next morning and they tried to make alternative arrangements. They even thought about an Air Force jet to fly in Mike Macauley who had done extremely well for Free State against the tourists, as a last minute replacement for Joe. But it could not be arranged. Joe was extremely blue and I not much better as we set off to the Wanderers that morning. It was a hot day and all we needed was to field first.

On what appeared to be a perfectly good batting wicket, Mike Smith won the toss and then suffered some kind of mental lapse. He sent us in to bat. What a tremendous relief. Joe went back to the hotel to spend the rest of the day in bed and our batsmen managed the reasonable total of 390/6. It was a great moment for Trevor Goddard when he notched his maiden Test century, a feat that had inexplicably eluded him for close on a decade. But he so nearly fell at 99, chasing a quick single which all but got him run out!

About three hours were lost to rain over the first couple of days and the inevitable draw loomed. A target was set – 314 runs at 78 runs to the hour. I managed an early breakthrough which included the prized scalp of Ted Dexter. There was even a faint sniff of victory, but snap went my hamstring. Deeply frustrated I had to watch the final two hours from the pavilion as Geoff Boycott, with a typically stubborn effort, spearheaded a recovery that earned another draw. It was a moral triumph for us, but those don't count.

In Test cricket you simply have to bowl the other side out twice in five days and we had failed. We had become the aggressors, for what that was worth.

The series ended in Port Elizabeth where the most notable achievement was a century by Graeme Pollock in a first innings total of 502. The pitch, once again, was a beauty – a batsmen's paradise – and England ensured that the game was going to die its inevitable death by responding 67 runs short, thanks mainly to another lengthy Boycott crease occupation! He loved the St George's Park pitch, for in the game against EP he was undefeated just short of 200 made in ten hours!

In my frustration I had actually been very naughty. I deliberately bowled two beamers at him. Worse, I didn't even apologise or make the excuse that the ball had slipped. Years later I finally asked his forgiveness, which he accorded with reservations!

We completed the first innings only after tea on the fourth day. What chance of a result! Rain thankfully intervened and the series ended on a symbolically correct damp note. Mike Smith was happy. He had achieved what he set out to do – beat the Springboks.

Unfortunately the series did have an unpleasant undercurrent. The home selectors, headed by Arthur Coy, wanted to make a change in captaincy. They had nominated Trevor for the series, but in Cape Town during the third Test they felt that perhaps they should reverse their decision. Apparently they felt that Trevor was not providing the dynamic leadership required to salvage the rubber. I don't for one minute believe that it was Trevor's fault, but the world is always looking for a scapegoat.

Complaining about pitches seems more like sour grapes, so Goddard became the target. They hoped that Trevor would give them an easy way out. They even prepared a statement for him. He was going to relinquish the captaincy because it was interfering with and affecting his bowling and batting. Trevor would have nothing to do with such ploys. He refused to play ball and told them if they wanted to drop him they would need to have the courage of their convictions. I admired him for that, but it ensured that he was most certainly not going to be available to tour England a few months later.

Certainly Trevor wasn't a leader in the Jackie McGlew, Richie Benaud or Frank Worrell class, but he deserved to be given his due. He had done a more than adequate job. To blame him for the summer of 1964 – '65 was unfair to say the least. And the way in which it was done – asking him to virtually sign his own death warrant – just added insult to injury.

The fact that the English only once in five first innings totals managed less than 400 and that five of the SA batsmen notched more that 400 runs in the series, shows something badly out of kilter. I was the leading wicket-taker for South Africa with a mere 12 scalps – four more than the next best Athol McKinnon. Only Titmus and Allen took more than 10 wickets amongst the English bowlers. In the light of what went before and what was to follow in England, the 1964 – '65 South African summer was won hands down by the curators!

4

SUMMIT

The Springboks in England – 1965

I f ever a team had the odds stacked against them it was Peter van der Merwe's 1965 Springboks in England. There was no Trevor Goddard, smarting after his run-in with the selectors, and to make matters worse, Tony Pithey withdrew from the original side, leaving Eddie Barlow without a recognized opening partner. I felt that the selectors had also erred in not picking Joe Partridge. Joe's control of swing and seam would have been perfectly suited to the English conditions. But he was getting old and his fielding was shoddy, so he stayed at home!

With the tour starting in mid-June, it meant that we lacked match practice. The England players had already enjoyed the opportunity of gaining confidence and running into form against the New Zealanders in the first half of that summer. To make matters worse, we were plagued by incessant rain almost from the moment we arrived. It not only reduced some of our opening matches on that tour to a shambles, but also continually interrupted net practices.

We lost our very first match against Derbyshire and skipper van der Merwe responded, "I am pleased about that. Now we won't have an unbeaten record to worry about." One way to look at it!

Three weeks of utter frustration, with bad weather our constant bedfellow, was all we had before the bus edged its way through the Grace Gates at Lord's for the first Test. We had only one victory in seven matches – and that against the lowly minor counties. The rain had won all the other fixtures! Even our practice on the eve of the Test was washed out. Not many pressmen gave us a chance, but though we had no right to feel this way, deep down there was confidence in our camp, typified perhaps by a remark made by Colin Bland.

Practice had been abandoned and we were just boarding the bus at Lord's when along came Fred Titmus, with his jaunty stride and a face full of smiles. He had every reason to feel chirpy because he had taken 15 wickets in the three Tests against New Zealand, including a hat-trick. "Well bowled Fred," said one of us. "It was against the blind school," replied Fred, attempting a show of modesty. "You couldn't be more bloody right than that," piped Bland and in the next two months proceeded to show Fred that he had been playing against no-hopers.

The South Africans got first use of the Lord's pitch which had a bit of grass, but didn't look particularly dangerous. It was a stop start innings. With contributions all around, including tail-enders Jackie Botten and me, the final mark of 280 was reasonable. England passed it by 58, thanks to the indomitable Ken Barrington who had become a real thorn in our flesh. Two run-outs virtually turned that match. Barrington's dismissal saw Colin run in from mid-wicket to mid-on to gather and throw without hesitation. A single stump was all he saw from his angle, but he threw it down with Ken yards out of his crease.

Jim Parks was the other victim. Realizing that he was in trouble with the ball already in Colin's hand, he tried to obstruct the path of the throw with his body. Dangerous, I would have thought. A ball in the kidneys from Bland is a high price to pay! There was a gap. Colin took it and a new national hero had emerged. His mere presence, patrolling the covers like a panther, saved us many runs. The batters refused to take the slightest risk and fielding had now been taken into a new dimension.

Certainly those two run-outs were match turning! In character with the fluctuating fortunes of the encounter, our second innings was full of ups and downs. England was left to score 191 in just four hours, by no means an impossible task.

In fact they should have "cake-walked" it. "We could have done it in singles," said Mike Smith ruefully after the match, but they paid the penalty for being too cautious. Why they were so tentative, heaven only knows. They pushed and prodded and finally were lucky to survive with a draw – at 145/7 wickets when stumps were drawn. In real terms they were eight down because John Edrich was in hospital with concussion, the result of ducking into one of my deliveries.

The incident had its roots back in 1963 when John toured South Africa with Richie Benaud's Cavaliers side. In the game against Eastern Province he appeared to have a lot of trouble picking up my bouncer and once or twice I nearly decapitated him! After the game one evening, as we sipped a couple of beers in the dressing room, John foolishly admitted to me that he had trouble picking my bouncer. In other words he found it difficult reading just when it was going to come. With most fast bowlers you see extra strain, bigger strides or some gesture that indicates the extra effort needed, but he admitted that I had him stone cold. It was a silly admission! But psychologically I felt I had it over him. Perhaps he didn't think we would meet again? John had made merry against the New Zealanders, including a triple century.

In the first innings I confirmed that I had the edge on him with an lbw decision following an extremely tentative prod. I remembered our discussion.

Then came the second innings. I sent down a bouncer, the very first ball. But shortly afterwards, obviously expecting another, he ducked prematurely. The ball was well pitched and it made a terrible thud as it crashed into the side of his head near the temple. The thudding noise – in those days there was no protective helmets – could be heard around the ground. He stood up dazed and wobbly, looked around, grabbed his head and then dropped like a log.

I was immediately pulled away and my team-mates gathered around to offer aid. One said to me, "You have lost your touch. He didn't drop immediately." Meant as a joke, no doubt, but nevertheless a rather sick appraisal of the situation. At that moment I must admit that I felt a bit hollow inside, but it was part and parcel of the game, a natural hazard. If you can't take it, there is no point in playing. From a fast bowler's point of view you can't allow yourself to be upset by such an incident. In fact, the killer instinct should stir to greater pace and venom, as indeed it did to me that afternoon.

The incident was soon set aside unemotionally, but the Test ended with the Springboks very much rampant. Tail-enders Titmus and Brown could hardly have been spotted by the spectators, being so encircled by close fielders. They must have felt as claustrophobic as General Custer on his famous last stand. Custer died, but Brown and Titmus survived!

David Brown and I were involved in a rather strange altercation. Early in the match we had shared harsh words. I hated the big holes that bowlers tended to dig with their footmarks. My ankles were not the strongest and the new front-foot no-ball-rule had ensured that all bowlers were now landing in the same spot and this annoyed me very much. Groundsmen tried to fix up the problem at the end of each day, but generally there were few who had mastered the art of replacing sods or filling in adequately.

The one morning I was batting and Brown, the bowler, had also lost his temper with the footmarks and started kicking out the sods. I suggested that he was acting like a schoolboy and he told me to get lost. So this continual sniping at each other went on. He tried a few bouncers, but I have always enjoyed the hook and my success as I dispatched the ball to the boundary only increased the acrimony between us.

The final afternoon had him at the crease. A bouncer was the opening salvo and it hit him in a painful spot, but earned him a leg-bye. He was furious. He got to the bowler's end glaring at me. Up I came for the next delivery and he moved over and actually bumped me in my delivery stride. Umpire Dusty Rhodes couldn't believe what he was seeing, nor could Peter van der Merwe. Afterwards one of the English players excused Brown by saying, "You know he is one of those rugby chaps. They are a bit physical. Perhaps he thought he was at Twickenham!" But it didn't happen again.

Turning-point at Trent Bridge

I believe Trent Bridge was one of the greatest and most significant Tests of the era and I say that despite the fact that it was a huge personal triumph for the Pollock family. It still stands as one of the most notable family performances in Test cricket history, but as the years have rolled by, I have become more and more convinced that it was not only a crossroads experience, but also a massive turning-point in the fortunes of South African cricket. It was a moment of destiny.

It also was just one of those games that had everything – drama, tension, uncertainty and the beauty that only a genius like Graeme Pollock can bring to any set of proceedings. I say all that humbly and with complete fraternal diffidence because the views, opinions and observations that were accorded during the match, have in fact truly stood the test of time.

South African cricket came of age that day. What a scene there was in our changing room after the game with the champagne flowing, the spirits high and a magnificent Test triumph under our belts. A memorable moment indeed, and as the years have ebbed away, its significance has become more and more profound.

It wasn't with any sense of destiny that Eddie Barlow and Tiger Lance strode onto the wicket that first morning to take advantage of their skipper's correct call at the toss. The inevitable butterflies no doubt accompanied them, but they were probably flying in formation! Not too many problems were expected from the pitch. It looked a bit grey and grassless and because the sun was shining the whole day prior to the game, it was a good toss to win.

But there were some devils out there! Tom Cartwright brought them into play as he wobbled the ball around most disconcertingly, both through the air and off the seam. By the time we had reached 40 runs, Barlow, Lindsay, Lance and Bland were back in the pavilion. When it got to 80 Ali Bacher joined them in the showers.

Doom and gloom abounded. I couldn't bear the tension. I locked myself in a backroom as the captain went out to join Graeme. My brother was looking good and taking the fight to the Englishmen. Whatever the cost, he was going to be the aggressor. Attack is, they say, the best form of defence! Graeme took the English attack in his teeth and shook it like a dog would do with a rag doll.

Before the innings ended, Graeme had become a legend. I was locked away, but to us, in those circumstances he was beyond any comparison. His total of 125 was brilliant, he had played with exceptional charm and grace. Even the doyen of cricket writers, E.W. Swanton, was lost for adjectives, such was the dominance and magnificence of the young blond South African left-hander. In 70 minutes after lunch Graeme and his captain put on 102 runs. I just heard the applause, but superstition prevented me from watching. Finally the team said it would be safe for me to come out of hiding. We were out of trouble and my little brother had his century. I came out just in time to see him dismissed!

Graeme wasn't happy about his dismissal, caught in the slips by Colin Cowdrey. He believed – and still does – that he hit the ground and that the ball had deflected from the footmarks. He was thus not in the happiest of moods when he arrived back at the pavilion. He was pretty abrupt with Sir Leonard Hutton who had come in to add his congratulations. Graeme, in fact, was still so flushed and sweating, not to mention annoyed over getting out, that he didn't recognise Sir Len. Hutton, who didn't often do this sort of thing, but once Graeme realized whom he was talking to, he turned on the charm and acknow-ledged the praise.

Trent Bridge had just witnessed one of the great moments of Test cricket. The Springboks finally totalled 269. Considering our predicament, it was a brilliant recovery.

That evening saw England needing to bat out 30 minutes. With the second ball I bowled, Boycott got an edge and the ball flew to Tiger Lance in the slips. There were palpitations all round as he fumbled and juggled with the ball. Finally he got it under control.

Before the England total had reached double figures, Ken Barrington had succumbed. It was my mother's birthday. What a present we had given her. The beers tasted good that evening.

The highlight of the second day was a faultless century by Colin Cowdrey. When he was in form he had so much time to play. As a bowler Colin made you feel that you were only operating at half-pace – he moves so quickly into line and timed his shots so effortlessly. What more could you ask for? A Pollock century on the first day, followed by a Cowdrey classic on the second. Five wickets was my contribution as England failed by 29 runs to reach our total. Eddie Barlow had hurt his toe, so Lindsay and Lance opened our second knock and immediately our backs were to the wall.

The third day see-sawed like a schooner on the high seas. Bacher, Barlow and Pollock all managed half-centuries and there was some lower order resistance to ensure a target of over 300. It was anybody's game, even though up till then, as the critics pointed out, England had never made 300 or more in a final innings to win a Test match. We were not prepared to put too much reliance on history. The wicket was still true and England had the batsmen to do the job.

Forty-five minutes of play remained that Saturday evening. We needed a quick breakthrough. It was absolutely vital. In my second over, Bob Barber got a neat edge to Denis Lindsay and in the final over Atholl McKinnon had night-watchman Fred Titmus caught. Two wickets were down, a few balls had to be played and out came a second night-watchman, this time John Snow. This was a controversial move, one that displeased the critics. To employ two fill-ins meant that top batsmen would be relegated well down the order and perhaps run out of partners. Also John Snow's presence meant that we would have a fresh go at an easy wicket first thing on the Monday morning. An early success would be just the right tonic, argued the experts.

The England camp was certainly not as happy as ours. What an exciting and momentous final day it proved to be. Fortunes fluctuated agonisingly, as if that maestro of suspense and intrigue, Agatha Christie, had written the script.

As expected, Snow fell early prey and it was 10/3. Three runs later Barrington tried to hook one of my bouncers and it was four wickets down for a mere 13 runs. We had to rub our eyes in disbelief as Cowdrey joined Boycott, but at 41 Denis Lindsay brought off one of the finest stumpings I had ever seen. Cowdrey, in attempting a leg-glance off McKinnon, missed the ball, but lifted his foot just a fraction of a second. Lindsay whipped off the bails and his most remarkable feat got the umpire's approving nod. Meanwhile, Boycott held on grimly, perhaps too much so! Though he was keeping his wicket intact, he was still allowing the opposition bowlers to dictate terms. Close in-fielders were retained and Boycott eventually succumbed.

Acknowledging a Greater Force

Then started the real fun as first Peter Parfitt and Mike Smith, then Parfitt and Jim Parks launched spectacular rearguard actions. It was time to attack and the Parks-Parfitt combination started to worry and frustrate us. There was some rain and drizzle and the ball was slippery. Their buccaneering approach revealed the folly of the earlier batters, who between them had occupied the crease for 270 minutes in scoring a paltry 127. In just one hour Parks and Parfitt added 80 priceless runs.

If I said we were worried, it would be an understatement. Our fielding and bowling had lost their edge and I was beginning to visualize the match slipping away.

For the first time in my cricketing career I secretly asked God to help. I was fielding at third man and I knew that a crisis was on hand. I bowed my head ever so slightly, that nobody would really notice, just in case they might think I was mad! I then desperately asked God to help. I even suggested that if He allowed me to come on and get those three wickets, I would not have a single celebratory drink that evening. That would be the cost, my penance! I would abstain totally.

A few overs later I was summoned to bowl. Success didn't come straight away, but when it did, it was spectacular. First Parfitt played across the line and was clean bowled. I don't think I have ever been more relieved to see someone head back to the pavilion. In the same over, Cartwright was leg before wicket. Larter got away with a few streaky shots and then, in attempting just one too many, he lofted the ball skywards in the direction of mid-off. Waiting under it was Peter van der Merwe, his big hands looking the size of the Grand Canyon, ready to swallow the offering. It felt like an eternity as he was waiting for the ball to drop out of the sky, but finally it was pouched and then tossed heavenwards. The whole team erupted. We had finally beaten England – in England!

It was one of the proudest moments of my life as I led the team off the field, having taken a further five wickets in the second innings for a match tally of ten. What pandemonium in our dressing room with well wishers and supporters.

But now was the hard part for me. I had to honour my promise to God. I could not have a drink. I was utterly determined. Half an hour went by and the merriment increased. I couldn't stand it so I went for a shower. The rest of the chaps were in their underpants, their jockstraps and some merely with towels around their waists. This was a moment to be sipped, savoured and enjoyed, except by me. I towelled down and changed and by then an hour had elapsed. The seconds and the minutes ticked by so slowly and everyone was so busy enjoying themselves, I don't think they noticed me, neatly dressed and so sober.

After two hours of this purgatory I had had enough. I sneaked back into the shower area. There I bowed my head, thanked God for the victory and then asked, "Isn't two hours enough, Lord?" I had at least honoured my deal. Now I was asking to be pardoned, or better still, excused for my human frailty! We all tend to believe what we want, but while I was still in the shower area, just after asking for latitude, I was joined by a London bobby who had been assigned to our side. His job was to ensure that no demonstrators or activists hounded us. He had a spare beer in his hand. Looking at me he said, "Peter why are you so glum? You guys have won a cricket Test. Celebrate. Have a beer." That was what I wanted to hear. I convinced myself that it was God's answer to my plea. Two hours was enough!

With a quick and very relieved "Thank you, Lord!" under my breath, I launched into that bottle of beer with the fervour of a man dying of thirst. Whether God had really said it was all right, wasn't the issue. I heard what I wanted and at the very least, I had acknowledged Him. That's the way I rationalized. And what a party! I made up for the two hours I had lost. We got up to the craziest of antics, including some piddling on the pitch! Fortunately in those days the media did draw the line somewhere!

Trent Bridge – this name still stirs emotions and memories, especially of those involved in 1965. It was an incredible four days. As the years have passed by, I have been convinced more and more that God's hand stroked that match in a mighty way! Not by way of a short term victory, but rather as one of those unprecedented moments of destiny. And in the midst of it all there was, even way back then, an acknowledgement of The Almighty.

So to the final Test at the Oval and the surprising recall of Brian Statham. What a great guy he is . We did consider it a great compliment that the selectors had to resort to resurrecting the old campaigners in an attempt to square the series. Why not Freddie Trueman as well? Though 35 years old, Brian was still regarded as the most accurate fast bowler in the country and we knew that his tight control would be a factor. Another newcomer, Ken Higgs, Statham's county new-ball partner was also included and between the two they captured all but one of our first innings wickets as we collapsed to 208 after being invited to bat first.

Once again it was my lot to answer that challenge and another five-wicket haul – the third in a row – saw England out for 202, six runs behind. A brilliant 127 from Bland spearheaded the second dig and with seven hours remaining in the contest, England had to chase a mammoth target of 399. I didn't think that England would even consider the challenge. But they certainly did and in the process produced their best cricket of the series. Ken Barrington and Colin Cowdrey were the main instigators. With seventy minutes to go and six wickets in hand, England only needed another 91 runs to secure a fairy tale and historic victory. The pitch had ironed out into a featherbed. Will I ever forget that final day? I did most of the bowling from the one end and for the first time in the series my role was that of a defensive bowler.

We also needed to waste a bit of time. "Don't rush through your overs," instructed the captain. All day the clouds, big heavy ones, had dominated the ceiling above us, but there was no relief. Several times we would see huge black clouds pass over, but there was no such luck of rain. We were getting a bit desperate. "You will have to bowl the rest of the afternoon," the skipper told me after tea. I wasted a bit of time and was booed occasionally. I didn't feel too bad because in the previous seven encounters against England they had wasted time and played negatively. This was our first time, with 91 to get in 70 minutes.

Fate, or someone, came to the rescue! The rain-bearing clouds had seemingly vanished, but along came one lonely little black cloud. It stopped right above the Kennington Oval and opened all its taps. The water bucketed down. What a relief. I didn't run off the field like the other Springboks. I was too weary having already sent down some 20 overs. I enjoyed every drop as I walked back very slowly. Irate members were shaking their umbrellas at me as I came through the gates. They obviously felt strongly that I had wasted time. But I could not have cared less. They were rude and angry and the brollies were menacing, but walking next to me was our own tough guy, Tiger Lance. I felt quite safe.

The rain became a deluge, much to our delight. Soon there were pools of water where fielders had been ten minutes before and the umpires called it quits. That evening saw a celebration second to none. The series was ours. For only the second time in our long history, we had beaten England in a series in England.

That evening we had to move on to Manchester for the final county game against Lancashire and I am told that we nearly had a big accident on landing. None of us were any the wiser. We had moved into the senseless zone of celebration. The next morning I had the inevitable hangover. I was sharing with Eddie. I got up to shave, but as I looked out of the country hotel window I saw a huge cargo boat moving across the meadows – or so it seemed! Was I seeing things? Later I was to find out about the huge canal in the area. That explained the illusion!

Brian Statham, in his book *A spell at the top* recalled an incident in the final Test:

I saw Peter Pollock once in my Tests, my farewell appearance at the Oval. He struck me as a good bowler, though like other South African quick men, Adcock and Heine, was inclined to bowl too many bumpers. Pollock however was the centre of a Statham tactical plan that misfired. South Africa was all out for 208 and with the wicket playing easy I thought England would bat a couple of days. Instead, Pollock and his fiery pace started to rip through us. That evening I invited Pollock to the Cricketers' Club in Baker Street, London for a chat about fast bowling. I thought it might be a good idea to give him a heavy meal and some drink. So much for the Statham softening-up plan.

Peter is a lone wolf even with his own colleagues. I could not get close to him. He remained aloof, never relaxed, sipping half pints at his own pace and left to go early to bed as fresh as when he walked in. He finished off the England innings the next day with figures of five/43.

Statham was out last with all three stumps knocked over by a yorker!

The Springboks were accorded hero status. Thousands were at Jan Smuts airport when we arrived home and Port Elizabeth came out en masse to welcome Eddie Barlow and their very own Pollock brothers. The Rand sportswriters chose Graeme and me as two of their six Sports Stars of the Year. The world was our oyster. Though nobody ever announced it officially, the people of Port Elizabeth had given us the freedom of the friendly city. All the money in the world could never buy that! All that remained now was Australia.

Against the Aussies in 1966 – 1967

When a critic of the calibre of Richie Beau suggests that only the 1960 – '61 Australia-West-Indies series produced more thrills and entertainment than the 1966 – '67 clash between Australia and South Africa, then something truly outstanding must have happened. It was a historic series, culminating as it did with our first ever triumph over the Aussies. We often had to pick ourselves up from the canvas to fight back against seemingly impossible odds and this ensured that truth was even more exciting than fiction.

It was a hard fight, with no holds barred and plenty of gripes about the umpires. Some of these complaints were justified, certainly in my opinion, but should not be allowed to tarnish the Springbok achievement. It's always argued that in a tight series, just a few vital decisions going the wrong way can make the difference between winning and losing. I will not contest that. The glorious uncertainty of cricket is a fact and it would be foolhardy to contest ifs and buts. But the home side surely earned and deserved their 3 – 1 success. It was to become a winning trend over Australia that finally produced credibility to the title of world champions.

This was the summer that saw Denis Lindsay emerge as the country's golden boy. Time and again he came to the rescue, but it was the aggressive manner in which he turned the tide, as much as the statistical significance of his efforts, that really captured the imagination of cricket followers worldwide. It wasn't a one-man effort, for in cricket it just doesn't work that way, but when all was said and done, Denis was the major difference between the two sides. His ability to inspire the bottom half of the batting turned mediocre starts into match-winning totals. Often Peter van der Merwe was involved. His guts and determination triumphed over his own technical inadequacies in a way that should have inspired many.

The daggers were out long before the tour got under way. The first thrust in the psychological warfare came from captain Simpson, "Dave Renneberg was far quicker than Peter Pollock." Obviously I was a target. They expected a bumper barrage and were suggesting that anything we could hand out, they could return better! I should have ignored it, but I swallowed the bait; hook, line and sinker.

Dad had always advised us that cricketers should only talk out there in the middle with wickets and runs. Pity I didn't listen. I had been working so hard during the winter with my coach Doug Fox, building up for the Aussies. I wanted to be faster than ever, and scarier than ever. As things turned out, it was to become the most frustrating four months of my cricketing career. Anyway, it was great to get the adrenalin pumping and the newspaper columns ticking. Interest reached fever pitch when they arrived and as usual the local press went overboard in proclaiming the virtues of the opposition.

But what really fired the enthusiasm was the tremendous triumph of Transvaal in beating Simpson's mob early in the tour. Australian teams enjoyed a tag of invincibility, but thanks to Ali, a 76-run defeat was the psychological boost we needed. Ali scored 235 while Tiger notched a century and both were key Test players.

So to the Wanderers and a packed stadium for the first Test. "Have you heard the latest van der Merwe joke?" Dougie Laws, the well-known radio announcer asked during the breakfast session on the second morning of the game. "No," replied his co-announcer. "We will bat, Bobby." The Test had taken on such wide interest that it even made the Springbok Radio funnies and the poor captain was in the hot seat. The media were critical. What had tempted him to bat first on a pitch so obviously full of life?

It had been raining quite consistently on the Rand and we as a team felt it was probably a good toss to lose and let Simpson rather make the decision. But it fell to van der Merwe and he took the brave line. It wasn't his fault that we batted so ineptly. At one stage the scoreboard said 41/5 wickets.

Garth McKenzie had been chief destroyer, as he was to be for the whole summer. But the rescuer who was also going to dominate the series, was Denis 'the menace' Lindsay. Helped by Tiger Lance, these two set about putting some sanity into the proceedings and their valuable partnership of 110 could not have come at a more desperate time. Denis was not scared to hit the loose balls and bouncers were potential sixes, especially when bowled by Dave Renneberg. Lance was more circumspect, but thanks to them, 199 finished up was a lot better than 41/5.

By close of play Australia had replied with 99 without loss, just to put the bow on a veritable nightmare. Our changing room that evening was as sombre as a graveyard. Worse, we had only ourselves to blame.

By lunch the next day, the Aussies were only three runs behind with nine wickets in hand. Thanks to the irrepressible Barlow, who on his deathbed would probably be planning his own reincarnation, and also the systematic Trevor Goddard, what looked like becoming a mammoth first innings lead was whittled down to a mere 126. Lindsay took six catches with his "sticky" gloves. Barlow's ability to come through when things looked dark and gloomy was becoming a new legend. "He lulls you into a false sense of security because he is not really regarded, nor does he look like a front-line bowler," was an Australian interpretation of his success. It was suggested that the more confident the batsmen were the more likely Barlow was to strike! Often he would be smacked for a couple of boundaries only to have the last laugh a few balls later.

Whether the secret lay in not being taken seriously or not, didn't bother us. The facts showed that he could administer a lethal dose when it was least expected. The beers tasted better that second evening and there were a couple of smiles.

The next ten hours of combat were nail-biting. Cigarettes were being smoked by the dozen in the unbearable tension. Silly little superstitions like retaining your seat for fear of causing a wicket to fall were being implemented and each time the capacity crowd of 30 000 roared, our hearts dropped into our boots. The Springbok gladiators were fighting back like men possessed in our second innings.

Barlow, though scratching around like a fowl searching for mealies, was definitely operating on determination alone. Form had deserted him. It was now just sheer guts. Bacher was run out controversially and that sparked the wrath of the spectators who then gave umpire Baxter the bird for the rest of the day. Graeme then played what I still regard as one of his finest innings. His first scoring shot was a soaring six off a Tom Veivers long-hop and the elegant left-hander smashed 90 runs in only 114 minutes – not even a session!

Lindsay and van der Merwe came together at 349/6 – still a long way from being out of the woods. Peter was never a good starter. He sparred at a delivery from Renneberg and the Aussies let rip with the most confident of appeals. The crowd waited in a stunned silence for the umpire's decision. He didn't move, nor did his finger. What a relief! Simpson was furious. He wasn't alone as others strutted about in anger, shaking their heads in disbelief. With the next ball the Bok captain got a huge edge. It went straight to Simpson in the slips and he grassed it. In the very next over he was dropped again.

One dubious decision was followed by two dropped chances. It was surely our day. Denis 's innings of 182 was positively outstanding. It earned accolades normally reserved for Graeme. He drove and hooked with power and interposed with a few delicate late cuts. By comparison van der Merwe was a beginner, pushing and prodding, but surviving! By the time the two had concluded their partnership the game had turned dramatically and a target of 495 stared the Australians in the face. We had eight hours to bowl them out.

The final day belonged supremely to Trevor Goddard. His control of line, swing and length was immaculate and his haul of six wickets for 53 saw us victorious by a massive 233 runs. Who would have guessed this result that first evening?

As we were celebrating I noticed that young Mike Procter was quiet. Something seemed wrong. To 'blood' him into the Test atmosphere, he had been nominated twelfth man. Colin Bland's tragic fielding accident, which saw him crash into the fence and damage an already suspect knee, had Mike doing service in the closing stages. In fact he pouched a couple of catches. But that was the problem!

He had dropped the final catch of the match! As he fell over, he spilled the ball, but his body covered the truth. The batsman walked, the spectators rushed onto the field and Trevor Goddard was being charioted from the arena. In all the excitement and hustle and bustle nobody had noticed the spilled catch. It definitely was too late to do anything about it. "Forget it," was the advice. It wasn't as if it was the last ball in the last minute. The margin and the time still available would have seen the Springboks win anyway. But it doesn't alter the fact that the catch was dropped.

The celebrations were hearty and jovial, but not for all. Bland was never to play Test cricket again and I had bruised my left heel. It happened that final afternoon. There was an exact moment of excruciating pain as I let fly a bouncer at Ian Chappell. The pitch had been extremely hard and I had erred in not taking my normal precaution of wearing two pairs of foam inner soles. I had bruised my heel once before and I recalled that it virtually put me out for the season. I just could not face the thought of being out of the action. I decided to grin and bear it. I wanted to be part of this fabulous series, even if I risked some damage to my reputation as South Africa's spearhead. A foolish decision in retrospect, but one that in the final analysis didn't cost the team as much as it cost me.

Newlands, the venue of the second Test, had never been particularly kind to me or to Springbok teams. It often started with losing the toss and sure enough we were out there fielding on the first morning. As usual, the pitch was grassless and the Aussies soon wrested the initiative. Simpson and Stackpole reached three-figure totals and the Aussies accumulated an impressive 542.

And we were falling like flies. The South African dressing room resembled a Red Cross station during the war. Richard Dumbrill and the two Pollocks were among the walking wounded. There were three substitutes on the field. If we were invalids in real terms, our batsmen soon became invalids in the figurative sense, thanks to an inspired spell by big Garth McKenzie. He was extracting life from the pitch that none of the South Africans had been able to manage and we were fighting for our lives.

The only good news was that Graeme could bat. For six hours he had been off the field and as such was fresh and eager to get among the runs. The Aussies were not charmed. They felt, and with justification, that this was just "not cricket," but there were no rules that prevented him batting despite being off the field for so long. One could see the anger rising as the runs piled up. There were a couple of blemishes that could be blamed on his leg injury and the consequent lack of mobility, but partnerships with Peter van der Merwe and me saw us scrape to 353. Graeme's contribution was a massive 209. As he passed the various milestones there were precious little words of congratulations from the Aussies. Every run burned deep into their resentment.

Simpson decided to enforce the follow-on, which suited us. Denis Lindsay had joined the injured list with several stitches in his head after being hit by a bouncer. Graeme's toe had turned septic and he had pulled a muscle. The follow-on did give us a semblance of a chance in trying to save the match. It would be a long haul. At close on the fourth evening we were 245/7 and things didn't look at all rosy. I was not out at 23, following my 41 in the first innings and with me was David Pithey who had an undefeated 38.

That evening, with defeat inevitable, we decided to drown our sorrows at a disco in Sea Point. We made a good job of forgetting about cricket and the predicament facing us.

Round about midnight Eddie Barlow and I decided to get back to the hotel. Fearing a hangover, we planned to get up early and head for the Newlands nets. Needless to say we didn't feel too bright on waking, but we left early as arranged. Eddie left a note for manager Jack Plimsoll that we had gone to practice. Eddie must have clean bowled me at least a dozen times. If anything, he destroyed my confidence rather than preparing me for a tough task ahead. He insisted that we carried on despite my protests. Then a nice shower and a cup of tea completed the preparations.

The first ball from Renneberg was a long hop outside the off-stump. I hit the ball in the meat and it screeched to the boundary. And I never looked back. When our innings finally closed I was undefeated with 75 runs, my highest Test score, and in the press box they were starting to classify me as a genuine all-rounder. The efforts of the tail-enders had put some fight back into the match and the Aussies needed 179 in four hours. I managed to send down 12 fiery overs and in the process changed my mind about a statement I had made about being unavailable for the third Test.

I knew that rest was the only answer for a bruised heel, but my batting had convinced me that I could still make a contribution as a run-getter. As for the pain I was going to try some cortisone and analgesics. Not a clever route, but I really couldn't face being out of the action.

The Australian win thrilled Simpson and helped breach some dissatisfaction in the touring camp.

Newlands had lived up to its reputation as a graveyard for home Test teams. We had lost to New Zealand, drawn with England and I recalled two thrashings dished out by Ian Craig's Australians and Peter May's Englishmen. Injuries, lost tosses and general bad luck firmly enhanced the 'hoodoo' status. For us it didn't matter how picturesque the setting or how awesome the view of the mountain, the Newlands ground was becoming an ogre of massive proportions.

There were a few changes for the third Test. Mike Procter, the blond speedster and Pat Trimborn, a tenacious seamer, would surely improve our attack on the bowler friendly Kingsmead surface. The pitch looked green and Simpson didn't surprise by sending us in. The first ball of the day saw Eddie hit a simple return catch to McKenzie and the big Australian snapped up the offering like a seal at the aquarium. A dejected Barlow made a slow return to the pavilion. While he was getting wickets, his form with the bat was dreadful. I was the converse, making runs but battling for wickets! "Don't worry Ed," I said, "even Bradman made ducks.""Who the hell wants to emulate Bradman?" came his sharp retort. Eddie sat there for ten minutes before taking off his pads. "I would not mind swapping with you," I teased. "You give me you bowling form and you can have my batting." Pity it wasn't as easy as that!

Despite a gritty Bacher, the pitch was winning. At 94/6, Simpson was smiling. Then – yes, you've guessed it – van der Merwe joined Lindsay. It was more or less a carbon copy of the previous rescue acts, Lindsay, the plunderer, van der Merwe the custodian. It was becoming downright uncanny. Just as amazing was how each time the Aussies contributed with fielding lapses. Lindsay and skipper added 103, but the real fireworks from Denis came when David Pithey joined him. Sixes and fours proliferated in yet another Lindsay century. Once again the last half of the batting had doubled up the first half contribution and 300 was a very healthy score on this lively pitch. The Aussies managed only 147 and were forced to follow on.

My meagre contribution was hitting Bill Lawry on the head with a bumper and forcing him off to hospital. He returned later, heavily bandaged to eke out a gutsy 44, the top score. The second time was much better for the tourists and at 266/3, things started looking a bit challenging. But two quick wickets for me, for a change, and a Procter nine-ten-jack mop-up put the game to bed.

I found it most refreshing to have an opening partner like Mike. He was young and fiery and certainly he helped motivate me. Despite the bruised heel I managed to regain some of the lost fire. Perhaps it was because I was not going to be overshadowed by this promising young colt. It was the first time in my career that I was sharing the new ball with a genuine speedster. Joe Partridge had been an admirable foil, as had Jackie Botten in England, but Mike provided a more complete answer. Now I appreciated the full meaning of fast bowlers hunting in pairs. A new partnership had been born.

Though we had to make 182, we got home comfortably and didn't even need Denis! The captain again took flack, this time for enforcing the follow-on. You just can't win, even if you do win!

It was Simpson's turn to boob in the fourth Test at the Wanderers. With rain around and a grassy pitch he decided to bat. Cowper top-scored with 25 in a total of 143. Lindsay did it again with a dynamic run-a-minute century. Typical of his arrogant dominance, Denis was five short of his century when an appeal against the light was turned down. No trouble to him, he walked down the pitch to the very next ball and smacked it high into the stands for a six! You just can't get more brazen. Australia needed 189 to avoid the innings defeat and when a huge thunderstorm washed out the match on the final afternoon, they were in a sorry plight at 148/8. The series should have been all over, but perhaps it was a blessing in disguise, for at least the final encounter had the Aussies still in with a chance of sharing the spoils.

The visitors were not a happy bunch. I had come to regard Bobby Simpson as a thorough gentleman. Maybe he had been a bit aloof with his team-mates. They were losing and though the umpiring had not been good, they had just not played well enough. Blaming Simpson didn't ring true. And I must admit that I respected the way he handled his dissatisfaction with the umpires.

There was always a high degree of decorum. In Port Elizabeth it was clear that the Australian batting line-up was just not equipped to deal with our non-stop attack. When McKenzie was not bowling, the Aussie attack wore its mediocrity like a badge. South Africa were taking wickets very much all-round and the pressure was relentless. If Simpson, Lawry and Redpath failed, it was trouble and in PE it was the same old story as they folded for 173. This time the first innings deficit was just over 100 runs. Australia failed to make a big enough impression. With their second turn at the crease the rampant Springboks knocked off the required 179 with seven wickets to spare. Tiger Lance finished the series with a mighty soaring six and by so doing typified the ascendancy the Springboks held in the final three outings.

The final was a tremendous occasion for Graeme and me, celebrating with a century and a milestone. Graeme, who celebrated his birthday during the five days, took his aggregate for the series to an impressive 537 with innings of 105 and 33 not out, while I became the fourth bowler in South African history to reach 100 Test wickets. It had been a painful summer, in more ways than one for me, but this cherry on top before my home crowd helped the medicine go down.

Keep it simple

Comparisons are odious, but it did please me that I reached this milestone in 24 Tests as against the 25 it took my former colleague and boyhood hero Neil Adcock. It had been an extremely frustrating summer for me, operating at three-quarter efficiency. Nevertheless, it had been a great thrill being there and playing a part in what turned out to be a historic series. South Africa had beaten Australia in a series for the very first time – and most convincingly! It's the results and the cold black statistics that count. The cricket world judges outwardly and even extenuating circumstances such as pitches and bad umpiring count for nothing down the corridors of time.

But a very simple truth came home that summer. Let me explain. While I was at school I wanted to follow in my father's footsteps and become a journalist.

He was an editor and I felt that writing was in our blood! I was soon writing articles under a by-line. I then felt it was time to develop my vocabulary. I got hold of a dictionary and kept it at my bedside with the intention of learning six new big English words each evening. I was out to impress. Every article included as many jaw-breakers as possible. One morning, after writing a rather lengthy article, my dad summoned me to his office. "Peter, have you swallowed a dictionary?" He had read my piece. I admitted and told him the story. "I thought so," he continued "the way you have used some of those words made it clear that you don't understand them properly." He then delivered the coup de grace. "We are in the communication business. We are not here to confuse. So keep it simple."

The summer had taught me the same lesson in cricket. God had gifted me as a fast bowler. From a young age I bowled faster than the other kids and coupled with the speed was a big out-swinger. It was a natural gift. At the age of 14, I was playing club cricket with the men, at 17 I was in the provincial scene and by 20 playing Tests. The speed and the out-swingers brought great success and I never really bothered to sit down and analyse it all. Then I decided to become more scientific. I got myself a trainer and moved into weights and gym-work. I started to experiment with in-swingers and slower balls. I started to read some books on positive thinking and psychological warfare. And I was ready for the world.

The Australians arrived and instead of blowing them to pieces, as planned, the away-swingers were not going and injuries were coming. At the end of the season I recalled my father's words. Get back to the simple basics.

Of course there is a balance in it all. Not for one minute am I suggesting that we shouldn't be scientific. There is need to measure and draw conclusions. But the greatest lesson will always be to acknowledge and adhere to the simple basics.

Richie Benaud said that it was a series to remember personally. I would have to agree, but for different reasons. Fast bowling also provides a certain loneliness. It's impossible to be friendly and chatty with the opposition, especially the batsmen, when you are expected to blast them at the crease. I found it incongruous to be congenial and a fast bowler at the same time. Opposition players had to be kept at an arm's length, lest I befriend them and lose that killer instinct. It was nice to have Mike Procter now, but in the past my contests with the Australians had me as the only bowler fast enough to genuinely frighten some of their batters. The Australians were compulsive hookers almost as if it challenged their very manhood to respond. People often talk about the loneliness of the long distance runner, what about the loneliness of the fast bowler?

I often used to sit in the dressing room watching the friendly intercourse with the opposition, but I always stayed distant and aloof, as Brian Statham noted. At one stage I was considered the fastest bowler in the world. Others said I was the fastest "white man" in the world! Perhaps I even enjoyed the fact that I was feared and that batsmen didn't exactly relish confronting my pace and venom. I remembered that magazine picture of those intense eyes across the front page and the banner headline: "The man who loves to hate." I had made the grade as one of the fastest and most feared, spearheading my country as I bounced and bruised my way round the world.

I had dreamed and fantasized about recognition and I had graduated. Even in a relatively poor series the expectations remained. They would never go away. I was breaking arms, fingers and wrists, hitting people against the head, under the heart and in the ribs and it was all part of the game, all part of a fast bowler's legitimate armoury. When I hit someone on the head, he was taken to hospital. I wasn't allowed to visit him just in case my hardened heart melted. I must admit this type of role-play rather bemused me. But if it was what was required, what the hell! While the tip of the iceberg was a façade there was no lacking for a genuine aggressive get-up-and-go nature in the engine room that was Peter Pollock. It would be a lie to say otherwise.

But I often meditated deeply about this fast bowling, especially in the down times. Many years later, a provincial match between Natal and Eastern Province provided my first real encounter with the consequences of hitting a batsman on the head. The victim was Berry Versveldt, of Natal. A particularly vicious bouncer crashed into his skull and he was groggily ushered from the crease. Normal sympathies were expressed and I was told not to worry. This time it was different because I was the captain and it was my duty to visit him in hospital. I was absolutely shattered.

The blow on his head had seriously affected his speech and he could hardly utter an intelligible sentence. He spoke very slowly as he tried to comfort me. Yes, he was trying to comfort me, the man who had hit him! I must say that the hollow feeling was deep and I didn't sleep well for a couple of nights. I just kept thinking about all the people I had hit and concussed. Indeed there were many times of contemplation.

Somehow the tough times get you thinking more than when things are going well. The 1966 – '67 Australian visit was relived again and again. And the politicians were to ensure that there would be considerably more contemplation than action over the next thirty-six frustrating months.

5

CLOUDS

Pawns of politics

A Nationalist politician once told me, "You are absolutely naive to believe that sport can change this country." He was responding to the pressures that were already beginning to mount in the mid sixties. He was arrogant in his conviction as he patronised my opinions. Similarly, my headmaster at Grey High School had once advised me, "Sport will get you nowhere, rather concentrate on your studies." He too was as inaccurate as that rather belligerent one-eyed politician. Sport was going to play a massive role in the destiny of South Africa and one of the key positions went to Basil Lewis D'Oliveira.

My first meeting with the man that destiny had chosen to deal with the iniquity of apartheid, was under rather controversial circumstances and involved some rather obvious journalistic sensationalism. I was a member of the Rest of the World team captained by Bobby Simpson and Scarborough, a delightful Yorkshire seaside resort, was the venue for a festival fixture against an England side. Dolly was in that team and had enjoyed a pretty successful season. He was now a fully-fledged Test player and his story had certainly captured the imagination of the cricket public.

The coloured man who had been snubbed by his own country had made good overseas – a classic fairy-tale story! I had never played against him and I was looking forward to the tussle. Towards the end of the first day I had to leave the field at the start of the England innings, because I had badly wrenched my ankle in the second over that I bowled to Geoff Boycott. Some rather nasty foot-holes saw me crumple in agony. The ball lobbed through head-high to the bespectacled Yorkshire man who neatly dispatched the full toss to the boundary.

Quick and efficient treatment enabled me to bowl the next day. The ankle was sore and it was pretty medium-paced stuff with the foot-holes a constant deterrent to anything at full pace. In fact I bowled utter trash that day and was carved to all corners of the field.

Then in came Dolly, the new hero of England cricket and there was thunderous applause. He started very slowly and after a while Bobby Simpson asked me to bowl. "Do I really have to?" I replied, "the ankle is sore and those holes are big." The skipper didn't have too many other options and his will prevailed. I trundled away a few balls at Basil with no action in terms of runs or beating the bat.

Then over came the arm, the front foot gave away and a full-toss, at slightly above hip level, culminated. Dolly obviously lost sight of the ball and played a rather weird shot with the ball hitting his glove and the handle of the bat and popping up in the direction of gully. "Catch it!" I shouted more in hope than anything else. A shocking ball like that doesn't deserve a wicket but I was bowling so badly that day that I would have taken any handout!

The main problem for us South Africans was the timing of these World XI festivals. September was still winter back at home and certainly I was anything but match fit.

Anyway, Dolly didn't get caught so I trudged back to my mark. Down I came for the next ball and Basil hooked me away for two runs. Why the rather rash shot? Maybe he was annoyed at hurting his finger. He clouted the next ball for a mighty six on the small ground and I was one of the first to applaud the fine shot. After this boundary Basil seemed to settle down and he blocked the next deliveries.

The rest of the afternoon ran its course with very little to enthuse over in the way of good cricket. It was rather tedious, to be honest. Certainly it wasn't the sort of cavalier stuff the crowd would have enjoyed. But in the press box controversy was brewing.

We had a few beers in the changing room, and then I went with Colin Bland for a few more in the Rothman's tent. There I met one of the South African pressmen and we chatted affably until he mentioned something about a beamer. "What beamer?" I asked and he told me that the press had decided that the one full toss I bowled at Dolly was an attempted beamer. They needed a news angle, a story for the day and this was it. "You can't be serious," I joked, but this was no joking matter. I was a pressman and I knew what this meant. "That's the way the press saw it," concluded the South African.

Suddenly I was a worried man. My imagination ran wild and I saw Fleet Street blowing this into an international incident. The South African writer wouldn't listen to reason saying that his story had already been filed.

If I slept an hour that night it was a lot and first thing in the morning I bought all the British newspapers to see what they had written and headlined. Nobody even touched the subject or even hinted at what my South African colleague had suggested. *The Daily Telegraph* referred to the full toss in passing. I was a relieved man.

The storm greeted me when I got home a week or so later and all because of the report by this South African who had a dreadful gutter press reputation. I took the issue up with some of the newspaper editors and was accorded belated apologies but, as always, the damage had been done. I recall that even Arthur Coy, the convenor of selectors, approached me to explain.

The following August (1968), we were back in England for another set of World XI matches. Gary Sobers captained our team. Australia was touring England at the time and we arrived during the fifth Test at The Oval. Roger Prideaux had been selected, but through illness withdrew at the eleventh hour and Basil D'Oliveira replaced him. Dolly had not enjoyed a particularly good summer, but in he came and took full advantage of some fielding lapses to record 158.

We were involved in a preliminary warm-up game down Canterbury way. In our changing room was a TV set and we South Africans watched with increasing concern and a sort of feeling of impending doom as Dolly piled on the runs. We looked at each other knowingly, but not talking about it. I knew that if Basil were picked, the tour would not take place. Arthur Coy had confided that the South African government would not accept Dolly in the team. I also knew that certain English administrators had been made aware of the situation.

The Dolly dilemma

What happened after this was pure farce and we were in England to watch it all first hand. First of all the England team was picked and there was no Basil D'Oliveira. How could they possibly omit him? I suppose we were a little relieved, but not for long. Immediately Dolly was offered a commission to cover the series as a writer for the *News of the World*. Premier John Vorster latched onto this as manipulation and mischievous philandering, using Dolly as the political football.

Then Tom Cartwright withdrew. He must have been amazed at being picked in the first place because his previous visit to South Africa in 1963 – '64 was conspicuously unsuccessful. As Eddie Barlow quipped, "I don't blame him for not wanting to come back for a second dose." Basil was picked to replace him. A rather strange selection decision both times! But now Dolly was in. Political intrusion and expediency were rife. South African cricket officials and some of their colleagues in England had been involved in this bizarre episode and I doubt if ever the whole truth will emerge. With so much ducking and diving, it was embarrassing.

John Vorster finally confirmed that Dolly was not acceptable, adding the usual political rhetoric as he denounced the enemies of South Africa. He was enthusiastically applauded at the meeting which he chose as the rostrum for his deathknell to South African sport. The politicians had seen the Dolly affair coming. After our government had chosen to leave the Commonwealth, South African cricket ceased to be a member of the Imperial Cricket Conference and it opened the way for renewed pressure on the government through sport.

Early in 1967 Britain's Minster of Sport was already looking ahead at the 1968 tour, saying that if Dolly were not accepted, the tour would be cancelled. Piet Le Roux, in South Africa, was approached and his response was that mixed teams would not be allowed. Vorster doused the flames at that stage by suggesting that some apartheid principles would be relaxed when affecting relationships with traditional sporting ties.

In March 1968 Sir Alec Douglas-Home had met Vorster in South Africa and had come to the conclusion that the chances were favourable for Dolly to be accepted. Lord Cobham had a different version. He announced that the tour would probably be cancelled if Basil were nominated. Opinions changed from day to day. It was touch and go. So other more subtle methods were tried. Basil himself related how a high-ranking official had suggested to him that he should rather choose to make himself available for South Africa and turn his back on England. Then a South African businessman, it was claimed, offered a huge fee and benefits if Basil came to South Africa to work and coach and not make himself unavailable for the South African tour!

What a right royal mess, involving men of reputation and integrity. One expects underhand tactics from politicians, but what sadness when others are naively brought into the picture and succumb to lies, cover-ups and deception. Some South Africans even became quite angry. "They should know that darkies are not allowed here. It's been the unwritten law for decades." What an indictment of a system that was in fact older than the Nationalist government's reign! England was expected to know and to accept the South African way of life. What utter arrogance.

I was brought up in a home that was very aware of political things. As a journalist it was in fact my dad's very lifeblood, especially when he became the editor of the *Eastern Province Herald*. Dad would often play the devil's advocate in his political discussions, much to the chagrin of my mother, but he was always strongly opposed to the Nationalist government, especially its policy of separate development. His friends were Donald Woods and Laurence Gandar, fellow editors who were passionate in their disapproval of 'that regime.' Braam Fischer's arrest shook him to the very core.

Dad had been at the Free State University and there got to admire the man. Then he was arrested and charged as an enemy of the State. That was a final straw for my father. "These Nats are going to mess up a beautiful land," he often commented. The philosophy of separate development was abhorrent to him. But worse still was the practicality of it all. "How do they possibly think it is going to work. Idealism aside, it's got no chance of succeeding. All it's going to produce is hate and bloodshed," summed up his view, so often shared with me in the many hours I spent in the editor's office. There are benefits in being the boss's son!

"They are supposed to be clever men. And men of God." That really exasperated him. Surely any bit of sense would expose just how short-term their thinking was. But idealism and power mess with men's brains and the result of it all would declare the truth of Alan Paton's well-known novel – *Cry the beloved country*!

I vividly recall my first brush with anything of political significance round about 1949 at Wakkerstroom. In the fateful election that saw Jan Smuts deposed and the Nationalists, under Dr Malan, come into power, this town's result was the first to sound a major alarm. Maybe that was only to my father because he was intricately involved. But the look on his face at the swing that he discerned, was quite frightening. Jan Smuts had spent too much time overseas enjoying the pleasures of Whitehall to give his attentions to his homeland and the disgruntled electorate was going to tell him that. You would have thought that the end of the world had arrived. Maybe it had in the short-term, like four and a half decades!

Then the Nationalists set about entrenchment and we as a family definitely developed anti-Afrikaner feelings and emotions. Unfortunately it seemed to develop along these lines; English versus Afrikaans. Elections just became "them and us" with nobody bothering to question what was really going on. Certainly I noticed more blatant abuse in both language and attitude towards the black people and it actually frightened me as a youngster. "Dad, they can't speak to people like that," I said and he just nodded and shrugged his shoulders.

Regularly we would spend holidays in Natal with my uncle who had a beautiful farm in the lush Richmond area. One evening my father went into the kitchen to find the trash can. The cook boy was there – he most certainly wasn't a boy! He could speak a little English. My dad complimented him on the meal and then tossed in an almost throw away line, "I hope they pay you well." The Zulu looked quite puzzled. "How much do you get?" was his attempt at rephrasing the question. The cook told him. It was a mere pittance. Dad was livid. Basically it was none of his business, but he certainly spoiled the coffee after dinner. Mom was upset, for it messed up the rest of the holiday. But that's how he felt.

Just after I had got my driver's licence there was an election and I offered my services in the fight against the Nationalists. My task was as a driver in Despatch, of all places! This was then a rather small town between Port Elizabeth and Uitenhage, but it was renowned for being extremely Afrikaans and obviously fervently pro-government. I borrowed my father's car and off I went feeling good about doing some political service. It was in fact quite frightening. I was threatened physically a few times.

I decided I was not going to speak Afrikaans, as a rather silly protest and this nearly landed me in hot water in my early days in the furniture industry. I had to call on Burgersdorp and there the manager of the one shop had an attitude rather similar to mine. He refused to speak English. There was no compromise and we just gave each other a miss. Ridiculous, but that's the way we are!

When I was a journalist, avoiding Afrikaans was not a problem. In the main you are granting favours. People love publicity or a good press, so they go out of their way to be accommodating. Even the politicians who might hate your guts will sacrifice everything before the altar of a good press. It's even regarded as an art, getting the press on your side! Most now recognize that it's not what you do or what you are that really counts. It's what you are perceived to be that really matters and the media are the guys who paint the picture. Journalism, particularly viewing so much of it through my relationship with my father, opened my eyes to the selfish motives of men.

"Don't rely too much on other people," Dad once advised. "Have goals and ambitions and be single-minded about them. But relying too much on other people can be a bit dangerous. You see, generally the only people who help, are those it will benefit to help." Cynical? Maybe, but uncomfortably close to the truth.

Anyway, the regime was in power, there was not much that could be done about it and we watched as the infiltration process began. Nothing clever about it. The formula is always the same. Simply get in and take control, Broederbond style. Of course, if you criticized, you were a communist, a traitor or a "black boetie!"

I am sure that the Government had a dossier on the Pollocks, but perhaps we were too high profile to allow them to do anything about us. Certainly we were not into subversion or anything drastic, so we didn't present too much of a threat I suppose. Geoff Dakin would organize cricket matches against the non-whites and we would even have lunch and drinks together at the Alabama Hotel. It was technically illegal, but again there was no intervention. Quite often I would venture into Korsten to the Adcock fields to watch the likes of Eric Majola and Maurice Wilson. I would park on my own and sit there for hours watching the cricket and nobody did anything about it. On occasions Graeme and I were honoured by the people of New Brighton at functions that were politically embarrassing, but again we got away with it.

In some sort of wonderful way, cricket elevated us above the lies, deceptions and intrigues that abounded. I well remember sitting next to Jan Pickard on a flight to Cape Town. We chatted most amicably. Then we got onto the subject of Eddie Barlow. Eddie had decided to venture into politics in the Cape. "Why has your friend done this stupid thing?" he asked. It's a free world I thought, so why not? "The problem is that we are going to have to get the party machine to work against him and that machine does not do nice things," he admitted. In other words, we have ways and means! He wanted me to warn Eddie. I didn't, because I knew that once Barlow had made up his mind, he would go for it, but what Pickard said only confirmed the dreadful truth of it all: politics and its players are involved in a dirty game. I would always stay wary of them.

I addressed a couple of Progressive Party meetings, but on the firm understanding that I was not a member of the party and that I was speaking purely as a sportsman. At one of these meetings I met Norman Elliott, famous for his Durban City soccer club. "Shame," he said, "that you are now beginning to suffer. What about us poor soccer players? We have been excommunicated for years. Welcome to the club." He smiled.

Naively we were trying to separate sport and politics, but that's not possible. What the politicians do affects everything, whether you want to believe it or not and Norman was just telling us to get our heads out of the clouds. His attitude was dreadful. I didn't want to hear it.

Meanwhile we were taking stick. Even before the Dolly episode there was constant overseas pressure. There were not many massive demonstrations, but from the time I first started travelling overseas as a cricketer, there were the inevitable placards and hippies, the constant reminders of the world's disapproval. Like it or not, the inference was always, "You are a racist!" Peter Hain was aggressive and rude, as if it was all our fault. You didn't dare go on radio or television, because you would be attacked personally. People looked at us sideways and in pubs we were often approached offensively. Initially it bothered us, but after a while you get hardened. It was gaming season and we were in the sights, a fair target.

Sir Learie Constantine was once commentating when my brother walked in to bat. He was asked to comment about this brilliant cricketer and he refused to say a word. He snubbed him. And it was okay! Nobody ever bothered to find out if we disapproved of apartheid – we had declared that publicly, emphatically and categorically so many times. We had to walk around treading on eggshells when we were overseas just in case an action or a word out of place would be turned into a political issue. And all because we were white and born in South Africa.

Initially we were always taken at face value – white South African face value! In time the opinions changed. I developed some wonderful relationships with cricketers from other countries. On the one world tour we even started a

West Indian - South African club and this produced some meaningful interaction. In fact, I recall arriving in England in the September of the 1966 West Indian tour. It had been an exceedingly tough one, especially for Charlie Griffith, the fast bowler with the suspect action.

On arrival at the Waldorf Hotel there was a message from Gary Sobers inviting the South Africans to their end of tour farewell function. It was to be a massive event, steel drums, Johnny Mathis and all! We renewed old acquaintances, one being controversial Charlie. Later in the evening Sobers joined a group of us. "Nice to see you all," he said and then looked at Charlie. "It's the first time I have seen him smiling on the whole tour." "Yes, these are my friends," retorted the big West Indian. And he meant it! Maybe he felt that many had deserted him on that trip, but he was very happy to see us.

During these testing times a double wicket tournament was organized in Australia and well-known Australian entrepreneur Jack Neary promoted it. He had brought the Beatles and then the Bolshoi Ballet to Australia and now it was our turn.

We were treated like show-biz personalities, something new and strange to us way back in 1968. TV appearances, in-store promotions and press cocktail parties – you name it and we were there for publicity's sake. It gave us a very interesting insight into the entertainment world, which to all intents and purposes was just a more lavish extravaganza with the dog eat dog formula hidden behind the footlights. But out front it was all smiles and glamour.

Graeme and I were paired and we finished second overall, the event being won by Gary Sobers and Wesley Hall. Basil D'Oliveira and Freddie Trueman were one of the England combinations while Rohan Kanhai and Charlie Griffith were the number two West Indian duo. Ken Barrington partnered Colin Milburn and they had a traumatic tussle with Kanhai and Griffith at the St Kilda Ground in Melbourne. Barrington had written a book and in it pronounced that Griffith was both a chucker and a cheat. This obviously didn't endear him to the West Indian paceman.

Bouncers and curses abounded, but after the match, right in front of me in the dressing room, Barrington had a heart attack. He collapsed, battling for air. It had all been too much for him. The strain and the tension had taken its toll and I know it shook us all – especially Charlie Griffith. Heart problems finally killed Ken and that set of events would no doubt have contributed greatly to it.

The media were on the lookout for any strained relationships between the South Africans and Dolly because again we were the ogres who had prevented Basil from playing for South Africa and made him seek glory elsewhere. Fortunately nothing happened, but Basil's part as a mere pawn in a unique set of circumstances certainly elevated him into a special spot in history. The fact that just about everybody else climbed in to take full advantage was to be expected.

The cost of apartheid had been massive, whichever way you look at it. Tours were cancelled. In my Test lifetime I was short changed on 15 Test matches, but that's nothing compared to the likes of Barry Richards, Mike Procter, Clive Rice, Garth Le Roux and Vincent van der Bijl to mention just a few. They didn't have Test careers. We never got against the likes of India, Pakistan and the West Indies, thanks to the policies of the ruling government.

Allan Lamb, Keppler Wessels and the Smith brothers would not have had to seek careers overseas. Worse, each found that despite being accommodated elsewhere they were never truly accepted into their foreign domains. But somehow we dare not mention any suggestion of cost, lest it be compared to the poverty and agony of millions!

Certainly in those days, and even now, any suggestion that the affect was more wide-spread than the black disadvantaged, is met with immediate disdain. All I can say though, is that if you happened to be born a cricketer anytime in the 50 years between 1930 and 1980, best you were not born in South Africa!

Blame whom you like, argue and debate whatever political and social agendas you fancy, but finally it revolved around a rather simple issue. Cricketers born in South Africa would pay a cost. Some considerably more than others! Thanks to politicians down the ages we landed in a mess that had cost everybody dearly. The fiasco, lies, manipulations and deceptions that accompanied the Dolly affair are unfortunately still all too prevalent.

6

GLORY

The Australians in South Africa – 1970

Those South Africans who had perhaps been a little over enthusiastic in celebrating the New Year, were probably still recovering from their hangovers when Bill Lawry's 1970 Australians arrived at Johannesburg's Jan Smuts Airport. They had just completed three months of campaigning in India and had successfully negotiated one of world cricket's more difficult tasks – winning on the subcontinent! Umpires, pitches and pestilence had been conquered and Lawry was full of confidence, claiming a better balanced attack than Simpson's side and certainly a better set of fielders.

Furthermore they were happy and motivated. The gem of all gems was his challenge that "Ian Chappell is the best batsman in the world on all types of wickets." This rankled immediately and was probably designed to do just that! The public and media reacted. How could he suggest that anyone other than Barry Richards or Graeme Pollock ruled the batting world?

Anyway, about two-and-a-half months later it was the Australians who were suffering from king-size hangovers after being thrashed so conclusively that the shame of the whitewash lived on for decades to come.

Even at the turn of the century it's a subject best left alone. Their valid excuses or explanations for defeat sounded hollow. Only silence would have provided any solace. Anything else was sour grapes.

For Ali Bacher's Springboks, each victory was easier than the previous one and by the end the Australians were so demoralized and dispirited that they had less fight than a wet chamois.

It had been three years since the Springboks had seen Test action while the Aussies had twelve months earlier put the skids under the West Indies, not to mention their most notable 3-1 Indian triumph. They had every reason for confidence, for wide grins and heads held high. They felt they were the world champions and they were happily patting one another on the shoulder.

Personally I had never visualized Bill Lawry as a skipper, perhaps because his cricket had seemed to me so dour and negative. I had come to know him a little on the Rothman's world tours and found him most likeable and amusing. But basically he was shy and withdrawn. Yet, you can't argue with statistics. On arrival in Johannesburg he stood with an impressive nine wins in 16 Tests, with only three defeats.

We were also told that his batting had blossomed, in that he was prepared to put bat to ball, rather than merely allowing the ball to hit the bat and glide off it. Well, we didn't notice much change that series. And as a leader he revealed his own emotions too often and that worked detrimentally in terms of the team's image and performance.

The series actually finished on a sour note when he refused to appear alongside Ali Bacher to make the traditional after-test address to the public. He also refused a sincere gesture made by one of the umpires, Charl Coetzee. He preferred to sulk. Quite frankly, his team had taken such a trouncing it should have been easy for him just to shrug the shoulders and laugh it off! If it's been a tight, evenly fought encounter, it's tough to acknowledge defeat. But when you are so out-classed it is easy to doff the hat and say nice things! But obviously not for Bill Lawry.

Anyway, let's not put the horse before the cart. The months prior to the arrival of the Australians had indeed been frustrating for me. I was battling with form. The years were beginning to take their toll, the rhythm would come and go and the media were talking in terms of my being over the hill. Dad was concerned, suggesting that I should perhaps think about retirement. Then a couple of weeks before the tour he died suddenly. He had also expressed criticism about Graeme. "You are not making the big scores. Top players get double and treble centuries!" was his rather direct challenge!

Newlands was a hoodoo ground, and the reporters were at pains to remind us of that as we gathered for the first Test. It's scenic beauty belies its hate for the green and gold and fast bowlers! Six times the Australians had been to this picturesque venue and six times they had won. Did we really need to be reminded? The Springboks had not won at Newlands for some 60 years and personally, with Currie Cup experiences thrown in, I had become quite accustomed to leaving the ground on the final day with my tail firmly between my legs.

Vital always is the winning of the toss, hence Ali's beaming grin as he strutted back to the pavilion. Lawry tried hard to hide his disappointment, but he would not have been a good poker player. Like me, his face conceals nothing.

The first day was a grind, but it was to pay rich dividends. Some vital catches were spilled and there was a lot of pad play as we employed our various tactics against the mystery spinner John Gleeson. Most found him difficult to read. His flick-finger action shot out leg-breaks and off-breaks with what looked pretty much like the same action. Aussie wicket-keeper Brian Taber reckoned he could "read" his team-mate, but the number of times he went the wrong way, missed stumpings and conceded byes, certainly defied his claim!

Barry Richards argued that he could detect the difference, but even he admitted that just occasionally he missed it. The general policy for us mere mortals was for the right-handers to play him as a leg-break bowler and vice versa for the lefties. This meant that the googly merely beat the bat into the pads and hence the abundance of pad contact and appeals. Getting out on the front foot was essential.

We could detect, almost from the start, that Lawry's men were looking to harass the umpires. Moans and head shaking started from the first morning and the visiting media also joined in the choir of discontent. I will be the first to admit that the umpiring standard in South Africa was not the best and that there were a few dubious decisions.

The home team had the better share of the luck in terms of mistakes, but that they would have made any major difference in such a one-sided contest was pushing it a little! In fact their attitude finally counted against them. They allowed themselves to become frustrated and even resentful and that not only affected their own concentration and application but it hardly endeared them to the men in question. They are after all only human beings with human emotions. It's fatal to get umpires against you. We had learnt that lesson the hard way and Lawry, as the major instigator, was leading his Australians headlong into self-demoralization, depression and cricketing suicide.

At the end of the first day the Springboks were 254/4 and applauding a Barlow century. Just before three o'clock the following afternoon we were all out for 382, by no means a mammoth total by Newlands' standards, but nevertheless useful.

But at three o'clock that Friday, January 22, a most momentous two hours of cricket that was virtually to set the seal on the remainder of the series began. Bill Lawry, until then undefeated in three weeks of batting on the tour, and Keith Stackpole strode to the crease, while being watched by a capacity crowd. Mike Procter started the attack coming downhill and down-wind.

Ali had said to me, "Take a few overs up-hill and then I will whip you off and you can follow Mike down-wind when he has finished his spell." That sounded reasonable. As usual Ali had everything planned. But it worked just a little differently.

The second ball of my second over pitched just outside the leg-stump to the left-hander Lawry. It hit the seam and tracked back but the Aussie skipper had shuffled into his wicket, preparing for the leg-glance. He had left the leg-stump unguarded. The ball just clipped the top of the unprotected stump sending the bail flying over wicket-keeper Dennis Gamsy's head. I couldn't believe my good fortune. The crowd roared and all the Springboks came rushing around.

Four balls later, Ian Chappell, the "best batsman in the world," was also back in the hut. He attempted to pull a bouncer, did not quite latch onto it and the ball flew at a height of about seven feet in the direction of Lee Irvine in the gully. Lee responded in cat-like fashion hurling himself into the sky and managing to push the ball into the air with his palm. Grahame Chevalier moved in from leg-slip to take the rebound.

Sheer chaos erupted. We looked like a bunch of soccer players hugging and congratulating one another. In those conservative days responses were pretty controlled, but we were like a bunch of kids.

I took my jersey and moved to mid-on. The crowd rose as one in applause that must have lasted a full minute. Tears rolled from my eyes. The emotion, the excitement and the thought that my father was not alive to see this, proved all too much.

Two hours later, at five o'clock, the Aussies were in a sorry state. Procter had joined the party and five wickets were down for 58. Spectators were rubbing their eyes in disbelief. By close it had improved to 108, thanks to a plucky but lucky Doug Walters who had chanced his arm. What a tumultuous day for the Springboks.

The next day their innings folded at 164 and Bacher, very wisely didn't enforce the follow-on. There were once again the inevitable critics who suggested that he had not driven home the advantage. But with so much time available we backed him. Bowlers always tend to want a rest between innings. It is never very easy to take up from where you had left off when forcing a team to follow-on.

Ali was not going to throw away the advantage of winning the toss. We didn't want to chase runs on the final day on a wearing pitch against the wily Gleeson. Our captain had read it right, we all concurred! The third day and fourth, while we piled on the pressure, were not spectacular but contained much excitement.

Umpire Wade and the Aussies were having their problems. Their bowlers were fighting, especially Mallett and Gleeson, the spinners and paceman Alan Connolly and their fine rearguard bowling restricted us to 232, with only Graeme reaching a half-century.

The controversy arose about a claim to have Graeme dismissed at 26. Australia's enormous target was 451 in ten and a half hours. Lawry and Stackpole were clearly not over-awed. They set about the bowling, particularly Procter, almost in Sunday-afternoon-picnic fashion. His bouncers on a then rather placid pitch, were being treated with utter disdain. The first wicket fell at 75 and when the score stood at 129/1, Ali must have had second thoughts about his follow-on decision.

But just as in the first innings, in a matter of 15 minutes the game swung dramatically. Mike came back into the attack after tea, this time concentrating more on line and length than speed and bounce. Suddenly it was 136/4 and the rest of the proceedings proved to be a mere formality, finishing just after lunch on the fifth day. Ten of the twenty Australian wickets fell to the Procter-Pollock combination and the Newlands' hoodoo had been broken. Celebrations continued well into the night.

Off to Kingsmead for the second Test, a match that will forever linger in the memories of those fortunate enough to have been there.

It was one of the finest days of batting that Test cricket has ever produced! All else, including a Springbok win by an innings and 129 runs, Eddie Barlow's 3 wickets in 9 balls and records galore, paled into insignificance when compared with the batting feats of the blond giants Robert Graeme Pollock and Barry Anderson Richards. They ravaged the Australian attack with such precision and timing that even the Aussies must have considered it a privilege to be the victims. It wasn't that Bill Lawry and company bowled badly, fielded badly or lost heart. They stuck to their guns gamely. But when two geniuses take control there is absolutely nothing mere mortals can do to stem the tide.

The visiting attack received the biggest thrashing in the history of Tests between the two countries. It was Barry who got the ball rolling with his picket-crashing during the pre-lunch session.

Bacher won the toss and out went Goddard and Richards. Usually there is a bit of life in a Test wicket on the first morning, so one would have expected a little careful play in the first 45 minutes, especially at Kingsmead. But no, Richards was not interested. He was going to prove a point and at lunch he was a disappointed man. Why? He had failed by a mere 6 runs to reach his century in the two hours before lunch! This was the sort of feat Bradman was renowned for. By doing so Richards would have joined a very elite band of batsmen.

Ali Bacher got himself out trying to give Barry the strike in the final over before lunch so that he could have a go. To give an indication of Barry's dominance, he and Trevor put on 88 of which Goddard's contribution was a mere 17. At 126/2, Richards on 94, Graeme strode to the crease for a couple of uncomfortable balls. He survived and the stage was set.

An hour after lunch, twelfth-man Ashley Mallett was ready at the player's entrance with the drinks and while he waited, he watched Richards being clean bowled by Eric Freeman's slower ball. But what happened in those 60 minutes, the Oxford dictionary and all its superlatives could not do justice to. In that hour, Richards and Graeme amassed an unbelievable 103 runs. Never had South African cricket enjoyed such domination, especially over archrivals Australia.

The early afternoon's format was pretty basic. Graeme took the one crease, Richards the other and between them they peppered the pickets with an array of shots that were both majestic and brutal. I just couldn't believe my eyes.

When Barry was eventually out, the poor shell-shocked Aussies stood and applauded Barry the whole way back to the pavilion. Lawry even waited until Richards had left the field before beckoning for the drinks. A mighty fine gesture. But such brilliance is indeed above the mundane aspects of Test cricket. It had a right to be bracketed! What a pity there were no TV cameras around to record those soaring 60 minutes.

The next man in, Barlow, lasted a very short while, got back into the pavilion and simply declared, "After the Lord Mayor's show, there was no room for me out there. I was embarrassed. Those two have made a mockery of batting." Indeed they had! The rest of the innings belonged to Graeme and he proceeded in the same classic vein to chalk up one record after the other.

Kingsmead had been an unlucky venue for the left-hander. This was his first century in ten years of first-class combat at the ground. At 210 he reached his personal highest first-class; at 233 he beat Dudley Nourse's record against Australia and an on-drive off Keith Stackpole saw him pass Jack McGlew's all-time best of 255 for a Springbok batsman in Tests.

As we were giving them a standing ovation, I just thought about Dad, tearfully wondering if he was out there somewhere, aware of this very special kind of graduation day!

It seemed as if Graeme was not going to stop and that for once he was going to allay his late father's fear about piling it on in massive totals, when a lazy, somewhat weary forward defensive prod was not quite to the pitch of the ball and consequently presented Keith Stackpole with an easy return catch. Graeme's 274 had been out of a total of 558 and he had also shared in a century partnership with Tiger Lance. At 622/9, Bacher mercifully declared.

Kangaroos with tails between their legs

Eddie Barlow is not the type to allow himself to be left out of the action for long. Having had to vacate the limelight to Barry and Graeme, he could hardly wait to make his own impact; 44/0 became 48/4. It was then 79/6, 114/8 and finally 157 all out, with Paul Sheahan's 62 being by far the biggest contribution. This time Ali had no hesitation with the follow-on and it was late on the fourth afternoon that we wound up proceedings.

Lawry again was not particularly happy about his caught-behind decision and just before reaching the player's gate as he left the field, he pulled out of his mouth the wad of gum that he had been chewing and in temper hit the blob of gum over the pavilion roof! Tiger Lance, master of dry wit retorted, "He has just played his most attacking shot of the tour."

Following this victory, we went to the Wanderers and a 307 run triumph. In the first two days the match did have its competitive moments when there was a certain amount of controversy over excessive bouncers from Mike and me. The Wanderers pitch did help quickies and I always enjoyed its bouncy qualities. It's fun, for a change, to be able to discourage batsmen who just simply like sticking out the front foot, sparing and prodding! The ball flying around their ears does tend to move them onto the back foot and as such presents a better test of real skill and technique.

We won the toss again and I was surprised that Lawry didn't suspect some sort of magic, or a jinxed coin! We made heavy weather of compiling 279, but it was humid and rainy and at the Wanderers that often spells trouble. Of course fans and the media don't always understand it and consequently I have always made it my business to avoid discussing the game with the ignorant. You only get frustrated.

Anyway, I had succumbed to a heated discussion to the extent that I even ventured a bet. Not with a bookmaker, but with an argumentative man. The bet, for the princely sum of R10, hinged on whether the Aussies would, for the first time in the series, pass our first innings total. Once again it was to be 8 wickets out of 10 for the Pollock-Procter duet and the bet was won by 77 runs. There was some fiery bowling into the bargain, even if I say so myself.

The main target happened to be Paul Sheahan, who bore the brunt of a fusillade of bouncers. Umpire Coetzee had some words with the captain because the sparks were flying, verbally and otherwise. Paul didn't enjoy bouncers. Nobody does. But he wasn't playing them very well. There was some poor slip-catching into the bargain. Twice in a matter of two overs Tiger Lance grassed simple catches, not that any slip catch is easy, mind you! My frustrations knew no bounds. The Sunday papers made quite an issue of what they termed "almost bodyline" tactics.

Our 77 runs first innings lead was turned into a final target of 408 to which Lawry's embattled troopers could only manage 178. It was another emphatic statement of strength and domination.

Nearly 120 000 people had clicked the turnstiles, but the taste of the champagne was not as sweet as usual. The sour note involved a decision by the selectors that Trevor Goddard would not be playing in the final game at Port Elizabeth.

Trevor had announced that he would not be available for the forthcoming tour of England – the tour that never was. So the selectors decided to drop him! Trevor had been a very faithful and successful servant and the players were noticeably upset. We all knew it was his final series and that his performances, though not up to his usual high standard, had more than justified his retention for the finale. It was a rather heartless decision to omit him from being a part to the very end of the most historic grandslam in our country's cricket history. Trevor's comment, "I would not be human if I didn't say I was disappointed. But that's life." Indeed it is the way the cookie often crumbles.

It was the same pattern for the final Test – Bacher winning the toss, a first innings lead, piling on the pressure in the second and victory by a huge margin. This time 323 runs separated the two teams at the finish of a game that was totally free of controversy, except for Lawry's unwillingness to say a few words at its conclusion.

Throughout the series I had shared a room with Mike Procter. It was at Ali Bacher's insistence. He wanted his two speedsters to get motivated together. For the final game Mike arrived in Port Elizabeth with influenza. This he managed to pass on to me. The flu bug had me leave the field on the second day and to add to the problems I pulled a muscle on the fourth! Poor Mike, anti-biotics and all, had to carry the attack. His strong young shoulders met the challenge and produced match figures of 9 for 103. I could only help with three wickets in the first innings because I only managed two overs in the second.

Joining Mike in what proved to be a great triumph for the three young musketeers, were Lee Irvine and Richards. Barry followed up his first innings 81 with a century in his second knock and Irvine notched his maiden Test hundred.

Ali had not been particularly pleased with our first innings of 311, but when the Aussies made 212 there was a shadow of a smile. Our second innings was declared at 470/8, setting an impossible 570 to win.

As the game died, some of the tourists – Doug Walters and Ian Chappell notably – were not even at the ground. They were playing golf! They preferred that to sitting through the agony and humiliation at St George's Park. There was so little morale and self-respect left, that it really didn't make any difference.

After the game I had to settle a wager made with Gleeson. He didn't like bouncers. Mike and I had not been selective in whom we dished them out to, even tail-enders. Gleeson appreciated this. But I could not read his googly. So we came to an agreement. I would not bowl him a bouncer. In return he signalled to me, by tossing the ball up once in his hands as he came in to deliver, whenever he was about to bowl an off-break! The rest would be leg-breaks. The one who dismissed the other the most in the series would win.

Gleeson won the wager by two to one and he did it fairly. He honoured his promises, as did I. But once I didn't believe him, and was rolled. The other was just a very good delivery. If I had trusted the opposition, we would have come out square! There must be some lesson in that!

Modestly, Ali Bacher suggested that the 1970 side was so good that it really didn't need a captain. An over-simplification indeed, because Ali played a very important role in his quiet and unassuming way. Graeme and Richards had topped the 500 mark in runs and Mike Procter and I had grabbed 41 of the 75 wickets that fell. The tag of World Champions was attached to the Springboks. But it was going to be a whitewash that would take the Aussies decades to live down, let alone try to explain away!

7

ISOLATION

Lost years in the wilderness

"**I**t was the best of times, it was the worst of times ... ," like Charles Dickens said in *A tale of two cities.* What could be better than being hailed as undisputed kings of world cricket, what could be worse than the rejection and the trauma of a cancelled tour?

When the 1970 tour of England by Ali Bacher's Springboks was finally called off, it shook me to the very core. Despite the Basil D'Oliveira fiasco and the aborted English visit to South Africa a couple of seasons earlier, somehow there was optimism this time. Maybe we didn't want to read the signs, maybe we had our fingers in our ears, but we were rationalising very positively about why England cricket needed us and why minority action groups should not be allowed to dictate to the great silent majority.

Peter Hain was public enemy number one for South African sports enthusiasts. Personally I never had a problem with the anti-apartheid movement's opposition to the iniquity of the South African government's ideologies, but why did the cricketers have to suffer? Sport was the soft underbelly and the demonstrators knew it. So did we, if we were really honest with ourselves. Cricket was far too vulnerable a game. It was just too easy to disrupt and what a summer it would have been for the British constabulary had we attempted to tour. Cancelling the visit was the only option, but there was much anger and resentment. South African cricket officials felt betrayed by their friends – a view backed by some of the more vociferous pro-South African campaigners in the UK.

For me, it was important to separate the issues. Apartheid was repugnant and indefensible. Cricket was the game caught in the middle, but it was unfair to expect cricket friends and allies to have to carry the can for our political baggage. The fault was at home with our own government and while that didn't for one minute alleviate the pain and frustration, it ensured harmony and understanding amongst the cricket fraternity.

We were angry and hurt and considerably inconvenienced. And we all had our own ideas and philosophies on how to cope. But it wasn't going to help. The door had slammed with a loud bang. The writing was on the wall!

A replacement tour was organized. A Rest of the World side, captained by Gary Sobers, the brilliant West Indian all-rounder, was picked and initially only included four South Africans: Graeme, Barry Richards, Eddie Barlow and Mike Procter. I was considered unlucky not to have made the original combination, but it was also suggested that to pick a whole team of South Africans would not have been wise politically. Some wag had mooted that to get around the demonstrators, the organizers should just have called the Springboks the "World XI!" They had, after all, just clinched the mythical world crown. No prizes for guessing where that suggestion came from!

The Morning Group Newspapers responded by deciding to send me over to cover the series for them – an offer I snapped up. I did work for the group and with retirement not far off, they felt it was a wonderful opportunity to train me as their cricket writer. It would be a great experience, working alongside a press doyen like Richie Benaud, the former Australian captain. The press boxes in those days were full of ex-cricketers and it was good fun. I would have the inside track because of my close relationship with the SA players and my presence was deemed to be good news for circulation figures. I actually felt quite honoured to be so widely acclaimed as a critic. It made up for my disappointment of not making the original selection, but it was the ideal launching pad for my cricket-writing career.

The series was originally billed as carrying full Test status, but that decision was later rescinded. For the record, the World side won the first Test at Lord's quite comfortably, but a draw in the second match at Trent Bridge, Nottingham saw the selectors succumb to constant pressure from the South African contingent – Eddie Barlow in particular – about my inclusion in Australian Garth McKenzie's place. I was called up and foolishly responded. Foolish? Well, writing articles in the press box is no way to prepare for front-line Test action!

I had about two weeks to prepare. It was nets in the morning and afternoon and a couple of two-day friendly matches and I must admit that Eddie was very helpful. No doubt his head was also on the chopping block. But who was I conning? There was no rhythm or zip and it didn't help that the pitch at Edgbaston was about as flat as a pancake. The game got nowhere near a result with a little more than two innings being completed in the five days.

As for my reputation, well it got buried in the run-glut and I was respectfully invited to return to the press box for the fourth encounter at Leeds. We were told that the Headingly wicket was likely to suit spinners – this helped to ease the disappointment for me, but as it turned out Eddie Barlow became the chief destroyer with the ball – taking seven wickets in the one innings, including an incredible hat-trick. It was a match-winning performance.

With another victory in the final encounter at The Oval, the Sobers troupe triumphed easily and Ray Illingworth's England side were left licking their wounds and wondering about the 21 players they had used for the summer's battles. Lanky Tony Greig was given three outings, but did enough to suggest that he was a future contender, certainly a man with a big match temperament. Besides Sobers, the other West Indians involved were Clive Lloyd, Rohan Kanhai, Deryck Murray and Lance Gibbs, the off-spinner. Farouk Engineer, of India and Mushtaq Mohammad and Intikhab Alam, from Pakistan made up the 14-man World XI squad.

It was a very interesting time. The biggest surprise for us South Africans was the apparent lack of planning and strategy amongst our highly talented team-mates. Most were professionals and the game of cricket was just another day's work! Or so it seemed. Certainly South African cricket sides were more committed to pre-match team talks and pre-planned tactical ploys. Barlow instituted such discussions and opened a few eyes and ears!

A luxury bus was always the means of transport and this meant plenty of time to imbibe and chat as we sped up and down the motorways. No subjects were taboo and we sorted out a lot of the world's problems in some of the discussions, but sadly only in words. We enjoyed the common denominator of being sportsmen with little interest in politics except how it affected the next cricket match. Tiger the Nawab of Pataudi, who captained his country many times, wrote in one of his books, "I wish it was as easy to solve the world's problems as it seemed for Peter Pollock and me in the back of the bus."

Conrad Hunte had always been a very righteous man. In his youth he had been quite a wild card, but on the 1960 – '61 West Indian tour of Australia he had seen a film called the *Crowning Experience* and this had changed his life.

At the time it shook his team-mates, but by the time I met him he had been walking a committed road for several years and was a mature and dedicated disciple of the Moral Re-Armament Movement. I found him fascinating to talk to, though we always skirted religion. We would tease him often, but he took it all in wonderful humour. It impacted on us. Whenever he felt that something was not right he was not afraid to say so and he once apologized to Graeme, Colin Bland and myself for the fact that politics had intervened and prevented us from visiting the island of Barbados in 1967. He apologized so profusely on behalf of his people that you would have thought it was all his fault!

One morning Conrad took me totally by surprise when he presented me with a book called *Remaking the world* written by Dr Frank Buchman. Inside he had written a message, "To Peter, with faith in your part in remaking the world. Best wishes, Conrad. 13/9/67." Prophetic!

One of Conrad's greatest hours was saving the West Indian flag on an Indian tour. The main pavilion was burning down. Apparently, irate fans had been sold counterfeit Test tickets. They decided to take the law into their own hands and burnt down the stadium. Conrad was the only one who gave thought to anything other than self. It was an act of some courage to salvage his country's flag as the pavilion was burning. He was a deeply committed man of God and he most definitely walked his talk, living his testimony.

Wesley Hall was another I got to know, respect and admire. We became very firm friends. One day he and I had been designated to visit a depot on behalf of the team to collect some items of clothing. Basil Butcher, a team member had asked us to get him some extras, but we forgot. When we got home and Basil found that we had not accommodated him, he became furious and let rip at us verbally. I responded with a few choice phrases and adjectives! Basil went off in a huff.

Then Wes turned to me and said something rather remarkable, "Now I know you are not a racist!" You could have knocked me down with a feather. I had just blasted a black West Indian cricketer and Wes responded that I was not a racist. South Africans did walk a tight rope. As high profile sportsmen we were always under microscopic scrutiny.

"Explain, please," I asked Wes. "Simple. I have been watching you guys over the years. The pressure is on you. You are always walking on eggshells. But just now you responded to Basil, not because he was black or coloured, but because he deserved it. You treated him as normal. You were not patronizing," concluded Wes. I listened, heard and took careful note!

Another fierce combatant I got to know better in the world teams was Bill Lawry. This Australian opening batsman and I had many torrid duels in the sun and as natural foes we did not spend much time sharing glad tidings in the dressing room after close of play. I think that all we managed were a few polite hellos at cocktail functions. However, when we were in the same team, I discovered a whole new person and his sense of humour really tickled me. Practical joking was his hobby!

It's a rather sad indictment, but illustrates that there really are a lot of nice people out there, but because of the barriers, jealousies and prejudices that abound we never get to find out whether a stranger is in fact just a friend you don't know.

Conversely, perhaps that's why it is not good to get to know your opposition too well. You might just begin to like them and that will take the edge off the competitiveness! It's far easier to stay a loner, treating the opposition very impersonally.

Ted and Sue Dexter became my good friends that summer. I played with Ted in 40-over Cavalier games, which were quite popular in those days. They were widely televised and Ted was the Cavalier's skipper. Often on the Saturday evening I would stay overnight on Ealing Common with the Dexters. The next day Ted and I would drive (speed would be more accurate) to the various venues! We spent many hours discussing various aspects of the game. The plane-crash after the Test at Headingly was the only nightmare during a delightful three-month interlude with the Dexters.

I managed to share many hours with Richie Benaud. That was not easy because the former Australian captain used to keep to himself. But I did rather hound him, for I regarded him then and still do now, as one of the greatest authorities on the game. Everything was always carefully considered and very seldom would you detect any private agendas or personal animosities. To me he was the personification of what cricket commentating and writing should represent, and I treasured his friendship.

Trevor Bailey was another wise counsel, as was Freddie Brown, former England captain and then manager of the World side. I wrote regularly for *The Daily* and *Sunday Telegraph*, with Michael Melford as my aide while I would also dare to count EW Swanton as a friend. That's name-dropping!

Except for my being out of form, politics and a rather dark and dank future staring us in the face, it was an otherwise very special summer for me. Everything about those few months brought experience and learning. Rather ironic, isn't it, that to all intents and purposes it was one of the darkest moments of South African cricket history yet, in real terms some buttons were being pushed. Not that I noticed then.

The reporting mission had been successful and I received some complimentary memos from most of the newspapers I served. In the Eastern Province the observations must have impressed some of the cricketing hierarchy because on returning home I heard there was a move afoot to have me captain Eastern Province. Geoff Dakin, who had been my skipper when I first played for EP as a 17 year-old schoolboy, was now on the executive council, and a prime mover in wanting me to replace brother Graeme.

This move wasn't designed to improve fraternal relationships and as things turned out it was tragic that Graeme had had one of his worst seasons ever. By his own high standards it was disastrous and he was even accused of not trying. My view is that he would have been desperately keen to do well, just to answer any knockers. But even a genius is entitled to one bad season.

After his success for England against the World side, Eastern Province were pleased, so was I as skipper, to have Tony Greig playing for us. Sadly, this too proved a disaster.

It all started on the morning of our opening away match against Transvaal at the Wanderers. While having early morning coffee with him in his hotel room, Tony had an epileptic fit. At the time I didn't know that he had once fallen off a truck and had been suffering from epilepsy since then. Anyway, he said he was okay and he took the field a few hours later. Early on I managed to entice an outside edge and the ball went straight to Greig. He pocketed the catch, but as we ran up to him he fell to the ground, writhing in another fit. We all gathered around him. I actually put my finger in his mouth – to be told later that I was fortunate not to lose a finger! Now we had a problem. Tony didn't want the world to know that he was an epileptic. What were we going to tell the media?

Manager Geoff Dakin and I talked it through. There was only one option. Tell them the truth. We told the media the whole story, nothing but the truth. We asked that they would keep from publishing it because it might affect his career. Now all we could do was wait and see whether the press and radio would honour their side of the bargain.

They did. It will always be to me a very precious illustration of what the media represented back in those days. Tony Greig's secret was safe with them and who knows what difference it had made to his career. Finally when it did come out, many years later, he was so firmly established that it became just another one of the obstacles in a career of a player whose trademark was guts and courage.

That summer had more controversy lined up. Transvaal, the Currie Cup champions, were due to play the Rest in a closing match that was part of the Republic Sports Festival celebrations. This was also a final trial for the team to tour Australia the following 1971 – '72 season and the touring party was due to be announced at the conclusion of the fixture.

Let Vintcent van der Bijl take up the story, as he related it in his book *Cricket in the shadows*:

Newlands, on a grey Saturday morning in April 1971, provided the backdrop for the most extraordinary protest in the history of cricket. The spectators at this three-day match had hardly settled into their positions when the players left the field. Mike Procter, opening the bowling for the Rest, delivered just one ball which Barry Richards, guesting for Transvaal, pushed to the off-side, scampered through for a single and then joined the other players on their quiet but purposeful walk to the pavilion. The expectant buzz of the crowd had given way to a bemused hush as the umpires, like two sentinels guarding the traditions of the game, stood alone out in the middle.

The inactivity on the field contrasted sharply with the feverish bustle off it as administrators and cricket journalists tried to find out what had happened to their game of cricket! Minutes later the players handed a statement to the press and returned to the field. The first political stand by cricketers was over. The background to the Newlands walk-off and the reasons for it are familiar to most South African cricket followers. The Springbok team to travel to Australia was due to be announced and the South African Cricket Association had asked the Nationalist Government to allow the best black players to be included in the touring party. Such a request now appears insignificant, but at the time it had enormous political implications.

The Government turned down the request, further damaging the flagging South African cause on both sporting and political fronts. The Aussie tour, already hanging by the thinnest of threads, seemed doomed. On the eve of the game Graeme Pollock, who was captaining the Rest side, his brother Peter, Mike Procter, Denis Lindsay and Barry Richards, who joined the group later, had decided over dinner that the players should show their support for the SACA. Initially they agreed that the Rest team should simply just boycott the match. As it was being staged as part of the Republic's 10th anniversary, it was the perfect platform for a political statement.

The respected Charles Fortune, later to become secretary of the SACA, was down in Cape Town to commentate on the game. He was staying at the same hotel and the players decided to consult him. He advised against the proposed action, believing that many sympathizers and cricket followers would be alienated by the refusal to play.

He did suggest, however, that if there was a genuine wish to make a stand, then a walk-off might be more appropriate. When the teams met the next morning, the remaining players were found in favour and the timing of the walk-off, and the wording of the statement were settled. It was decided that only the umpires and team managers would have prior knowledge of the walk-off and that to achieve greater impact, the Rest would have to field first. Careful thought was given to the wording of the statement. It read:

'We cricketers feel that the time has come for an expression of our views. We fully support the South African Cricket Association's application to include non-whites on the tour to Australia, if they are good enough, and furthermore subscribe to merit being the only criterion on the cricket field.'

Left wing commentators later described the protest as window-dressing and simply a last-ditch effort by the South African cricketers to save the Australian tour. To an extent this was true. But it was also an unequivocal and independent plea for equality in sport and selection totally on merit. It was not the first stage of a well-conceived plan to alter the state of

South African cricket, but was the spontaneous reaction of a frustrated group of young cricketers who had already seen two international tours cancelled for political reasons. It was the first time the players had made a public stand against racial and political influence.

On tours to England in the sixties, South African teams had been subjected to small but vocal demonstrations at grounds and airports. But the players never involved themselves and the future of South African cricket had been left solely in the hands of the administrators. They in turn believed that the International Cricket Conference's sense of fair play would ensure South Africa's speedy return.

The statement made by the players at Newlands in fact indicated only qualified support for the SACA. The cricketers did not want to see the token selection of Blacks, but simply wanted to see selection on merit alone.

The response to the walk-off was remarkable. Support and criticism came in abundance and often from unlikely sources. I was amazed at some who condemned us, and conversely the support base shattered me. It shook South Africa. Prime Minister BJ Vorster was to have presented festival medals to the players, but he failed to fulfil his commitment while an invitation to attend a braai at the house of Frank Waring, the Minister of Sport, was abruptly withdrawn. Waring dismissed the walk-off as merely a gesture for local and particularly popular overseas consumption. Helen Suzman, lone liberal voice in Parliament, remarked, 'Good for them. It's nice to see they are coming along so well.'

While reaction from the politicians was predictable, the response from the cricket administrators was not. There was annoyance that the cricketers had stepped out of their domain and a witch-hunt began to find out who had been behind the protest. Talented Don Mackay-Coghill, captaining Transvaal, was a strong contender for the Aussie tour, but was told by a national selector he would never be picked for South Africa – a forecast, which proved horribly accurate. Efforts were made to find the ringleaders in the South African side.

The selectors clearly felt Peter Pollock was to blame and Graeme was summoned before them and asked about his brother's involvement. Graeme told them it had been a team decision. On the day after the walk-off, a concerned Arthur Coy approached Peter and told him that he may be a scapegoat.

The inference clearly was that the selectors were considering leaving Peter out of the touring party. But the message quickly went back to the selectors: that they would have severe problems with the other players if Peter was omitted. Springbok captain Ali Bacher and his understudy Eddie

Barlow, who had both missed the Newlands match, immediately pledged their support for the players' stand.

The reaction of the media and public was intense and varied. As Vince concludes, there was cynicism, aggression and bewilderment. But the players had taken their stand. My role in it all probably ensured that a file was opened up with the Special Branch and I subsequently did address a few public meetings as well as gaining banner headlines in condemning Sports Minister Frank Waring. Even cricket administrators were now threatened, for clearly the players were fed up with rhetoric and what politics and politicians were doing to their game.

The dust settled, but the Australian tour was duly cancelled. Again there was the 'on-off' uncertainty and it was a relief when finally it was called off.

In September a Gallup poll showed that 63 percent of Australians approved the tour, 23 percent disapproved and 14 percent were undecided. It was doomed and Sir Donald Bradman announced the decision "with great regret."

A Rest of the World Series was to replace it, a team again to be captained by Gary Sobers. South African cricket was not too keen to release its players for the tour, but finally it was agreed that Hylton Ackerman, along with Tony Greig, could be available for the whole tour and that the two Pollocks could join the party from New Year's Eve 1971 till the end. The SACA insisted that we had to meet our commitments with Eastern Province until Christmas and then we could fly to Australia for the final three Tests of the series.

So it was two weary Pollock brothers who touched down in Melbourne on New Year's Eve to be met by a beaming Tony Greig, Hylton Ackerman and manager Jacobs. Twenty hours of flying would be no excuse. "The two of you have to play in tomorrow's Test at the MCG," pleaded Tony. "Of course we would. That's why we were there."

In the first two Tests of the series, the World team had been annihilated at Perth, thanks to some brilliant bowling by Dennis Lillee on a very helpful pitch, after a draw in the encounter at the Gabba at Brisbane.

But the Aussies were confident and rampant and the World team needed some new courage and rejuvenation. In fact, the critics were starting to damn the venture. Percy Beames wrote in the *Age* that the tour was the "biggest blunder" in recent years and that the World stars were being "grossly overpaid." Injury didn't help the tourists, the biggest blow being Clive Lloyd injuring his spine in a heavy fall. Lillee stood like an ogre. He took eight wickets for 29 in the first innings at Perth and then followed up with 63/4 in the second, making the match a financial disaster. It was all over in two days and 90 minutes! "Only the Pollocks can save this series" – that was the daunting message! No doubt the Aussies were also keen to settle some scores.

I knew that they were looking for me. It was pay back time for all those bouncers I had been dishing out for 14 Test matches since 1963. Now they had someone to give me my own medicine – fiery Dennis Lillee, Australia's new hero.

Lillee started again like a tornado, picking up where he had left off at Perth; taking five wickets for 48 in just over 16 overs – the World was wrecked for a mere 184. He bowled Graeme and Gary Sobers with successive balls leaving Greig to fend off the hat-trick!

Australia replied with 285. That included an undefeated 115 from Greg Chappell.

But the historic event, the innings that will remain one of the greatest classics ever seen at the Melbourne Cricket Ground, came when Sobers returned to bat a second time. Gary had been battling and critic Benaud had even suggested that he was Lillee's "bunny!" That didn't impress the brilliant West Indian. His innings started at 14:04 on the Monday and he was dismissed at 14:20 on the Tuesday for 254.

Sir Donald Bradman described it as one of the finest innings ever and a special video was produced of the performance, with Sir Don himself commentating. Ian Johnson, former Aussie skipper, rated it "the best I've seen." Doug Ring said, "Words escape me." John Snow said, "Bowling to Sobers is a gamble ... like a runaway train ... buffers are no good ... you just have to wait for him to crash or run out of steam." That's what the critics said and wrote. It was one of the great moments of my career.

I came in at number nine, having been dismissed cheaply in the first innings. The score was 319, our lead a mere 218 and in the pavilion were two veritable tail-enders, Norman Gifford and Bishen Bedi. Sobers was there on a century but Australia had control. Lillee, Massie, Jenner and O'Keeffe needed only to put on the finishing touches. But 319/7 wickets were destined to become 505, before the next wicket fell, Sobers was caught by Doug Walters off the bowling of Greg Chappell. Nearly 200 runs came from that partnership and I watched Dennis Lillee being unceremoniously hit out of the attack with the third new ball.

I still get goose bumps thinking about that innings and the privilege of sharing so personally in one of cricket's great moments. Gary and I both departed on 505, my contribution being 54 and the team innings closed at 514. Australia lost the match by 96 runs, but most importantly, it had been one of the truly great cricket matches. Colin McDonald commented, "This was a game that made me proud to talk about cricket again."

The World team never looked back. A deluge of bad weather spoilt the fourth Test at Sydney and the fifth Test at Adelaide gave Sobers his second win. So after all the dire predictions early on in the tour, the Rest of the World won the series and the public was back applauding cricket.

Sir Donald Bradman, whose brainchild was the replacement tour, allowed himself a smile. He had been well and truly vindicated. Almost as a reward, the four South Africans were invited to dine at the Bradman's home – a singular honour. What a fascinating evening and the greatest cricketer of all time even reminisced about the infamous bodyline series. In the early hours of the morning, the four of us, entranced by the incredible experience of a night with legendary Sir Don and Lady Bradman, made our way home, smiling like Cheshire cats. What more could I ask of cricket?

My last over

I had been thinking seriously about retiring. I had discussed it with Inez, but the timing was the issue. That morning I knew that I had arrived at *the moment.* It was time to say cheers. Once again we had put it over the Aussies. The record was simple – four series, three won and one drawn. In all, 16 Tests had produced ten mammoth victories and only two losses.

Indeed it was time to say farewell. Dad had always warned that we should get out at the top. "Don't wait until you are old, bitter and making excuses," was his advice. So from Adelaide, the wires tapped the news, "Peter Pollock has retired from cricket." A couple of more games for Eastern Province would constitute the final lap. I had also decided that retirement would be once and forever. No come backs!

Bill Woodin, president of Eastern Province cricket was not too pleased to hear the news. But he was certain he could change my mind. Even the official farewell function was low-key because he was sure I would be back next season. But it was not to be.

My last few games for Eastern Province provided a dream finish! In the Currie Cup we finally managed to persuade the ground man, Piet Bester to leave a bit of grass on the pitch. For a decade he had steadfastly refused, but he granted our wishes. The pitch proved to be a real green top. We beat both Western Province and Natal in a day and a half, the one by an innings and the other by ten wickets and this ensured that we came within a whisker of the Currie Cup.

Then the highlight of my career followed. Eastern Province had never won a trophy. It was March 18 1972 at a packed Wanderers Stadium and it was the Gillette Cup final. Eastern Province, after a pretty useful start, had been pegged back. At 158/6 I strode to the crease for my very last appearance at the Wanderers. The crowd rose as one to applaud me all the way to the crease.

I was overwhelmed as tears ran down my cheeks and it took me a while to restore my composure before I faced my first ball. Thirty-six runs later (second top score) Eastern Province had recovered to post a total of 225/9. Competitive, but not a winning score, especially with Barry Richards in the Natal line-up. I got an early wicket, but the turning-point of the match was Richards edging a widish delivery from me into the gloves of Ashton Galpin. The defining moment had come and gone and Eastern Province had clinched their first major trophy.

So the curtain came down on my cricket-playing career. I also knew that the timing was perfect. Even in those days I often suggested that maybe God had decided to bless my final hours on condition that the decision remained final. It all just went far too well. It was a fairy tale, too much so for it to be a coincidence. I couldn't have written the script better myself!

To ensure that I would not be tempted, I cut all ties with cricket, even at club level where they had promised that I could play just as a batsman. I knew it had to be a complete break. It would be too easy to take up the ball and start bowling again. So I decided to take up a biased bowl and start a different bowling.

Billy Woodin finally realized that I meant business. My sports career had seen me get very serious about hockey. I finally gained selection for the South African Country Districts team and then it was squash. Provincial representation in several Jarvis Cup tournaments and even a ranking in the top twenty in South Africa was the reward.

Then to bowls. From the start I took it seriously, spending much time rolling bowl after bowl. Very soon I was the Mill Park bowling singles champion, finished runner-up in the Eastern Province junior singles and then in 1974 I reached the quarter-finals in the singles at the South African championships.

When I thought it was safe, I allowed myself to get involved with an organization that I named the Knight watchmen. I wanted to get cricket enthusiasts and businessmen together and convince them to contribute financially to keeping Eastern Province well supplied with foreign imports. The game was going this way, as the Kingsmead Mynahs had found in Natal with Barry Richards. I was determined to utilize whatever limited financial resources were available in Port Elizabeth. Our first import was England spinner, Phil Edmonds and he was an unprecedented success.

Later I became an Eastern Province selector and managed a few of the teams, one of the occasions being a Gillette Cup final when Eastern Province was beaten by Rhodesia.

In that match I had a run-in with my very dear friend Charles Fortune. He had then become secretary of the SACA. He had a strong personality and liked things done his own way. Anyway, the first attempt at staging the above-mentioned final was hopelessly washed out. The deluge ensured that we couldn't continue the next day. We had to come back the following week.

Joe Pamensky was the president, but at the meeting to finalize all the rearrangements, Charles Fortune seemed to be doing all the talking and all the organizing and it wasn't going our way at all. It annoyed me very much. At one stage I looked at Joe Pamensky and I simply said, "Joe, I thought you were the president. Charles seems to be running the show." A dead silence followed. The rest of the meeting was staid and stilted and Charles didn't speak to me for years!

My retirement saw me change jobs. In fact, I just moved into the next-door building, home of the *Sunday Times* regional office. Some 14 years at the *Eastern Province Herald* had served me admirably, but now was the time to venture into the big league. The *Sunday Times* was just that. I was to be involved with more than just sport, and the nature of the new animal I now worked for meant that stories needed to be more controversial and certainly a lot juicier.

For a story to be published, it needed to be eye-catching or head-turning. I met some incredible characters in the short time I worked for *The Times*. There was a weird guy who could predict the future and who was always around to help the police find missing persons. I had a lawyer contact who exposed some embarrassing aspects of the legal system.

One afternoon I was invited to interview someone who promised me the story of a lifetime! I pitched at his office to note that he had been drinking heavily, had a loaded double-barrelled shotgun on his desk and wanted me to personally witness him shooting an archrival. "Have you ever witnessed a murder?" he asked. Most certainly not! I was scared out of my wits. After a couple of hours of hell he left the room for a brief moment. I took the gap, dived out of a window and screeched off in my car.

When I got home, before I could even begin to tell the story, my wife let loose. She was furious that I was late and had forgotten the money for the gardener! When I told her what had happened she thought it was a concocted excuse. Later she apologized!

The last straw for me involved a well-known Port Elizabeth family. The one son had psychiatric problems, but against medical advice the family insisted that he stayed at home with his mother. It became a rather gruesome story when he killed his mom. Naturally it made national headlines and the *Sunday Times* wanted the best story. I was their man in the area and they asked me to do the investigations and tabulate the story under a big by-line.

There was no way I was going to get involved. I knew the family too well and I also didn't want to get tangled up with all the gory details. I asked a colleague on the *Evening Post* to do the story for us. He would be suitably rewarded.

His story was good and when they phoned me prior to publication to congratulate me on my journalistic efforts, they were very annoyed to hear I hadn't written it. In fact, I got a roasting.

This made me reconsider my position. Most certainly I didn't want to spend my life writing about other people's problems and digging up dirt. In fact I had become a little disillusioned by what was being paraded as journalism. My dad would turn in his grave! Besides, I was also pretty poorly paid!

Cricket had a question mark. The doors were closing. I could become an international traveller, but was that what I wanted? Certainly digging and delving into private lives, seeking smut and scandal, was out! Not long after that, I met with Stan Anderson, chief executive of a furniture group in Port Elizabeth. He was not only a top businessman, but was also very involved with cricket. I told him my reservations about journalism and he offered me a position. Just like that. "I will come and see you in the morning," I promised.

When I arrived, he was very surprised. "What are you doing here," he inquired. "I have come for that job." He seemed a bit embarrassed. Maybe the beer had been talking, for both of us!

But Stan made a plan. He created a position for me, gave me a decent car, an impressive marketing title and off I went, a glorified sales representative. But I discovered I could sell!

Soon I was a director and truly earning my keep. As national sales executive I established a clientele that was to serve me well for the next fourteen years. The furniture industry was to become my home and I kept my hand in writing columns, initially for the *Saturday Evening Post* and then later for the *Sunday Times* and *Natal Mercury* when we moved down to Durban in 1978.

Sales opened a whole new realm in terms of having to give of oneself. Everything had formerly revolved around my sport and my opinion as a writer, but now I had to sell myself. I was surprised, not only at the results, but at how much I enjoyed socializing. Admittedly alcohol became more and more the catalyst, but I was enjoying work, selling and jostling around the world of big deals and promotions. To offset the socializing, I had become a long-distance runner, sweating out the toxins.

I enjoyed my 27 years in Port Elizabeth, but got into a rut. So the move to Durban was a most welcome change. New friends, a new environment and a new challenge – the Comrades marathon. It's addictive and soon I was hooked. I must add, however, that it is truly a magnificent event, presenting a unique challenge to the individual. The first time I crossed the finishing line to complete a Comrades, it was a moment unparalleled in my sporting career. Though there are thousands on the road, the battle is against yourself. Those moments when you ask inside, "What am I doing out here?" have to be dealt with all by yourself.

Bruce Fordyce, the Comrades legend whom I got to know well, confirmed that whether you are out front or right at the back, it's the same intimate challenge: you, your will and a long, long road! The bug had bitten me and running became my daily fix. It was an antidote to social excesses. Or so I thought.

The Kingsmead Mynahs had approached me through Brian Booth and Clive

Conyngham to become a member with the view to taking over as president. They needed some clout in their dealings with Natal cricket and obviously they thought I had the right credentials.

I served for two years, the maximum stint, and then ended up on the Natal executive in my own right. With my weekly column in the Durban newspaper I was enjoying a strong voice in Natal cricket. Occasionally I would get a call from Mike Procter regarding some of my views and comments, but there were seldom any serious challenges. I suppose to challenge the media or a critic is foolhardy, for the last word always rests with them. Apologies or corrections are usually neatly tucked away or worded in such a way as to virtually deny culpability. Back-handed admission of error or misinterpretation is a skill that the media has perfected over the years.

The pen is powerful. Indeed it's mightier than the sword. When we are sitting behind our typewriters, we feel it's our duty to hold others accountable, but we don't like the same rules to apply to us. The media take instant offence to criticism, usually suggesting that freedom is threatened.

Sadly, it is the inevitable lot of sportsmen to become the target of criticism or controversy. When you reach the top you become public property and fair game for critical opinion. The controversial issues might be big or small, constructive or destructive but misdemeanour, real or perceived, on the field or off, seldom escapes retribution.

Sometimes, however, I wonder whether writers quite realize the tremendous influence they wield as they sit down to write their stories, particularly when they are looking for an angle or just thumb-sucking to fill space! Too often controversy is born out of a perception or a misinterpretation or just plain and simple mud raking. Once the story has been printed, the seed has been sown, irrespective of vehement denials or explanations.

The Pollock philosophy, born out of inside knowledge and first-hand experience, was simply never to argue or contend with the media. Rather just keep your mouth closed and answer the critics with action and deeds on the field. That's not always easy, but it is the right strategy, the only option.

In my playing days the media were relatively tame. We knew whom to avoid in England and Australia, but at home the press was extremely supportive. Radio commentators, Charles Fortune and Gerhard Viviers, were fantastic. They were always positive and parochial. I believe that they were major contributors to the South African cricket cause. Negative remarks were seldom heard and this ignited wonderful support from the public. The two of them were the game's best public relations officers. And the fact that people still talk in legendary terms of the feats and personalities of those times – the 60s and 70s – is testimony to the incredible influence of Fortune and Viviers.

Ali Bacher has always been a respecter of media power and has cleverly harnessed it over the years. One thing I always knew when I was writing my column, was that Ali would read it! As a cricket administrator he made it his business to keep in touch, so I knew I had his ears and eyes.

Those were interesting times. First there was the Kerry Packer controversy and that huge mess! Of course, views differed and depended upon which side you were on. But it definitely birthed the "pyjama game" and made cricketers a lot richer. Tony Greig was a leading light in the action and I found myself pretty supportive of the venture. South Africa was isolated, so it didn't affect us. In fact, with so many South Africans involved, it gave the fans and the writers much to talk about. In our country Ali was building a "mean machine" – the Transvaal side. This was to become his platform into cricket leadership and governance. I didn't like the principle of such utter domination and wrote that.

Then came those rebel tours. Again full marks to Ali and Joe. It was a battle for survival against great odds and while I was particularly disturbed about the way a rather hapless group of Sri Lankans were used politically and racially, the good doctor got my support and backing. When you have to write a column every week, at times you battle for a topic. It's then that you often play devil's advocate or take up a cause just for the sake of filling some space. That's generally when you tread on corns and then are loathe to apologize.

Those were good times. Business was flourishing, cricket-writing was a pleasant hobby and road running had become a passion.

I had been appointed executive director of Edblo (Africa) – a multi-million concern – and the sales staff that I controlled in Durban, Port Elizabeth, East London and Cape Town were winning sales incentive prizes like crackers at Christmas dinner. Trips to Mauritius, Beacon Isle in Plettenberg Bay and Sun City were virtually becoming the annual festive holiday.

It was the best of times. That's what I wanted them all to believe. My social drinking had become excessive. As an after dinner speaker I was much in demand with my dry sense of humour and bawdy stories. Some of them were plain crude. In fact, Eric Dalton, former South African cricketer walked out of a dinner at which I was speaking, in protest against my language usage. I must say I was a little hurt, but others convinced me that it was a prudish overreaction. That's what I wanted to hear.

Then came another one of those defining moments. I was chief organizer of a banquet to be held at the City Hall in Durban to fête Vintcent van der Bijl. It was his benefit and we had arranged with Kim Shippey, a well-known broadcaster, to do a presentation of "This is your life" based on the BBC model.

It was a mammoth undertaking. The banquet had two guest speakers; Tony Greig and Prof. Chris Barnard, of heart transplant fame. My job was master of ceremonies. What a day of preparation. Exhausted and anxious, I had little to eat and towards evening too much to drink. "An unprecedented success," was the unanimous rating of the evening. The only glitch – the master of ceremonies had had too much to drink. In fact, he was downright embarrassing.

I knew it had been a disaster, but I didn't want to hear it. Up stepped Tony Greig. "Peter, what happened to you last night? You were drunk. You were very embarrassing. What is happening? You need to pull yourself together."

His words hit me like a thunderbolt. It was the truth, but I was angry that he had said it. Who did he think he was! Tony had the guts to tell me straight to my face.

8

REGENERATION

The moment of truth

I t was Sunday evening, August 1, 1982. It had been an ordinary day and as my wife Inez busied herself with the final touches in smartening herself for church, I grabbed an ice-cold dumpy of lager, unscrewed the cap and flopped onto the TV couch. Inez was humming a tune I assumed was one of those melodic new songs they were singing at the churches lately. It was all part of the happy-clappy charismatic movement that I found all too threatening. "Why should she be so happy?" I thought. After all the weekend was over and for me another week of business pressure lay ahead.

When you have nothing to be happy about it is annoying to see someone else seemingly happy about nothing. What joy could she possibly find by going to church, even if she was "born again?" I decided that I was going to investigate what went on at that church because she would leave at about 18:15 and return home even more joyful some time near nine o'clock.

It was a Presbyterian church and from what I could recall of the services they were strictly one-hour affairs, somewhat boring and to me totally devoid of any intelligible message. Pastors were preaching from their pulpits six feet above understanding and thus the same height above contradiction.

It always intrigued cynical me that as churchgoers passed the pastor at the entrance, they would invariably nod politely and say, "Thank you," and compliment him on a lovely message, a message that they usually didn't even understand. To me it was always verbal hieroglyphics! It almost seemed as though the pastor set out to defy comprehension, speaking in a language only God understood, as if to prove his super spirituality. Perhaps it was just that I had not practised enough to listen during my rather chequered career as a churchgoer.

Anyway, there was no doubt that Inez was looking forward to the service as I nestled into the couch, savouring a beer.

Oh no! Horror of horrors, I heard that tell-tale music signifying a religious programme and there it was: the dreaded "Cross Questions" – a Christian discussion session. This type of stuff wasn't for me and almost as if I feared anything with a Christian connotation, my instant reaction was always to switch it off. I could not tolerate epilogues or anything religious. Maybe they stirred some deep guilt in me?

But I kept the TV on this time and in fact immediately became interested, because the topic under review was the charismatic movement and the issue of being born again. On the panel was Reinhard Bonnke, the well-known evangelist, and Stephen Grenfell, critic and self-confessed cynic. He immediately showed himself to have the same sort of views as I did on those self-righteous people who claimed to be closer to God than the rest of us.

Inez had been a Christian for just over a month and on a couple of occasions I had expounded to her about the hypocrisy of her new-found faith. Because I remembered a smattering of Sunday school stories out of the Bible, I reckoned that I knew all about religion and I felt that I was very convincing in exposing this as just a passing phase in her life. She was after all over 40 and women get neurotic and emotional as they go through a change of life!

But perhaps the most impressive part of my argument was the loudness of my voice and the fact that I arrogantly did not permit any counter assaults. You just can't win against this type of bloody-minded aggression.

But now on television Stephen Grenfell was saying most of the things that I propounded. I called Inez. She was putting the finishing touches to her make-up in the bedroom. "Come and listen!" I shouted. She came. She listened, obviously not too impressed! "You see, it's what I have been telling you all along," I blurted. I was simply suggesting that it was her prerogative to believe me or not.

But now that my views were being confirmed on TV, she had no option but to agree! I think she was a little disappointed by what Grenfell was saying, but deep down I was smilingly and triumphantly adding my quiet little "I told you so." She was, however, spared much more agony because a car drove up the driveway and a hoot suggested that her lift had arrived. She could now escape my clutches and those of Stephen Grenfell and seek the haven of her church. I thought to myself, "Typical. These Christians can't see the blunt facts and reality of life. They are always just running away living pipedreams."

This left me on my own in front of the television. Suddenly, I found myself deeply transfixed. Slowly but clearly it was as if the whole TV set was speaking only to me. Looking at Reinhard Bonnke I saw clean-shaven freshness and innocence and deep tranquillity and I saw a power, strength and confidence which seemed so out of place, hidden behind that smiling countenance.

In fact, I never heard a word he said as he joined the debate. His face just shone at me. It was quite remarkable. Then I looked at Grenfell and suddenly in his place, I saw myself transposed on the screen and there, rudely exposed, sitting in his seat was the ugly real me. Yes, there was the fast bowler whose intense hard eyes were once pictured and headlined in a magazine article under the banner of "The man who loves to hate." I saw the cynic, the know-all, the ego so full of pride, the selfishness and the one-track ambition that sought recognition and gratification no matter what the expense. Yes, I had a killer instinct and I understood that 'nice guys came second'. Those are the rules of the rat race. It all came before me like a flood and what I saw was ugly.

Had anyone been sitting in the room they would not have heard a word, but it was as if I was challenged: *You are in the process of trying to gain the world, something you will never do. But tragically you are also losing your soul.*

A thunderbolt! From heaven?

Worse, I was still arrogantly daring to question Jesus Christ. There I was, seemingly pointing an accusing finger out of the mud and darkness of my pigsty of a life. Inside I felt sick, sick, sick, the type of nausea that is empty and soul-destroying. Indeed I had never before seen myself so clearly exposed, cut through the middle by a surgeon's scalpel. On display, those disembowelled innards. Oh so ugly! It shook me to the very core. It was as vivid an experience as I have never had before and that ordinary Sunday was starting to become very extra-ordinary.

Time flashed by, for the next thing I remember was the telephone ringing and my wife inviting me to come up the road to Arnie and Lorraine Gilchrist's house to have coffee. Normally I would have been in bed and asleep by this time, but somehow I knew this phone call was coming and I was drawn to them like a magnet.

When I arrived, Henry Hauser, the former Springbok soccer skipper and his charming wife, May who was a counsellor at the church of the Good Shepherd in Durban North were there. Henry read from the Bible. May set out to explain to me how wrong I was in some of the blasphemies that I often resorted to in my arguments. Poor, frustrated Inez really deserved a medal for what she had gone through, but being so fresh and newborn as a Christian, she couldn't be expected to provide adequate answers to my barbed questions. There are none so deaf as those who don't wish to hear.

That experience in front of the TV set had opened my ears. They pricked up like a frightened rabbit's, keen to hear and perhaps fearing the awesomeness of the message. I was still very aggressive, but at least I listened. Very much later, somewhere near midnight, as we got up to leave, May slipped a little piece of paper into my pocket with a tender "Just in case you need it," and a smile.

Peter Pollock – the gifted young cricketer. At the age of 14 he was playing club cricket with the men. At 17 he was introduced to provincial cricket and started playing Test cricket when he was 20 years old.

Peter made his Test debut against New Zealand at Kingsmead in December 1961 in spectacular style. He took nine wickets for 99, single-handedly snatching a Test out of the jaws of defeat. This Test was regarded as the starting point for a cricketing era that was going to take South Africa into a new dimension.

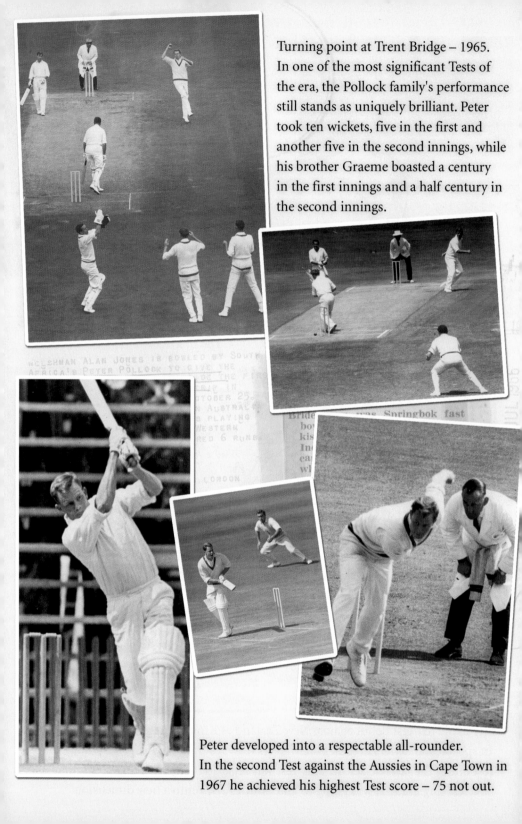

Turning point at Trent Bridge – 1965.
In one of the most significant Tests of
the era, the Pollock family's performance
still stands as uniquely brilliant. Peter
took ten wickets, five in the first and
another five in the second innings, while
his brother Graeme boasted a century
in the first innings and a half century in
the second innings.

Peter developed into a respectable all-rounder.
In the second Test against the Aussies in Cape Town in
1967 he achieved his highest Test score – 75 not out.

Victory for the World XI at Lord's 1967.
Sharing in the glory are Graeme Pollock, Barlow, Lindsay, Kanhai, Peter Pollock,
Sobers, Gibbs, Hunte, McKenzie, Bland and Nurse.

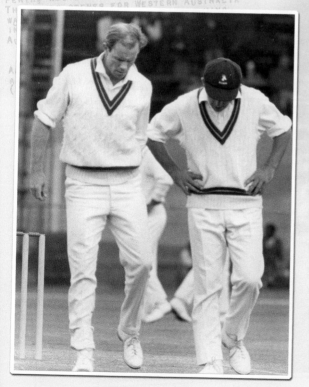

Peter has just bowled his
final ball in Test cricket – he
pulled his hamstring in the
Test against Australia in
Port Elizabeth in 1970.
On 18 March 1972 he played
the last match of his career for
Eastern Province at the
Wanderers. The highlight for
him was that Eastern Province
had won the Gillette Cup.

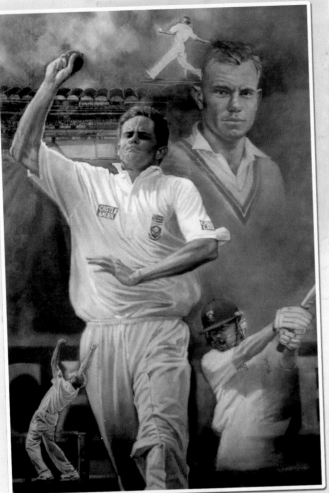

This striking painting was commissioned by the UCB to commemorate Shaun Pollock's 100 Test wickets and 1000 Test runs. Both Dad and Son achieved 100 Test wickets!

The two unique father and son combinations who have each taken 100 Test wickets. Peter and Shaun with New Zealanders Lance Cains and his son Chris.

In a class of their own: the terrific Pollock trio! Shaun received his 200th wicket presentation at Kingsmead, the same ground where uncle Graeme had scored 274 against Australia and his dad had taken 9 wickets in his dream Test debut.

Peter as chairman of selectors at the World Cup 1999 at Edgbaston.

World Cup 1999. Bob Woolmer gets to grips with a technical point at Edgbaston prior to the semi-final against Australia. Peter Pollock is keeping a fatherly eye.

Peter Pollock married Inez Benson in July 1966.

The Pollock children:
Gavin and Shaun,
Nicola and her husband Cliff,
Anthea.

Peter Pollock the journalist at work.

Peter and Inez with Colin Cowdrey
in Adelaide – World Cup 1992.

Honouring radio commentator
Charles Fortune. Peter made the
presentation at his farewell banquet.

God's fast bowler – Peter the evangelist spreading the message of hope, true glory and victory.

At the Cape Christian Celebration at Newlands on Human Rights Day, March 2001, Peter bringing the Gospel to 50 000 people.

I don't know if the others noticed that gesture, but only later, once I got home and Inez was in the bathroom showering, I read the note. It was The Sinner's Prayer. I had no doubt at all. It was time to give my life to Jesus.

I went down to a quiet spot at the bottom end of the garden and I committed my life. These are the words I prayed:

> Lord Jesus, I come to you today just as I am. I thank you that you accept me just as I am. I admit that I am a sinner and repent of my sins of the past. Thank you for dying on the Cross for my sins and please come into my life and become my Lord and Saviour. I surrender my will to you right now. Thank you for coming into my life and forgiving my sins.

What had started as a very ordinary day suddenly became the greatest day of my life. My forty years of wandering in the world's wilderness had come to an end. I was now 'born again.' Conversions don't come more sudden than that. I had opened the door, taken my first step and my life was never to be the same again. I was a growling lion transformed into a lamb.

I will never forget the moment of conversion. I didn't hear any bells or trumpets, there was no singing in my ears but there was a distinct awareness of a giant burden being lifted from my shoulders. I sobbed like a baby. It was the sobbing of a child who had been trying to take on the world on his own, trying to satisfy those self-consuming, never-ending goals and yardsticks.

Often as a child I remember finding out that things often were not what they seemed and that people didn't always mean what they said. Success and failure too were fickle impostors separated by a very thin red line. Often nothing is more consoling and healthy than a good honest sob! Of course as you get older you are not supposed to seek such relief. Cowboys don't cry, they say. You have to learn to fight your own battles. You learn to build a cocoon of protection around the little child within. You enjoy success, despise weak people and failures and become a self-sufficient, self-indulgent bastion of man's durable and unquenchable will to exist and survive.

Little do we know that it's a self-destroying time bomb that leaves a trail of heartbreak and misery. The horrible truth is that while you are travelling that road, you won't let anyone try to tell you that you are wrong.

"I did it my way," the refrain of Frank Sinatra's classic song brings me goose bumps. I knew I was too conditioned to the world's value system, I couldn't see the wood for the trees, the light for the darkness and the right for the wrong.

My role as husband and father

Manfred Hartslief at the St Columba's Church in Port Elizabeth married Inez and me on 30 July 1966, after we had been courting for just under two years. I will never forget our first date, a film called *The Guns of Batasi*. It was a tense story and at one stage Inez grabbed my leg in her deep involvement with the exciting action on the silver screen. She does have this tendency to get really involved when she watches films and her grabbing my leg had no ulterior motives. She was quite startled by my reaction and how I virtually brushed her hand away. Showing affection wasn't one of my strong points!

It was the way we were brought up. Inez admits that her family was much the same, so obviously it was par for the course in those days. Victorian, I believe!

Anyway, the following evening we were going to date again, but Inez was not quite sure that she wanted to see me again. In fact, she made some excuse about attending another party and suggested that perhaps we should go along. She obviously felt more comfortable in a whole crowd than at an intimate dinner with me. At a party she could also ditch me, I suppose. Anyway I insisted that I had already made the booking, which I hadn't, but that turned out to be the night that we switched on to each other and the relationship struck up strongly.

Inez was a divorcee and this did not particularly please my parents. When they saw matters were getting serious, they intervened. In fact, I was prohibited from seeing her, which resulted in clandestine rendezvous. It was highly secretive and exciting.

On one occasion, when I phoned Inez from the club, I accidentally dialled our home number. Dad answered and before I had time to realize what I had done, I asked to speak to Inez. Dad immediately recognized my voice, but when I got home later I denied it, saying it must have been a coincidence. I didn't fool him.

Matters then reached a head and in making it quite clear to my mother and father that I was going to marry Inez, I moved out of the family house, spending a few days at a local hotel. Once they realised that I was serious and had made up my mind, they finally accepted Inez, even if just superficially in those early days.

Cricket officials had also got involved with trying to break up our relationship. There was an attempt to get Inez transferred to another city. During our time of courtship Inez was blamed for my run of bad form. Probably my ducking and diving to avoid detection was a contributory factor. The family did their best, especially Dad, but I don't think that Inez ever really felt totally part of us all and with good reason. During the secret meetings I felt like a naughty schoolboy and at times it was quite harrowing. It was certainly not a firm foundation for a marriage.

There were a couple of problems about the wedding. Inez was an Anglican and would have liked to marry in that church, but the priest refused because she had been divorced and they were still pretty strict about that in those days.

So it was off to the Presbyterian Church. At least they seemed to be more understanding, but this incident didn't enhance the image of the church in our eyes. Nobody enjoys rejection. All's well that ends well, and we were finally married with Graeme and Eddie Barlow as the best men.

It was a great day, a lovely reception and the honeymoon was aboard the *Transvaal Castle* for a week as we sailed from Port Elizabeth to Durban and back. An amusing aside was that Inez developed what seemed to be mumps and the ship's doctor, who was obviously better looking than he was qualified, diagnosed that it wasn't mumps but an allergy – an allergy to me! Would you believe it! It made some good reading in the newspapers.

Our eldest child, Gavin, was born about a year later in July 1967 followed by Anthea in February 1970, Nicola in December 1971 and Shaun in July 1973. In between there were quite a few other pregnancies – a total of eight in all – but four were lost in midstream. Big families seemed the in-thing. Our closest friends all seemed pretty committed to building a nation.

We came very close to losing Anthea. Apparently it is quite common in Caesarean births for a hyaline membrane problem to develop and I must admit that at one stage we had resolved ourselves to accepting that we might lose her.

She went from incubator to respirator and was literally being kept alive by the machine. Inez didn't even stay on at the hospital. It was a traumatic experience knowing that her little daughter was in there, battling for her life.

Everything turned out well except that the whole experience certainly left its psychological scars. All incidents, however big or small, affect perceptions and consequently the lives of our children. Those formative years saw much pain and heartache. But we blundered on, regardless.

It had always been my custom to allow Inez to make all the decisions around the house because, quite frankly they were in my opinion too small and inconsequential to require my valuable time. I kept all my thinking and decision-making to running the business, writing my articles and any other issues involving the fulfilment of my career. I was, after all, the provider, the breadwinner and as I often said to them, they were totally dependant on me for the basics and luxuries. I expected to be accorded my rightful respect as head of the house when I came home. Any actions of mine which were queried or criticized, brought instant reaction and when I launched out verbally, I could be very scathing, pointed and hurtful.

It was in my nature to lose my temper quickly, but I was just as quick to forgive and forget. However, what seemed to me a quick blow-up, remedied by a quick sorry, didn't always slide off so easily with the family, especially Inez. Verbal ding-dongs didn't and never do get anyone anywhere. Inez just clammed up and kept her hurts inside. I arrogantly thought I was doing a great job as a husband.

I felt too that children should be seen and not heard and that discipline was something sadly lacking in the world today. My upbringing had been pretty strict and I had always felt that I had not suffered through being tightly disciplined.

My career was a top priority. Being a firm believer in either doing something properly or not at all, whenever I got myself involved I set my course straight and true and the family was always the last consideration. They had to fit in with my plans, not I with theirs, and I guess that though they might not have liked it particularly, they settled for it. They never complained.

I travelled quite a lot, both for sports and business and I always sensed that when I went away, it reduced the strain at home. I was not easy to live with.

My selfishness and single-mindedness did not apply only to work or writing, but also to my sporting interests. There can be no more selfish commitment than long-distance running; so much time is involved in the arduous preparations. The heavy training, involving the alarm clock ringing at 05:00, certainly didn't enhance relationships at home. Later in the day, with guests visiting, I used to nod off to sleep at the most inopportune or inconvenient moments. I was a dead loss as a participant in any family fun, especially around Comrades time. I hated to feel caged in. I was restless in the home environment. "Stop prowling around like a caged lion," Inez would often say.

I treated family like an appendage, a social cross we had to bear. I knew all about the carnal type of love and that side of the marriage, but as for tender loving care, that wasn't my game. Inez' commitment was the result of many years of searching for something. Believing that if she gave her life to Jesus, she could hand over all her problems, such as an impossible husband, Inez made her decision at Lorraine Gilchrist's house. She was challenged and led by May Hauser and said that when Inez got down on her knees and invited Jesus to become her Lord, she felt an incredible warmth totally surround her. She too wept uncontrollably.

It took her a couple of days to tell me. I don't remember exactly how I responded. If I recall correctly, I congratulated her as if she had joined some club. I tried to show good husbandly interest, but you know how patronising that can be. I felt that that would be one of those passing emotional experiences that seem to beset women in the fearful forties. I was extremely condescending.

But I immediately noticed changes in her. She was more loving, pleasant and accommodating and she started agreeing with me on such issues as disciplining the kids. Immediately our relationship improved at home. I was being loved, honoured and respected. Even the kids noticed a change. So did the animals if they could have spoken! A miracle! I thought she was just putting on a great act. It was mind over matter. It was nice. There was no more nagging from her. But there would have to be a simple explanation.

I had a habit of interrupting Inez's stories, adjusting her facts when she was

116

relating an incident, exposing any exaggerations and I often belittled her in company. Despite it all, she stuck it out. She came in for a heavy barrage for being born again, especially if I sensed any effort to try and convert me. She had been a perfect silent evangelist. The changes in her had impacted me. My anger or verbal retaliation only emphasized that I was feeling threatened by a truth that was daily becoming more real, though I would not admit it.

I kept telling myself that it was just a passing phase. Her change had been enough for me to even suggest to my running mates at the Hangover Harriers that they should send their wives along to this church! I told them that born again wives are definitely better than ordinary ones. We laughed mockingly and downed a few more pints. "At least she knows now who is the boss at home" – a testimony to her new spirit of submission!

Wives often try to bash their husbands over the head with their new-found Bibles and they just drive them further back into the wilderness. Inez just allowed her love and attitude to do the talking. But there were slip-ups.

One Sunday morning, after a rather heavy night, with too much red wine, I wasn't exactly joyful when I awoke. The portable radio had been turned on to a religious programme and I was getting a sermon in my bedroom. This was pushing it. I gave her a piece of my mind. Had she gone crazy? I told her in no uncertain terms that I was the provider, and I was in charge, not Jesus. If she wanted to go and sing hymns and listen to sermons, she was welcome to attend church, but she was not to bring any of that religion into my home. I was also not going to have the kids brought up as a bunch of street corner Bible-punchers and that was that!

Such strong verbiage would have rendered any Christian either angry or emotional. She listened. I noticed a couple of reluctant tears in her eyes. She didn't reply, but those tears spoke volumes. How dared I speak in such terms about her Jesus? Inez seldom cried, but that tear of grief at my attitude and response was a beautiful indicator of the spirit of God resident in her.

Christ also speaks through ordinary people. The kingdom of God is seen when evil lives change, when defeated lives become victorious, when embittered lives become sweet and when family units are restored to each other. It's easy to recognize Him. That tear was one of the irresistible calling cards. Like the mighty walls of Jericho, something was disintegrating inside me. Those tears ministered so profoundly. The five-week period between Inez's commitment and my eventually seeing the light, was an indescribably tough time for her.

Total commitment

Inez and her friends had been praying, but more and more abuse came from me. I was running away on the inside, but the bravado outside was saying that

Jesus is only for weaklings and failures. Then that night everything changed.

After having her spirits dashed by my absolute relish at what Stephen Grenfell had had to say in the early part of "Cross Questions," she was soon among friends at the church. It was a splendid service. The sermon was challenging and the praise and worship was deep and meaningful.

After the service she and Lorraine and the Hausers went for hotdogs and coffee. But alas, there were none. Lorraine suggested that they should all go to her place. Inez discussed the dreadful programme she had watched and my reactions to it. They suggested that she should invite me over so that they could attempt some answers "There is no way he will come," she said. "He is usually in bed by now. He also doesn't drink coffee." But they finally convinced her to call me.

My eldest son Gavin answered the phone and she immediately asked if I was in bed. She was most surprised to hear that I was still up and about. I came to the phone, she invited me to come over for coffee and my instant acceptance completely dumbfounded her. She, of course had no idea of my experience before the TV set.

When I got there, my attitude initially was aggressive, but at least I listened. Slowly but surely I ran out of questions and arguments. I was as meek as a lamb as I left that evening, with May sneaking that piece of paper into my pocket.

And so I committed my life to Jesus all on my own, in the darkness of the bottom corner of the garden. There was just enough light to read May's prayer.

I didn't admit it for just over a week. Inez had already got herself involved in orientation classes at the church and a week later she was still uncertain about whether or not I had made a decision.

There was almost immediately an irresistible urge within me to read the Bible and the tracts that I had so arrogantly ordered out of the house.

One evening I was browsing through one of my wife's books when I came to a page that listed about forty words which described what a Christian should not be. I studied the list long and hard. It was the first time in my life that I had got 100 percent in an examination! I was the lot.

Despondency struck. They were all inside words: hate, revenge, pride, jealousy, lust, greed, selfishness, anxiety, fear and the list seemed endless. Each one of these sins was inside, deep down. That was the real me! Not the one I pretended to be to the world. That was the me God knew.

I picked up the telephone and shared my disillusionment with May. "If I have got to be without all these things to be a Christian, I simply can't do it. It's a waste of time," I told her. There was a moment or two of silence. Then May responded. "Have you given your life to Jesus?" she asked. "Yes, with your little piece of paper," I sheepishly confessed. "Praise God," came her reply. "Don't worry about those words. You just keep your eyes on Jesus," was the advice.

"And if nothing has changed in three months we will have something to worry about," she added.

The plane crash – in retrospect

There was another profound aspect of my decision that night at the bottom of the garden. Tears flooded and this meant that I had to stay out there for some time because I wasn't about to tell my wife what I had done or let her see that I had been crying.

But as I was standing there I was rather vividly reminded of that air crash with Ted Dexter, almost as if to underline that it was a miracle – an answer to prayer. I had, after all, cried out to God in flight, but after scrambling to safety, I never took even one second to thank Him or even acknowledge that He might have had a hand in it all!

I had been very quick to call on Him, but not to give a word of thanks. I was more interested in getting the story into the newspaper – like a good reporter.

Twelve years later, memories of the incident flashed back. But what agony those twelve years had been for me as I travelled the world and South Africa for sport and business. I was neurotic and claustrophobic about air travel.

Anyway, as the crash came back to me, it was almost as if to confirm that God had answered a prayer and that His hand had been upon the event. After all, not too many people survive air crashes! At that moment there was both acknowledgement and sincere thanks.

I didn't think much more about it, but five days later I left on one of my monthly chores to attend a meeting in Johannesburg. It was the early flight up and back in the evening. I got to the airport, boarded the plane and was strapping myself in, readying myself for the take-off and the next nerve-wracking hour when it suddenly hit me: all the fear and tension had gone! I was as relaxed as a baby in its mother's arms.

From that moment on, my neurosis about flying disappeared and these days I am one of the calmest, happiest passengers around. Later a very important insight challenged my intellect. Simply this: I had always known about God. In fact, though I never took much interest, there was never any doubt in my mind that He existed.

Then came that crash. In my most desperate moment of need I prayed. I cried out to Him. And a prayer was answered. I walked away from an air crash, physically unscathed. God had revealed Himself to me, but I walked away arrogantly. For twelve years I had been fearful, anxious and a total neurotic.

Then at the bottom end of the garden something profound happened. I had always known about God, but that night I changed *knowing about God* into *knowing God*. Now there is a massive difference between the two. It's the difference between religion and intellectual acceptance and a spiritual relationship. It's the latter that changes lives and value-systems. Additionally, the air crash probably underlined that man and his science are also fallible. I still don't understand how airplanes fly, but I had accepted air travel as one of man's ultimate scientific feats. I probably never imagined that I could ever be involved in a crash. Man and science are certainly not infallible, as disappointing as the dawning of that truth might be to accept!

A couple of weeks later, Inez and I were eating out at a nearby steakhouse, which had become a regular haunt for us on Saturday evenings. Ron, the manager, was always very kind and accommodating and we loved visiting the place. We were almost part of the décor, though sometimes he must have found our parties a little rowdy, especially when I was there with my running mates. Anyway, he never complained. We were good for business! This particular evening was one of the quiet nights, just Inez and me.

After the meal I had lit up a cigarette and taken a couple of puffs when suddenly it tasted bitter and horrible. I had this burning conviction, excuse the pun, to give up smoking there and then. I had tried on and off for many, many years. A good friend John Ferrant and I had often had bets on giving up smoking, but though we managed for short periods, we didn't ever win the 'battle of the weed.' We sometimes set the stakes high financially, but even that didn't work. One of us would cheat or opt out with a good excuse. I don't remember ever having a payout either way! We just accepted finally that we were both hooked on the weed. Inez hated smoking. She really did.

As a child she had to share a room with a sickly mother who was a chain-smoker. Inez was almost obsessive in her dislike of smoking and often after our guests had left, she compulsively cleaned out the ashtrays, counting the butts. She knew exactly how many I had smoked!

Anyway, I stumped out the cigarette and symbolically handed over the half-empty pack of cigarettes to Inez, telling her it was over. I was going to give up smoking.

I had felt prompted, but I simply handed the problem over. I even had the cheek to ask, as I prayed, that I would suffer no after-effects. I wanted no withdrawal symptoms. I had been smoking for 23 years. I also requested that I would not become irritable or put on any weight – the normal fears of the repentant smoker!

That Saturday night was the last time I have ever touched a cigarette. More importantly, it was the last time I have ever felt inclined to smoke. I was instantly rid of an affliction that had been with me for 23 years. I didn't feel a thing, I did not even have the slightest craving for nicotine.

Inevitably, my drinking had to be addressed. I had this strong conviction that I had to quit, but I didn't want to listen to that inner voice. I looked around for justification and found it. Elders at the church were drinking beers and some pastors I knew enjoyed their wine. Nowhere could I find in Scripture that drinking was condemned. Drunkenness I saw as wrong, but who will admit to being motherlessly drunk. Most drinkers will acknowledge being tipsy or merry, but never out of control.

I was happy to find in the Bible that Jesus turned water to wine at Cana and that Paul suggested to Timothy that he should have a little wine with the meal and that finally it wasn't what you ate or drank that counted, but the "circumcision of the heart."

I knew I was just fooling myself. It had been such a big part of my life that I felt it was impossible to socialize without alcoholic stimulation. I did much public speaking and a couple of noggins under the belt did free me up. Dutch courage, they call it, but I needed it.

Finally I made a deal. I would give up hard tack and wine, but I would continue to have a few beers. I promised God that if I ever got drunk or disagreeable on beers I would quit immediately. Needless to say, that day finally arrived.

I ended up in a rather pointless but very personal argument with some cricket officials after a Natal cocktail party. The party had concluded, but the stayers were there. I was then the president of the Kingsmead Mynahs and I was also a columnist and through both channels I had said some disagreeable things about the administration. They tackled me that evening. The discussion actually started objectively, soon became subjective and then romped into being personal and vindictive – on both sides. I was told a few things – including my being a hypocrite if I thought I was a Christian – and I managed my own fair share of verbal retaliation. It was not very nice.

When I got into my car to drive home I felt most ashamed. And I was reminded that it was a pretty poor show. I thought about the deal and knew that I had well and truly blown it. I had disgraced myself and the cause had been, once again, alcohol. It was the end of the road. I would have to honour my word and give up drinking.

I hardly slept that night. Because I had arrived home late, I was not popular with Inez. First thing in the morning I phoned those involved in the heated words the previous evening and apologized for what I had said. I asked them to forgive me and told them I was giving up drinking. "That's a bit harsh," was the comment of Vic Hohls, but they were most surprised by the phone calls, especially the apologies!

It is not the done thing in the tough world today to apologize or admit that you were wrong. I must add that some of them also had the good grace to say they were also sorry and that it was best buried and forgotten.

The decision had been taken and needed to be honoured. You just don't play games with God. I phoned the office and told my secretary that I would be a little late. I had decided on my plan of action. First, I was going to the gymnasium to sweat it out in the sauna, then I was going to get on my knees at the church, apologize and ask God to help in delivering me from alcohol.

The sauna was fine. At the church I knelt before the Cross. I began feeling very nauseous and developed a massive headache. I felt so downright rotten and sick that I went home and lay on the bed. I couldn't move and I could not satisfy the nausea even by vomiting. I don't think I have ever felt worse. But it was all for a very special reason. It would always serve as a reminder to me of the day that I was delivered from alcohol.

At the time I had wondered why, as a reasonably high profile believer, I had not been invited to testify publicly. No newspaper had interviewed me and publicity had given me wide berth.

But within 24 hours after I had given up alcohol, the telephone started ringing incessantly with requests to speak at breakfasts, schools, guilds and women's association meetings.

Within 48 hours a reporter from the *Sunday Tribune* contacted me and asked for my story, blazoning it across a full page, just five days after the deliverance. That story was also published in most of the Argus papers. The doors had been opened to testify.

I lost some good friends. Not that they didn't stay friendly, but the bond and close relationship we had once enjoyed was now severed. The drinking had been the final nail. "He has finally flipped," agreed the Hangover Harriers as they laughed and quietly mocked. They actually had a meeting about me and sent me a get-well card! It read, "If you drink you get drunk. If you get drunk you fall asleep. When you sleep you don't sin. If you don't sin you go to heaven. So if you want to go to heaven then DRINK."

Obviously my decision had made an impact. It had searched a few souls, but had finally been rejected as too high a cost! Henry Hauser, ex-Springbok soccer captain continued attending the Saturday morning running sessions that I had abandoned. "It's great to see that you are still one of us," he was told. "Peter has become a freak. He doesn't drink any more. You are also a Christian, but you still have a few beers. You are still one of the boys! You are a far better testimony than he is," they assured him. Initially, Henry says, he was quite flattered to receive this compliment, but then he realized it was a backhander. It dawned and he too turned his back on alcohol.

I wanted a silver chain with a cross. I had stuck a fish emblem on my car and also wanted to wear a cross. I asked Inez to try and find me one, but they were either too small or too expensive. I had to have one! A bright idea came from Inez, "Melt down one of those silver medals you won in the Rothmans series." So off I went to the silversmith and three lovely crosses were made, one was far too big, but the two smaller ones were just right. I donned it proudly.

Rather interesting, but disturbing, was the fact that every couple of weeks I had to clean the cross. It was tarnishing badly. The heat and humidity of the tropical climate in Durban was to blame, I reasoned. I thought nothing more about this constant tarnishing. Then came my quitting alcohol and the deliverance. Suddenly, amazingly and unbelievably, the cross was not tarnishing any more! Scientists and the learned will no doubt proffer explanations. I just know what I saw and experienced!

Kruger Day (October 10) was a public holiday in the old South Africa. It is no longer, but for me it will always be a most significant and memorable date. And it also does involve the old and the new, but, in a totally different context! As the president of the Kingsmead Mynahs supporters' club I had planned to spend Kruger Day 1982 at the Kingsmead ground watching the Computer Sciences cricket competition – a quick-fire weekend of instant one-day combat. But there was an earlier date – 07:30 at the church for baptism by full immersion.

I had been christened by my grandfather – the Presbyterian pastor and moderator – but though I had been sprinkled as a child, I really felt convicted to be dipped. Not for one second did I have any doubts. If it was good enough for Jesus then it was most certainly good enough for me. Inez felt the same. It's a controversial issue and my mom was totally opposed to what I was doing. But I had total peace about it. I was forty-one years of age, but I was as excited as a little kid. I was even a bit nervous when asked just prior to the baptism why I wanted to be baptized. I said something like, "I want to openly confess that Jesus is Lord of my life and I can think of no better way." That was my public testimony. Simply, the service symbolically represented to me the death of the old man and the birth of the new creation – the regenerated me.

Inez and I went into the water together. I didn't hear bells ringing. But as we stood there singing at the close of the service, I felt a deep emotion surging within and my eyes became clouded and misty with tears. I think it was the first time that Inez had seen tears in my eyes for she would have testified to my being a rather unemotional type. But there were tears streaming down my face and I didn't mind if anyone saw. Yet while there were outward signs of emotion, deep inside I felt calm and peaceful. I stood there deeply lost in joy and thought and the whole world seemed like such a beautiful place. My senses were so sharp and the inner joy defied explanation. I had drowned the old man. It was a powerful and meaningful experience.

At about the same time, I was down in East London on business and often spent time with Trevor Goddard and his wife Lesley. One evening just before I returned to the hotel, Trevor asked if he could pray for me. During the prayer he asked for the manifestation of the Holy Spirit in my life, and you can imagine my elation the next morning when I woke up in my bedroom in the Holiday

Inn and in my quiet time started speaking in tongues! It wasn't just one or two words, but a merry babbling in a language which, though very foreign, sounded pretty real to me. Certain words seemed to recur, but my mind had no control over what my mouth and lips were saying. It was a strange but beautiful sensation. I had control of the language. I could stop and start as I pleased, but what I was saying was foreign, even though it literally slid off my tongue. Needless to say my intellect got involved.

How could I be sure it was the Holy Spirit? I had been very cynical, but now it was happening to me. I needed verification. I needed an absolute test. The test was simple and yet quite incredible. Speak in tongues and read a book at the same time – that's the challenge that came to me. I tried it. The one didn't affect the other. Speaking in tongues didn't disturb my ability to concentrate on what I was reading. It would if you had to think about what you were saying. Quite brilliant, I thought. Part two was along similar lines. Speak in tongues and write a note to your wife – again it worked.

The mind wasn't involved. It was Holy Spirit language through the normal human channels. With our worldly backgrounds nothing escapes testing, but God had answered clearly and very precisely.

It was also in East London at a youth rally when I happened to pray for a whole lot of youngsters who had responded to an altar call. I closed my eyes as I prayed, but suddenly I heard such a commotion I had to open them. In front all I saw was bodies lying all over the place. I had prayed for God to touch them and the whole lot had fallen over. I had been seriously questioning these things, wondering about whether any pushing and shoving went on. That night I was definitely the most surprised person in the audience – and I was the preacher!

How we battle to believe. Before my conversion, I was once rather neatly manipulated into attending a Christian outreach luncheon in the Northern Natal town of Ladysmith. One of the local retail furniture managers had invited my business colleague Mike Beattie and me to hear Trevor Goddard, who was the guest speaker. I had always respected him and had a soft spot for him as a person. He was an utter gentleman, a really nice guy.

He had committed his life to Christ and for this reason Mike and I were just a little wary about what to expect. We felt distinctly uncomfortable upon discovering no liquor would be served at the luncheon, for if anything could have provided some much-needed Dutch courage, it would have been a couple of frosty ales. Alas, no such luck!

People hugged one another, called one another "brother" and often just shouted out "Amen" or "Praise the Lord." Indeed we were two uncomfortable fellows. We were locked in, as it were and we would just have to grin and bear it.

Trevor gave his testimony and I must admit I listened intently. Any other reaction would have automatically made me look rather conspicuous. Unfortunately though, his testimony seemed like a whole lot of soppy stories and did not make a lot of sense to me. I didn't really want to listen. But right at the end he told a story which stuck. Trevor related how difficult it is for the unbeliever or the cynic to grasp that the Lord always provides.

His illustration involved his being without cake once when guests were expected for tea. Trevor had to go to the airport to pick up friends, but before he left a prayer was said for a cake! Off he went. When he returned, lo and behold, there was a cake. I looked at my colleague, Mike and he looked at me, each of us reflecting total disbelief on our faces. How could Trevor expect intelligent human beings like us to swallow a story like that! That took the cake! When it was all over, we ducked out as quickly as possible, hurriedly shaking Trevor's hand and seeking the refuge of our motorcar.

As we sped out of Ladysmith it must have been some ten minutes before the silence was broken. "Mike," I said, "it's very nice to know that Trevor has found something in life. I am so pleased that he is content and happy. But what about that cake?" I asked in total exasperation.

Mike burst out laughing. "Yes, how did the cake get in there? Did it fly through the window?"

Of course I now know how it got there, but to the two of us then it was silly. It became a source of mocking and scorning until finally one day we realized that the joke in fact was on us.

9

Renewal

God's fast bowler

It really was a beautiful morning as I puffed up the extra pillow, placed it comfortably under my neck and lay in bed absorbing the wonderful view. I was ministering in Margate and Trevor and Joy Evans were hosting me very kindly at their beautiful home in Southbroom on the Natal South Coast. I had been accorded the guest flat – a rather plush understatement! A large stretch of undulating lawn seemed to merge into the beach some half a kilometre away. From the beach line to the horizon, the sea looked more like a still, calm lake.

It was an incredibly beautiful sunrise. The golden sun had only just become a complete ball of light and radiance, but it had a sharpness and definition that was awesome and magnificent. I had never before appreciated the daily phenomenon of sunrise to this keen, titillating degree.

As I was staring out of the bay windows, it became a whole new dimension before my eyes. It just lifted me from within. This was all part of God's rich domain and I just thanked Him for allowing my senses that morning to be so acutely aware of the absolute beauty that surrounded me. In all directions it was indeed awesome. It was my time of prayer and meditation, but that morning my soul leapt inside like an unborn baby in a pregnant mother.

It had only been a couple of months since I had left secular employment. I had swopped my fancy Mercedes sedan for a clapped-out second hand Skyline. I reflected on my business career and also my cricketing days. Why did it all seem so long ago? Granted, that morning it was some 14 years since I had last bowled a ball in anger and that's enough time to relegate cricket to the history pages of one's mind. My business days had been happy and I had established some wonderful friendships and relationships and cricket had helped to open many doors. But as I was meditating, a strange sensation overcame me. It was not agitation, anxiety or frustration; it was just a wonderfully cool and collected peace.

It was then that a profound thought struck me, almost as if God had spoken directly to me, *"You are wondering why it all seems so far away. You are amazed that while it seemed so important at the time, it's now just a pleasant memory. It was all part of my plan for you. You had to go through all of that to get here. My real purpose for your life will start now."*

Just after I had finally come to terms with my calling from the business world as an itinerant evangelist, and having had severed cords with secular employ, I met with Charles Gordon, head pastor of the Church of the Good Shepherd in Durban North one evening. I had been travelling much, sharing testimony and preaching. I knew it was time to get out there and live by faith because the ministry was getting so big that I couldn't do justice to my secular employment any more.

I didn't want to cheat the company, but time constraints were such that there was only one decision. But when you finally have to make it, it's a massive decision! I don't think the step surprised too many of those who knew me. Even my colleagues in the business world sensed the seeming inevitability of a new course in life.

The meeting with Charles was to finally confirm it all. "I am not one to glibly make these sort of claims," said Charles, "but the Lord has spoken to me about you," he announced.

"You are God's fast bowler," he pronounced with conviction. In terms of how I understood my calling into the ministry, his explanation was so beautifully simple and lucid. There was nothing presumptuous about it. I was His servant, had given my life to Him and was once a fast bowler of some reputation.

God's fast bowler – out in front as an evangelist, attacking with courage and conviction at the rock-face! Fast bowlers can't compromise, they are born, not bred and they have to subject themselves to more rigours and disciplines than the other cricketers.

As Charles continued with the similarities and comparisons, I was convinced of its higher origin and inspiration! A fast bowler is more prone to danger and injury, strongly self-motivated and single-minded and a type of loner – all straight from the shoulder! Fast bowlers are expected at all times to give their utmost, even on dead wickets they are expected to pound in and produce results. They need to stay focused and fired up.

We were on the same spiritual wave-length. Charles' simple description and understanding was enough to convince me that the analogy was divinely inspired. All that I had experienced, in my 40 years in the wilderness, was in fact preparation. A platform had been established. It's one life, not a whole lot of segments and the best lessons are only taught and learnt the hard way, through tough experience.

What Charles had said was confirmed a short while afterwards while I was on a mission in the Eastern Transvaal. David and Loreen Newington, who have spent virtually all of their long lives in the mission field, were a tonic to me. David's humour and sincerity, not to mention his incredible knowledge of the Bible, really blessed me.

"Cricket, what a game," said David over the cereals one morning. "God brought you through it for a reason. Don't ever forget that. You are God's fast bowler. Stay that way. Don't become just another preacher!" – a prophetic confirmation if I have ever heard it!

And so the exciting adventure got under way. *God's fast bowler* has been the label. Even after 18 years I daily experience people's surprise when they are told that I am a full-time preacher or evangelist. Surely, they know I am a Christian and that I speak all over the world and write articles. But I have no dog collar or religious tag!

My conversion surprised many. Kim Shippey, once a well-known radio personality, interviewed Trevor Goddard on one of his shows and commented that he had heard about my commitment.

Yes, there were many in business, sporting and social circles that found it quite a stunning "turn-up for the books" as they say in betting parlance. Trevor's response was that of all the cricketers he had toured with, he would have thought I would be "the last that would turn." Trevor said:

Having had the privilege of being Peter's captain on the tour of Australia, I got to know him well. In Australia as spearhead of our attack he was very quick and aggressive, a good chap to have on your side! His youthful enthusiasm wanted to see every batsman flattened, with every ball. The success of his cricket is well-known and runs parallel to the success of the South African teams during his playing days.

After giving my heart to Jesus in 1970, I realized that some of my old team-mates thought I had gone crazy. Peter, I am sure, thought I had gone all religious and crazy. The result was that I was given a wide berth. I was a chap to stay clear of and so Peter and I had very little contact. For my part I listed the players I had played with, especially on that Australian trip. I used to pray for them often, going down the list praying for each one in turn, eventually coming to Peter and thinking, 'Phew, Lord! You have really got a tough one here. I don't know how you will ever get him changed.'

One ex-Springbok, when asked what he thought about my conversion merely commented, "Perhaps he needed to change!"

On the first day of the opening Test on the rebel tour undertaken by Kim Hughes' Australians, I was strolling across the Kingsmead turf during the luncheon interval. I was keeping an interested eye on the numerous little cricket matches that were taking place around the circumference of the field. Out of the blue I bumped into an old friend, Alan Hector. Alan and I had for many seasons opened the bowling for Eastern Province and had become pretty good friends. Our ways parted when I left Port Elizabeth back in 1978. He had subsequently got divorced and remarried and I had not seen him for years. I must say that my first impression was that he looked a bit on the thin and gaunt side but I assumed that he was one of the many distance-running fanatics. They look lean, mean and sick, but are actually very healthy!

I asked him how he was keeping and he said that he hadn't been feeling well of late. A year ago he had succumbed to jaundice and he felt that this was a recurrence. Tests were being conducted.

I learnt too that his son Paul had just recently been chosen for the South African Schools cricket side and Alan was justifiably proud. Anyway, we parted, promising to get in touch again, the way old friends usually do!

About a week later we heard the bad news. The tests on his liver revealed that he had the dreaded cancer. And he was given about three months to live! What a shock. I sent him a copy of the book I had written. *Clean bowled,* my testimony. It was the option Inez suggested and I wrote him a note inside.

Ten days later Alan phoned to say thanks for the book and mentioned that his brother Rupert had also sent him a copy. Two books! Some sort of message! Anyway, he read it, twice in fact, and asked if he could come and see me because there were some questions he wanted to pose. "Peter, I have been looking for God," he admitted "and maybe you can clear up some issues for me." I readily agreed and the next morning he came into my office, along with his dad.

I shared some testimony and answered some of his queries. Then I was confronted by three big questions. Firstly, he had done some things in his life that he would be too ashamed to admit to anyone. Could he be forgiven? God hates divorce and he had done just that. And finally, making a decision for Jesus with just a couple of months left in his life was like trying to sneak in the back door. "Are you allowed to come at the last minute?" he asked.

He was embarrassed to be thinking about Jesus only now in his final hours of desperation and need. He felt it was kind of backhanded and most certainly not acceptable!

I assured him that his worries were unfounded, that Jesus had died for all of us irrespective of our problems and that He welcomed all who sought him. With most of us prodigal sons it required tragedy and setbacks to highlight our own inadequacies. There was no doubt in Alan's mind. He wanted to make a commitment and I led him in a simple prayer as he surrendered his life. There were sobs and tears, from Alan and his dad. I also prayed that God would reveal himself to Alan in a special, tangible way.

The following Sunday Alan was at church and enjoyed the service. But as he sat at the service that morning he was blissfully ignorant of the drama with his son Paul. The previous evening he had been involved in a motor accident and was fighting for his life in a critical condition in an intensive care unit. Prayer chains were informed and God only knows how much intercession ensued. There was need for an operation to remove damaged brain tissue and it seemed a pretty hopeless case. Initially Alan went up to Pretoria to be alongside his struggling son, but he returned to Durban. Paul was still unconscious.

Every couple of days I phoned Alan to find out the latest on Paul and the cancer treatment. The outlook on both fronts just got dimmer and dimmer. Then one Monday morning there was a whole new story. "Paul has regained consciousness. He's up and about," blurted an excited dad. "You remember when you asked God to reveal himself to me in a special way. Paul's recovery is that sign," said Alan with more than just a hint of emotion. I couldn't answer. We just put the phones down. Paul had survived. God's hand had been on the recovery.

Alan's earthly commitment was to last only 36 days. On Thursday March 13 at about 11 o'clock in the morning Alan passed on to Glory. I had the privilege of being at his bedside in his final hour. The peace and strength that shone from him was awesome. There was no fear of death, just a peaceful anticipation as those near and dear to him gathered to bid their final fond farewells.

The previous Sunday Alan and his wife Sally had come to church and afterwards we had prayed for healing for Alan. Afterwards as I sat with him in the vestry, along with Henry Hauser, I happened to remark, "Al, we don't understand these things. It's now all in the hands of Jesus." To which he replied, "Peter, I have been healed!" Obviously I looked a bit startled at his statement. "No, not in the body," came the reply. "I have been healed because Jesus Christ is Lord of my life." Indeed that's the truth of it. "I have found God. I know Jesus. I am at peace with Him." What a declaration!

At the Highway hospice the morning of his death, a well-known Natal sportsman approached me. "When you are involved with death like this it's impossible not to be a Christian," he commented.

What did he mean? "When you see a lifeless body representing the end, then you have to believe that there is something more. If life is just about ending up in death, a lifeless body, then it's meaningless. There must be something more," he concluded.

Indeed I had never felt closer to God than in the short time I spent with Alan on his final day in the hospice bed. I had always feared death. I had been too frightened to go to funerals. But now death had lost its sting. For someone who had so feared death to be sitting alongside Alan, represented a complete turn-around. That hospice experience was life changing, awesome to say the least.

Rev. Philip Jourdan conducted the funeral at the Frere Road Presbyterian Church. Alan's friends flew in from all over and included many well-known personalities, such as Nicholas Oppenheimer and a whole heap of cricket superstars. You could have heard a pin drop throughout the service. Nobody left that gathering untouched or unchallenged. His story has been told over and over again and many lives have been changed by it. Inez wrote this lovely letter to his wife Sally:

> I really believe that through Alan, God has touched many lives. The people who have been drawn into the experience of the last couple of weeks have come out of it far richer. I believe God's purpose for having called a beloved son home was only a small portion of what his overall purpose has been during this whole time. When Alan said, "Peter, I know God," I really believe God had already allowed him a glimpse of his final love and purpose for him. Nobody could have failed to be overawed by the peace that shone from Alan and if it has touched one life to the extent that they would come to the knowledge of the saving grace of God, then the angels rejoice in heaven and all has not been in vain.

Jaundice was the start of Alan's problems, but way back in 1956, I was in bed for two months with this same hepatitis. At the same time my sister, Helen arrived. She was twelve years younger than brother Graeme. I helped a lot in caring for Helen because being stuck at home, I was able to be nurse-maid when Mom needed a break. With a young baby, especially if you are over 40, a mother needs time to relax! Mom however, really struggled and sadly depression finally overcame her. It became so bad, she ended up with a psychiatrist and later she left PE for a special mental hospital in Cape Town where shock treatment was administered.

She was away many months and returned a lot improved, but certainly not healed. It was quite eerie, for the treatment had blocked out certain areas of her memory. She was also on regular medication. We got accustomed to her memory lapses and to all intents and purposes we regarded her as cured.

For some 24 years she managed, being a pretty strong-willed person and even when Dad died in December 1969, she was able to keep soldiering on. I know that from time to time loneliness did get her to admit, "I wish I still had Dad," but whatever she felt deep inside was carefully guarded.

She moved to Durban with us, but about the time that I was born again, the symptoms of her old depression started afresh. Off she went to the psychiatrist and the whole process was re-enacted – medication, deliberation, consultation and the inevitable shock treatment! I must say she went downhill fast. It was quite frightening trying to make sense of it all and certainly it was impossible to try and reason with her, especially during treatment periods.

"You will never understand depression unless you've had it," she kept saying as I tried all sorts of tactics. "The feeling of hopelessness and doom is devastating," she kept telling me. I was trying to cajole her into being more positive and telling her to "snap out of it" – the worst thing I could do! I read many books on the subject of depression and it intrigued me more and more. I also looked at it from the Christian counselling viewpoint, but I was getting nowhere. How can a few electrodes or pills fix up the mind? Surely only God is sovereign in this area? There were questions galore, but no answers. Things just got worse.

Then one evening Mom came along with us to a church meeting. George Dillman preached about faith and healing and at the altar call, Mom felt led to go up front to let the pastor pray for her. "Why did you go up?" I asked. "I don't know. I just felt I had to," was the simple explanation.

Well, something did happen. She improved almost immediately. A few weeks later we were absolutely convinced that she had been miraculously healed.

Charles Gordon asked me to share this testimony at a Sunday morning service. I shared the facts. Needless to say there was an enthusiastic response, but not from Mom! She was in fact most perturbed and was very cross that I had dared to tell the story. She was uncomfortable about claiming a healing. I was stunned by her reaction. "Don't you ever tell that story again," she insisted. "It was not Jesus who healed me, it was these pills," she added as she pulled out a bottle of nerve restorative tablets. It was an old remedy that she thought had been taken off the market but she accidentally found them at a local pharmacy a few days after that meeting she had attended with us.

"Mom, do you know what you are saying?" I asked and there was horror in my sister's face as she witnessed Mom's denial of Jesus. But Mom was adamant. It was those pills! Well, the healing didn't stay long. The depression returned almost with a militant vengeance. Her path backwards and then downwards was rapid and severe.

There were more bad days than good days and for sister Helen it was a nightmare because Mom was staying in their granny flat. There was a constant barrage of depressed thoughts, moods and action. Mom even attempted suicide and had to be rushed to Addington Hospital for a stomach pump. Again she went to the psychiatrists and all the experts. All efforts were fobbed off with the chestnut, "They just don't understand depression."

Out of frustration and even hopelessness I often got quite angry and irritated. I had read all the right books, done all the right counselling, called in all the right experts and yet we were getting absolutely nowhere. In fact there was major deterioration.

It was getting through to all of us. Having Mom around for the day was a terrible strain on the family, but we endured it dutifully, although not without a few outbursts. Mom would often ask me about Jesus. She knew all about Him, having been a churchgoer all her life. But she wanted to find Him. She wanted a real experience like we had before she was prepared to believe.

"How can you be so sure about Jesus?" she would often ask me. It was an incredible question! Yet it explained everything. She was trapped by unbelief. All the counselling in the world, all the Christian advice and all our best intentions merely knocked at the door of her unbelief. Quit those tactics, just love her and pray for her – that's what I felt we should do.

So we prayed and endeavoured to love and understand. In despair and frustration we finally surrendered. We gave up. It was impossible. She was sent to Town Hill in Pietermaritzburg on the advice of the psychiatrist. She was going to be certified! A padded cell! It had come to that. I contacted the other members of the family to give them the bad news. It was the only road left to us, for her own good and protection.

When you have reached that point with your own mother, you truly know what it is to be in life's cul-de-sac. We rationalized. All sorts of thoughts produced various degrees of guilt. We had finally given up on Mom.

With man it was impossible, but not with God. God could now take control and He did. Mom was never certified or institutionalised. God restored her to secular sanity. In a wonderful way God had miraculously revealed Himself to my mother. To what depths did she have to go for that experience, but she was never to be the same again. Jesus became Lord of her life, the Bible next to her bed was her most treasured possession and a few years later, in May 1986, she died of a stroke.

A fisher of men

We still don't know who blessed us, but that same year Neil Freimond, then a pastor at the Church of the Good Shepherd, gave us the glad tidings. Someone had sponsored Inez and me for a ten-day visit to Israel. It was an incredible time, certainly for two excited young Christians who absorbed every minute. We visited all the popular and famous spots and what really intrigued me was that all over nobody denied that Jesus had been there. His deeds and His existence are irrefutable, by Christian, Jew, Moslem and even the studied atheist. There was more proof concerning Him than any other part of history. Sure there are those who questioned His deity, but the fact that he came and did the feats and miracles that the Bible claims, was not questioned. This was most reassuring.

We travelled all around, finally finishing up with several days in Jerusalem. And naturally we visited the Garden Tomb. A plaque declaring, "He has risen" stimulates hard swallows and goose bumps. Led by Dave Smethurst, one of the touring party, we shared Holy Communion as the sort of grand finale to our visit.

But while we were partaking of the elements a very strange thing happened to me. It was almost as if a voice told me, "Go back to Gethsemane." We had been there a couple of days before, but the command was clear, almost as if I had missed something very important. The next day several of us decided to retrace the steps of Jesus on the day He was crucified. We were going to walk it out, starting in the Garden of Gethsemane. We were going to get everything into the right sequence of events, as described in the Bible.

Immediately there was a problem. At Gethsemane they would not let us in. Our shorts and bare knees were not allowed! Fortunately there was another, less official garden at Gethsemane. A local, seeing our disappointment, approached us with the good news about this alternative, but for the gate to be opened required a small consideration! No problem, we parted with some shackles! In this particular garden there is a statue depicting Jesus at the time He sweated blood in anguish.

We decided to break bread right there. As we shared communion, I happened to look up at the statue.

In one of my greatest moments of revelation, some profound basic truths hit me. Firstly, that Jesus sweated blood, not just for the sins of the world, but very specially for me. It was private, intimate and very personal. Secondly, it was my sin and iniquity that nailed Him to the Cross at Calvary. It was no good blaming anyone else. He is my personal Saviour because of my sins – a vital truth! Thirdly, and finally, I had put Him there, but His response had been to ask His Father, "Forgive him, he doesn't know what he is doing." What a profound moment of biblical truth. What a revelation.

My life would never be the same again. The trip to Israel was worth it just for those few moments in Gethsemane, albeit the unofficial one! The one other very special moment was by the shores of Galilee at the place where the apostle Peter was called. As I was standing in that spot, I felt an unmistakable conviction that just like Peter, I was called to be a fisher of men!

Another nagging thought that kept bothering me was the issue of debt. I had spent most of my life in common debt, not the sort that leads to jail sentences or streams of lawyer's letters, but the credit malady that plagues our society, simply living beyond our means. We all want to keep up with the neighbours or the peer group and the main problem is that to stay there, you need to borrow on the never-never!

The Bible tells us that you are in bondage to whom you have borrowed from, whether you want to admit it or not. For years you pay the bond on your house and yet really make very little impact on the capital amount. I looked at my financial situation and saw that after six years – with a few hassles here and there – I had reduced the original loan of R46 000 on our house, by a little less than R2 000. I had paid interest in the region of R35 000 or more. To purchase my house I had to borrow money from my brother and mother, the result of having lost a small fortune in my move from Port Elizabeth to Durban in 1978. Unlucky? That's what I told myself, but now it was a case of ducking and diving with overdrafts. Robbing one to pay another became the accounts system. It's a story as old as the hills and involves the great majority.

Of course we can rationalize and justify our actions, but it doesn't relieve the stress and anxiety. I was in bondage. I wanted to go into the ministry full-time, but debt hung around my neck. I had a bad dream, a rather vivid one with floodwaters rising to window level. "Get out of debt," was the simple interpretation. The message was as clear to me as if God had sent me a fax. I told Inez. She was a little dismayed.

Sell the house and settle the debts! It's terribly unfair to tell that to a wife. It goes against all maternal instincts. A woman, mother and wife, needs security. But Inez was supportive, certainly outwardly though inside her stomach churned.

The house went onto the market and we set a price. A well-meaning builder suggested that before I sold I should paint, touch up and even think of spending on improvements to make a handsome profit. I just knew that there was to be no wheeling and dealing! That's the price, I insisted.

A few days later a cash buyer came along and that was that! No hassles and no problems, except friends who said I could have got more. I had made a healthy profit and cleared my overdraft. The selling of the house and the ridding of debt was an incredible relief.

If someone had told me in those days that one day I would sit in a position of being debt-free, I wouldn't have believed him. It's a way of life. I always thought that the brotherhood of man was a brotherhood of debt. I didn't believe that, in this credit-mad society, you could escape being in bondage to a card or an organization. It's become an accepted mode of life. But the borrower is indeed servant of the lender. God's provision does tend to boggle the mind.

April 1was the date of our entry into full-time ministry, living by faith. At the time Inez had been working mornings only as secretary to Charles Gordon at our church. I felt strongly though that she shouldn't work, but rather be available to travel and minister alongside me. She wasn't so sure, but complied with my wishes. She had been earning a small salary. "Enough to buy bread and milk should we get in trouble," she argued. "But if you are sure God will provide, then I will give up my job," was her dutiful response.

A month later I was ministering in Johannesburg when I got a call from a businessman whom I had helped in his search for God. He wanted to see me urgently. I responded and this was his simple story, "I don't know about hearing from God, but I am sure He has spoken to me. I know that I must send you a certain sum every month." He told me the amount. It was exactly what Inez was earning. A cold shiver went through my body. It had to be the exact amount just to confirm!

The five years it took me from commitment to going into full-time ministry saw much tugging and pulling as my views and perceptions came under the microscope of God's value system. To dust out some cobwebs I had to visit an ex-Springbok team-mate whom I had slandered some dozen years before. I had to see him, take my pride and trample it in front of him. I apologized for what I had done, asking his forgiveness for the heartache I had caused.

One of my leading business accounts asked a direct and very embarrassing question. I had no option but tell the truth, which resulted in uncomfortable and anxious times. A lie would have sufficed. It would have been the easy solution, certainly in the short term. I was castigated for being self-righteous!

I started to care and carry a burden for what companies were not doing for their people. Big companies boast personnel departments, training courses and incentive schemes – not to mention pension and medical aid – but when it really gets down to the crunch, when the choice is between people and profits, the people suffer. People are the greatest resource, but too often it's only lip service that's paid when the choice is between legitimate hopes and aspirations and the company's bottom line. Christians find that they are inwardly bombarded with doubts and questions about their jobs and working environments.

So much of what happens in the cut-throat, highly competitive business world stands directly opposed and in open contradiction to biblical principles. These differences become more and more obvious and intolerable. There is even revulsion to the extent that many Christians then become one thing on Sundays and at home and then put on a new hat every morning as they head off to work.

Two-timing and double standards have severe consequences. We often talk jokingly about the 11th commandment – the business commandment – "Thou shall not get caught!" Businessmen are actually considered smart and wide-awake when they con some extra profit or outsmart a rival with a fast one or an underhand tactic, or smartly outmanoeuvre on a big contract with inside knowledge or insider trading. Bribery is couched in the most acceptable terms these days, disguised as incentives, study tours or what have you. It's a veritable minefield in so many respects.

I often found myself meditating and pondering about these business issues. I had reached a particular point when I felt it was time to go preaching. I became a little bored with what I was doing and felt that maybe this boredom was a sign! I needed more of a challenge and certainly a change of boardroom scenery.

I was in the right frame of mind for change and along came an offer. In a strange twist, the new offer had me seriously considering something that a few years ago I would have grabbed with both hands. It had to do with Natal cricket. The big job! Not only to take charge of the playing and coaching, but also the marketing and public relations. I was the obvious, ready-made candidate. Although I had not applied for the post, it was mine for the taking! Even the financial package was raised to meet my requirements and all that remained was the mere formality of the right channels and due authorization.

Fortunately it didn't have to be an overnight decision. There had to be a delay. My initial reaction was that it would be the right place for me and that my background and qualifications were ideal. I actually got quite excited as I started to formulate strategies and plans for how I was going to rejuvenate Natal cricket.

But slowly, intuitively I started to have doubts deep down. I consulted Christian friends. Would I be compromising?

May Hauser, who had written out my conversion prayer, had no doubts. "I think it's a test," she stated emphatically. Her explanation? "It's cricket or preaching. That's the decision God has placed before you," explained May. I didn't want to hear that, but I knew it was the truth. I approached others for advice and finally consulted Derek Crumpton, a man of integrity and stature in Christian circles. He posed the same direct question, "Will this job involve compromising God's word in any way?"

I instantly knew the answer. Yes, it would! I gave it a weekend of further thought, but the answer was clear.

On the Monday I phoned the cricket officials with my decision. "What a pity there was a delay," said the cricket official "A week ago we would have got a yes." I denied that, but deep down I knew he was right. I might well have rushed in.

Full-time ministry was beckoning. I was down the final straight in terms of honouring my calling and out of the blue comes this gift-wrapped incentive to stay away. Interesting. Perhaps even frightening! Things are not always what they seem.

Cricket as a platform would return at a later date, but now it was time to focus elsewhere, at least for a season or two!

10

REVELATION

The power of prayer

T hough the eldership had recognized my ministry as an evangelist, had prayed for me and sent me out as it were, pastor Charles Gordon was nevertheless rather shocked and dismayed when I first told him that I was going full-time.

"How are we involved?" he asked. "I mean what are we in for financially?" as he clarified his question!

"Nothing!" And my reply shattered him even more. "God is going to provide," I stated emphatically, underlining that I was not relying on the church financially. He didn't have to worry about that!

"Bucks, Peter, bucks," – I will never forget his words. "Excuse me if my Presbyterian petticoat sticks out here, but I am talking about the simple issue of bucks to pay the bills," added Charles. God was going to provide – I was absolutely sure about it.

I shared my vision with Charles and Dudley Daniel, leaders of the New Covenant Group, how I saw the ministry panning out and what I envisaged. My enthusiasm and my dream they respected, but the question of what will happen after a couple of years when the church circuit tires of my testimony and something much more substantial is needed to survive, bothered them.

Charles was honest enough, and up-front enough to speak it as he saw it. I appreciated the views, but it didn't change my resolve or conviction in terms of God's calling for me. I was absolutely sure that God would both provide and open doors for preaching.

As for finances, Charles assured me of the church's much valued prayer and spiritual support, but that financially the best they could do was give me R1000 a month for the first six months – just to get the ball rolling! Charles did say that I could rest assured though that if I was ever in any trouble I could always come to them.

I thanked him, but assured him that if God wanted the Church of the Good Shepherd to supply me He would tell them! Charles just smiled. Many months later Charles phoned me and asked me to come and see him. "I don't say these things lightly," he said, "but God has spoken to me about your finances. He is going to supply you. I don't have to be involved." That wasn't just passing the buck! He really meant it. From time to time over the years, Charles would ask, "Pete how are the bucks going?" "Fine thanks, Charles," I would assure him! "I know," would be his inevitable closure!

It has not been about fancy cars or fancy homes. Second hand cars and rented homes and many month-end tight squeezes all helped to build the faith and the testimony in those early days as I moved around South Africa. I have travelled interdenominationally almost uniquely, perhaps because of the cricketing background, and it's been going for just over two decades. I have covered South Africa extensively and also went to Namibia, Malawi, Botswana, Zimbabwe and Swaziland, not to mention Australia, New Zealand, India, Britain and the United States. And God has provided!

In 1996, I was in the subcontinent for the World Cup cricket competition. One Sunday morning I preached at the massive Anglican Church in Calcutta, but after the service while sipping a cup of tea with two of the clergy, a thought came to me, "Why don't you go and visit Mother Theresa?"

I asked my friends whether that would be a problem. They checked first to establish that she was in Calcutta and off we went across the city. It took the best part of an hour through the hectic traffic, but we finally made it. Mother Theresa was in, but was busy upstairs with a group of students. So the three of us climbed the stairs. I was in front and as I reached the top I looked across this room and there she was addressing the youngsters. As she looked at me she stopped talking, pondered a few moments and then obviously told the students just to excuse her.

She then walked over to me, took me by the hand and led me off to a little alcove that had a bench. She started talking. She told me first that I was from Africa. I mean was that so obvious with my white skin! Nobody had told her who I was or what I did. She then confirmed that I was a preacher of God's Word and proceeded to give me a sermon. First she underlined that the greatest in the Kingdom of God shall be the servant, not the king or the ruler. After about five minutes on that subject, she finished by expounding, "What you do for the least, you do for Me."

She spoke about Jesus and told me just how wonderful He is. "You will never know that Jesus is all you need until Jesus is all you have." What a powerful statement! Finally some grave prophetic news. "Africa is dying of AIDS. It's urgent. People need to find Jesus."

She then prayed for me. It was a simple prayer asking God's guidance and protection and she sent me on my way back to Africa to preach the gospel. It lasted twenty minutes in all, but as we drove back to the hotel afterwards, the two pastors were still dumbfounded. They had both stood within earshot. What an incredible experience.

One evening I was standing in my garden. We have a house on top of a mountain called, believe it or not, Mount Moriah! A couple of vacant plots alongside ensure our privacy and seclusion.

A veld-fire was heading our way, aided by a stiff wind and there was not much we could do about it. It was moving so fast and it was coming straight for us. We had phoned the fire department, but they would not make it in time. We were advised to button down the hatches and move the cars out of harm's way. It was all great advice but too late! I stood there watching.

My son Shaun stood next to me and asked, "What are we going to do, Dad?" "Nothing. God will look after us," I replied. I closed my eyes and prayed. I felt a hand on my shoulder. Thinking it was Shaun, I looked up, but there was nobody. A shiver went through my body. "Is that you Lord?" I thought.

The fire came. It was pretty fierce, but it never touched the house. It went around and then on into the nature reserve behind our property. Not a single flame even shot over the wall.

The fire department arrived too late, but the trouble had passed. They ensured that the pockets of smouldering outcrops were doused and then went home.

The next morning the young man who had led the fire department's crew came back to check on everything. Then he asked me to come and see "something rather amazing." The wall facing the previous night's onslaught was about 30 meters long, but there was absolutely no evidence of charring on its white surface. What's more amazing, was that a metre from the wall was an area of untouched grass and shrub. It was almost as if an invisible wall had been put up in front of our vibracrete fence. That was the young man's observation.

"That was God," was all I said. He smiled nervously and bid farewell. I remembered that hand on my shoulder!

Our youngest daughter Nicola was having some women's problems. An operation was going to require financing that quite frankly wasn't available. Inez moved into action with her friend Marietjie Mostert, an anaesthetist from Pietermaritzburg, and she made arrangements for Nicola that would cost considerably less than the original estimates. Her friend also arranged a gynacologist and the date and venue were set. The morning of the operation Inez and I prayed together, as is our daily custom and we specially highlighted Nicola's predicament.

Inez drove Nicola the eighty kilometres and on the way told her daughter that we had prayed for a miracle! "Thanks Mom," said Nicola, "but I can assure you the problem is still there." She dressed down for the pre-operation check-ups. The gynaecologist arrived, donned his gloves and started the inspection. "Where is this problem?" he enquired. "Down there on that side," reiterated an embarrassed Nicola! He looked, he examined, rubber gloves and all.

"I can find nothing. If there was something there, it's gone. It's clear. No problems," as he slipped off his gloves.

"My mom prayed for a miracle," Nicola blurted out in her delight and excitement. Sheepishly he just shook his head. Who knows what he thought that day! But it was gone and it never came back. And all it cost was some petrol and some rubber gloves!

Promise Keepers

One Sunday evening I was due to preach at the Christian Victory Lighthouse fellowship in Durban. It was part of the World Cup 95 rugby crusade and as I was about to address the Bluff congregation, Pastor Andries van Schalkwyk, when introducing me, paused and then shared that God had just given him a vision of sports stadiums full of men "praising Jesus and not their sports heroes."

I was a little non-plussed. It didn't ring a bell with me. It did not have much more significance than that it would naturally be nice to see sports stadiums housing giant crusades for men.

Anyway, I shared the incident with my wife and left it at that. About seven weeks later some books arrived at my home, sent by Danie van der Heever, of *Focus on the Family*. The instructions were simple, "Please read and respond."

I was away on mission at the time and Inez allowed her curiosity to get the better of her. She browsed through the material and then phoned me. "That vision at the Bluff. It's on your desk," she pronounced. I needed to read for myself. I did and as I avidly consumed all the book had to offer, God spoke to me clearly and profoundly, "Bring Promise Keepers to South Africa." That was a tall order.

On Friday, August 18 1995, I had a breakfast meeting with Danie and a good friend Terry Rosenberg. I shared my interest and excitement about what I had read and what the Promise Keepers stood for. Danie admitted that during his previous visit to the United States he had attended one of these men's gatherings and during the meeting God had spoken to him. Simply a name had been slotted into his mind: Peter Pollock!

In October Danie and I had an international telephone conference with Dr Glenn Wagner and by January of the following year a PK delegation arrived in South Africa. The three key figures were Bishop Philip Porter, the Chairman of the Board, Peb Jackson and Glen Wagner. They visited Johannesburg, Cape Town and Durban and the show was on the road.

In July that year I flew to the United States and met with Glen in Denver, Colorado, and I visited *Focus on the Family* at Colorado Springs. I also attended my first PK gathering at Pittsburgh. What an experience. The most moving aspect was seeing 65 000 men applauding Jesus! The praise and worship had just finished and as the men sat down to prepare for the first speaker of the Saturday morning, the master of ceremonies simply suggested that he felt led to ask us all to stand again and give a round of applause to the unseen Guest of Honour – Jesus.

The men rose and started clapping. It just got louder and louder. No shouting or yelling. Just clapping. What a crescendo. And as all these men stood there clapping, tears were rolling down their faces. For five minutes it continued. Unplanned. Totally and utterly unorchestrated, it was one of those great experiences. The Holy Spirit had taken charge!

This clinched it for me. The long process of registration and legitimisation got under way. It was often frustrating, for constantly groups and individuals in South Africa wanted things to happen faster. We live in an instant world, with glib answers and instant solutions.

Focus on the Family was magnificent, so too was Jack Eans, but it was a process that needed to be slow. Given the conditions and nature of South Africa it had to be slow and steady and all about patience. Glen Wagner and Tyrone Kemp were the contact men in America but their hands seemed to be tied, which only added to the mid-course frustrations.

The organization was young and even in America they were encountering opposition and their own teething problems. Nothing worthwhile ever comes the easy way. While never questioning that I had a role to play in the initial process, it was always crystal clear to me that I was not to get caught up as anything but a facilitator. I saw that it had to start at ground roots with small groups around the country. But we had to avoid trying to sell it as yet another Christian "method!" Unfortunately methodism and religion abounds and I knew we had to avoid it like the plague.

Those initial stages cost plenty and Terry Rosenberg bore the major brunt. To get all the churches involved, to grow from grass roots and to find God's leader was the mission. However, I was to stay an evangelist and just a catalyst in the PK process. It's not always easy to explain these things!

In June 1997, a month before I was to go in for major surgery – a hip replacement – I met the right man, David Molapo. I knew it the moment I met him.

Ray McCauley and the Rhema Church were very supportive and so Promise Keepers became official in South Africa. It wasn't an easy road. On September 8

1999, a massive outdoor meeting was held at Loftus Versveld rugby ground and estimates ranged between 20 000 and 30 000 as the attendance figure. But it's really not about facts and figures and methods or strategies.

Those five years opened my eyes and really allowed me a wonderful glimpse, overview and perspective that no educational institution anywhere in the world could offer. I have travelled uniquely interdenominationally and of course the reason was my cricketing background.

In 1998 I was privileged to be invited by St Margaret Lothbury, an Anglican church in London, to lead an evangelistic outreach to the Square Mile, as it's known. 'Holding out Hope' was the title which seemed appropriate at the time with so many people in Britain asking questions, particularly since Princess Diana's death. At that time the volatility of the markets, redundancies and insecurity had made the Square Mile business population (about 250 000 people) very unsettled.

Tom Farrell, a former British athlete of note, had invited me and the plan was to utilize non-church venues – large firms, banks and civic meeting places. Also included were large churches like Holy Trinity Brompton. The Bank of England and Linklaters were among the hosts over some 18 meetings.

Many responded to the gospel message and most interesting were the way doors actually opened to me. Simply being a well-known South African cricketer and not wearing a dog collar, intrigued most listeners. I could not be pigeon-holed the way the British do to their own, and that ensured that there were no preconceived barriers or objections.

Interesting too, was that most were very keen to hear testimony and were very open to being told about God, Jesus Christ and even being born again. What they did have a problem with, was the church. "As long as you don't try and sell us the church," we often heard.

That was the forthright comment of one man who summed up a pretty general opinion. Don't try and sell us the church! That's not marketable!

Once I was in Kuruman and I visited the Moffat mission. Many years ago David Livingstone had been connected to this place and I found it intriguing. Chatting to one of the missionaries, I asked about how the preaching of the gospel was progressing.

"Well, initially there was the problem of God and the chiefs!" he related. "You see, the chiefs don't relish the idea of a superior authority, so we decided the best strategy was education. Educate the masses. The age-old formula! They will read and that way we can circumvent the bottleneck at the top," he explained. "But the problem is that we are still educating and have not got round to the gospel. Certainly we don't dare take on any issues like witchcraft and ancestors," he admitted.

It's the soft-soap strategy! It's the method and organization versus the simple life-changing truth. It's the church again acting as if it's omniscient. This was the often repeated lament of the Square Mile!

This friend of mine once belonged to a well-known sect. He was winning people to his cause and the churchgoers in his area felt they needed to do something about him. One of the elders approached him, hoping that they would be able to meet and discuss the error of his different gospel. He agreed to meet them, seeing this as the opportunity to convert some Christians!

They met on a Monday evening and talked and argued for an hour and a half. They returned to the debating floor the following Monday for another 90 minutes and this extended into a third session. But nobody was winning. At the conclusion of each session the Christians went home thinking they had won. Needless to say he also thought that his case had been strongest.

The following Saturday he happened to be in the supermarket waiting for his wife. He started chatting to a young girl. She was full of bounce and life and related to him how she has just been born again. She shared her story. It changed his life.

"I had been arguing, debating and selling religion. What this young girl had, was life!"

In a nutshell, the process of regeneration is the awakening of the spirit in each of us. The latent spirit is reborn. Then God begins to work and change us. It's a relationship, not religion.

The great conflict revolves around the impression and perception that it's all about the church and that this organization only caters for the religious and the super spiritual.

Take the sportsman who becomes a Christian for instance. He has success behind him, but often admits emptiness as well. He has found that there is still something missing despite all the fame and accolades. He has found that obsession with success produces depression with failure. In seeking fulfillment he finally comes to Jesus, but finds himself with the challenge of having to live in two worlds. He is almost a foreigner in each! Some Christians frown upon his sport, especially if he plays on Sundays, while his worldly contacts give him uphill for his Christian stance. It becomes a struggle. Usually he ends up trying too hard to act like a Christian.

Christianity isn't an act, it's a reality. But to the immature, aided and abetted by the worldly, it becomes a pressure to perform or avoid the inevitable criticism. There is an inner turmoil as he is dabbling in two worlds. It's a confusing time.

Finally there is an answer! It's not about two different worlds. God is in every minute of every day! True Christianity is an everyday on-going relationship with Him that changes your life and affects those around you. It's most certainly not a religion! But it's a revelation that took me forty years of searching in the wilderness of life.

It's about a change of heart

God often works in strange and mysterious ways. We are the products of our environment and experiences, and our philosophies and thoughts are shaped by these events. One particular Christmas lingers in my memory. We were a long way from home and you are never more aware of home than at this time of the year.

Christmas Eve 1963 was spent in part at the Launceston Airport in Tasmania. As we stood around waiting for the delayed flight to take us to Hobart, we tried to engender the right seasonal spirit with a few draughts of beer.

Over the loudspeaker system, carols and hymns provided the background and no doubt thoughts of loved ones back home ruled supreme. Eventually the plane arrived, but the flight to Hobart was not without incident. On landing we had a narrow escape. Apparently some truck driver, under the influence of alcohol, decided to take a short cut across the tarmac runway just as we were coming in.

At the last minute, our plane had to abort the first attempt at landing. We were none the wiser in our Christmas merriment and stupor. When we were told what had happened, there was delayed shock.

Anyway, the next morning, Christmas Day, Graeme and I were among the first down for breakfast to be told that there had been a small problem. The chef had been involved in a disagreement with management and stabbed his boss! What a way to start Christmas Day.

At the team breakfast table were the two Pithey brothers, David and Tony, togged in suits and looking very smart. They were going to church. We decided to join them, hoping that perhaps it would help change our fortunes on the playing field. We rushed upstairs, put on our glum looks – because nobody ever looks happy about going to church – and off we went. A few blocks away we came to a beautiful church and in we walked.

The service had started. In fact we were probably quite late because we immediately joined a queue that led to the altar. I was always a little scared about getting up front at church, regarding it as holy ground. But there was no turning back now! We received communion, something totally new to me and I must say I felt pretty good about it. I just hoped that the Lord was taking note!

We sang a few songs; the sermon was highbrow and complicated and then finally it was all over. There was a sigh of relief, but I did feel good inside. Outside the Pitheys asked how we had enjoyed the service – as if you are supposed to enjoy these things! We nodded our reverent approval, as hypocrites often do. Then I asked about the communion.

Imagine how shocked they were to find out that we were Presbyterians, didn't understand the significance of communion and had not even been confirmed in our own church. But we had had the cheek and audacity to share in the breaking of bread and the drinking of the blood in the holiest of holies – the Roman Catholic Church! Had we committed Holy treason?

We survived, but I recalled the very odd occasion that my father had talked religion and how he had warned about the Catholics. They were to be avoided like the plague. He would tell a story about a great friend of his who married a Catholic. They tried all his life to convert him and then finally on his deathbed he succumbed. Dad would relate that story in almost horrific proportions. By the end of that tour I was to find out more.

At Newcastle in New South Wales I met a delightful girl named Jenny. I fell in love with her. It was a whirlwind romance and I wanted to marry her. The flight back to South Africa at the conclusion of the tour was sad because I had left her behind. But I was going to come back and marry her. My intentions were most noble, genuine and sincere.

We corresponded and even got down to ring sizes, but my family was totally against it. It didn't matter that she was beautiful and charming and even brother Graeme approved. What did matter was that she was a Roman Catholic. Mom and Dad were strongly opposed to that.

To cut a long story short, the relationship died, helped largely by the great distance between us – some 6 000 miles – but aided and abetted considerably by this anti-Catholic prejudice. When it finally collapsed, I was consoled by platitudes such as "It's for your own good, even if you don't understand right now." It was hugely amusing and annoying to me that parents who showed so little interest in the things of God could be so strong in their conviction on the Catholic issue.

My later understanding and conviction has far more to do with changed lives than doctrines and denominations, accepting always that there is need for a clear understanding of Scripture and what you believe.

Juan Carlos Ortiz described it so beautifully and aptly at a seminar I once attended. He compared human beings to a lemon tree growing at the bottom of the fruit garden. Lemons are not very tasty. They are in fact very sour! They are not as popular as oranges that are sweet and tasty. So what do we do figuratively when we want to change someone? We just lop off the lemons with our various religious formulas.

But what happens next season? Back come the lemons. That tree does not produce the sweet tasty oranges you were hoping for, it produces lemons. It will never stop producing lemons. To change the fruit you have to dig out the tree at the very roots and replace it. It's the same with people. It's about a change of heart, the replacing of the roots, not about religion and dogmas.

I read a most unforgettable analogy, told by Dr Ernest Gordon in his book *Miracle on the River Kwai*. The morale of the men in the allied prisoner of war camp was very low. It was so low in fact that men forgot the common decencies and were prepared to do each other down – anything for survival! It was a case of every man for himself and they grovelled and snarled like starving animals in the jungle. It was a sick situation. They even ate vermin – what degradation! Such was the terrible atmosphere at the camp, man at his lowest ebb.

One day after work, a count was taken of the tools. There was one short. So all the men were paraded and questioned about the missing implement. The man who had taken it was ordered forward from the ranks to own up. Nobody stirred. The Japanese sergeant in charge became livid with fury, he raved and ranted at the prisoners and threatened to shoot the lot if the guilty party didn't own up. It was obvious to everyone that he was serious.

Suddenly, very deliberately one man stepped out of the ranks. The Japanese immediately clubbed him to death. The squad was marched back to camp and the tools were checked through again. It was found that a mistake had been made with the first count – all the tools were there!

That incident made a tremendous impression on the camp. It revolutionized the morale. There was a man who was completely innocent, but he had died voluntarily in order to save his doomed comrades. This was self-sacrifice out of the normal run, it was fantastic. Mankind is similarly doomed, like the men in the squad, but the innocent sacrificial scapegoat has stepped forward. Suddenly I understood the analogy almost as if I was there at the camp!

I was once sent a book *C T Studd,* the life story of a famous cricketer who had turned his back on worldly fame and gave his life to serving Jesus. Written in the inside cover was a Scripture, *"Preach the Word, be prepared in season and out of season; correct, rebuke and encourage – with great patience and careful instruction."* He had quoted 2 Timothy 4:2. Was it a coincidence?

A passage from this book was to change my life:

Christ's call is to feed the hungry, not the full; to save the lost, not the stiff-necked; not to call the scoffers, but sinners to repentance; not to build and furnish comfortable chapels, churches and cathedrals at home in which to rock Christian professors to sleep by means of clever essays, stereotyped prayers and artistic music performances, but to raise living churches of souls amongst the destitute, to capture men from the Devil's clutches and snatch them from the jaws of hell, to enlist and train them and make them into an almighty army for God.

But this can only be accomplished by a red-hot, unconventional, unfettered Holy Spirit religion where neither church nor state, neither man nor traditions are worshipped or preached, only Jesus Christ. Not to confess Christ by fancy collars, clothes, silver crosses or gold watch-chain crosses, church steeples or richly embroidered altar cloths, but by sacrifice and heroism in the foremost trenches.

When in hand-to-hand conflict with the world and the devil, neat little biblical confectionary is like shooting lions with a peashooter. One needs a man who will let himself go and deliver blows right and left as hard as he can hit, always trusting the Holy Ghost.

It's experience, not preaching that hurts the devil and confounds the world because it is unanswerable. The training is not that of schools, but of the market; it's the warm, free heart not the balanced head that knocks the devil out. Nothing but forked lightning Christians will count. Those strong words, from the heart of a missionary in deepest Africa, had a profound effect on me, almost as if God Himself had spoken.

Christ wants not just nibblers of the possible, but also grabbers of the impossible by faith in the omnipotence, fidelity and wisdom of God Almighty who gave the command "to go out into the world and preach the Gospel to all mankind."

The Rev. Emlyn Jones was very close to our family and had in fact christened Shaun. He also married my sister Helen to John Gardiner. They are both strong believers and in forefront ministry. *Joy* magazine and the Jesus Factory fellowship in Howick bear testimony to God's grace and anointing upon their lives. Just after our conversion decisions, Inez and I wanted to find Emlyn and tell him the good news. We had not seen him for some time. We found out that he was very sick, in fact dying, and we were eager to visit him. I will never forget going into his little room and as we got close he recognized us through his watery old eyes.

"To what do I owe this honour?" he asked as he clutched our hands. "We have good news for you. We are born again."

"Oh, the power of prayer," was his response and we realized immediately that he had been praying for us for some 18 years. We sat on his bed chatting for about an hour and though he was in pain, he managed to keep talking.

He told us that prayer was the most powerful weapon in the world and he talked about how much he adored Jesus and just couldn't wait "to go home." He mentioned how each day of his life he re-travelled the world in his mind, praying for everyone but wondering why God was still keeping him alive for he so wanted the peace and joy of the final home-coming. "It's frustrating hanging on down here," he admitted with that wonderful smile.

The last words he had shared with me were, "Peter, I have lived long. I have done much and seen much. Some things I have reason to feel good about, others not so. I have understood much and yet finally realized that we all know so very little. I once thought I was so clever. I can leave you with one truth though and I know it's the absolute truth in this very confused world of ours.

Nothing, Peter, absolutely nothing is worthwhile if you have not found Jesus."

Emlyn died a few days later and that wisdom was his parting gift to me. Just like mighty King Solomon, he had found that not even all the money and wisdom in the world suffices if you have not found God. Not just know about him. But actually find him.

It's not about accidents, and it's not about coincidences. The destiny of your life always remains in your hands and revolves around the decision you make. God of course knows in advance how you are going to respond, but that still does not alter the importance of the individual role in the decision-making process.

Way back I experienced that precious moment down Southbroom way when I really understood for the first time that I had to go through everything, the cricket, business and the normal ups and downs of life to provide the platform for ministry. Wisdom and experience come with years, not with degrees and diplomas!

I recall at about the same time another rather amazing experience. One morning in my quiet time I happened to be thinking about my testimony and how I often referred to my grandfather in jocular fashion, suggesting that he represented an excellent start to my Christian Curriculum Vitae!

That morning a whole new complexion was revealed. In my mind I heard these words, "You joke about your granddad, but there are two things you need to know about him. When he christened you, he dedicated you, as the eldest, to serve Me. He also had a major hand in your being called Peter."

What was the significance of this information? Two weeks later I was ministering in White River. I shared my testimony at one of the meetings and then afterwards I noticed a little old lady who had stayed behind. She battled her way to the front and addressed me, "Young man, you mentioned your grandfather tonight. I have a message from the Lord for you. You need to know two things about him. First, when he christened you he dedicated you to the service of the Lord Jesus Christ. And secondly he had a hand in your name, being called Peter."

My heart thumped and I knew this was just confirmation of my quiet time a few weeks ago.

Forty years was the time that elapsed between my christening and my final conversion. Biblically, 40 years seemed the appropriate time to spend in the wilderness and indeed it had been just that for me.

11

RETURN

The road back to international cricket

The 1990s had begun and I was still involved with cricket, to the extent that I was writing a regular column in the *Natal Mercury* and I was a member of the Natal executive. Life in the main, however, was all about preaching and winning souls. I had helped my friend and associate Ian Gourlay plant a church on the Berea. It was aptly enough called the Berea Christian Fellowship. My calendar was full with speaking engagements, missions and crusades. I had watched and commented strongly on much that had happened in the cricket world. I had never been scared to speak out and tell it as I saw it.

I recall an incident in the ladies bar at the Kelvin Grove Hotel way back in 1964, while we were battling to put it over the English. It must have been about ten o'clock in the evening when I went in for a nightcap. Roy McLean to whom I had always been very grateful for what I had learnt and experienced on the Fezela tour, was there. Roy had been recalled for the series, but things were not going well for him. Anyway, he was holding the floor and the listeners were hanging on to his every word.

One of the guys then posed a question to me on a subject that had obviously been discussed a little earlier. My answer obviously didn't agree with what Roy had said and he took it up with me in front of the packed bar. I stuck to my view. "How many Tests have you played, sonny?" was his response. "How many more are you going to play, Roy?" was my immediate retort. There were some chortles and half-laughs, but you could have cut the atmosphere with a knife.

I really wished I had not said it, but it was too late. It turned out to be the very last Test he had played. He was dropped for the next encounter at Newlands.

The remark hurt him and it wasn't very nice, nor was I proud of it, even in those days. Perhaps we had been a bit sensitive because one of the issues that really bugged the likes of Eddie Barlow, Colin Bland and myself as youngsters in the Springbok team, was the issue of having to keep quiet. Don't dare speak until you have got some Tests under your belt! You needed to earn the right to have a say or to be respected in the hard school under Jackie McGlew.

In retrospect I don't think it did us any harm, but we did overreact sometimes. As a journalist, I always tried to stay objective, but was never overawed by circumstances or who had said what! There were issues that had wrought my journalistic disapproval. While respecting the efforts of those who were fighting the odds to keep South African cricket alive, the Sri Lankan visit really switched me off.

The Arosa Sri Lankans, under Tony Opatha was a disgrace. Not only were they hopelessly inadequate as players, but also the efforts made to try and sell this huge mistake to the public did much to damage the credibility of the SACU. It was a total embarrassment.

When Lawrence Seeff scored a huge century on his debut he never tried to pretend that his feat deserved Test match recognition. "We all know it's not the real thing," he said and was immediately fined for his honesty. His career was short-lived.

It was argued that being non-whites as such, this tour provided the forerunner for the West Indians. That in itself was an admission of manipulation and sadly most of the media went along with the deception, rationalizing that it was for the good of the country and the game!

International exposure

The initial Graham Gooch English visit had captured the imagination and the way it all came together was quite exciting and novel. The public admired the tenacity and sheer nerve of it all. We were of course picking our opponents, but there was not much option. And money was making the difference. Kerry Packer had proved the point and cricket administrators world-wide were shocked into understanding and acknowledging the power of mammon.

The cheque-book ruled supreme. Lawrence Rowe's West Indians were a nightmare. My great friend Atholl McKinnon served them in a managerial capacity, but actually died on the job, in his hotel room. Everything was done to appease them, including preparing the right pitches for their fast bowlers – something that really rankled brother Graeme.

The West Indians had to win for the gates and so everything possible was done to that end. Graeme felt that even the administrators were secretly backing the tourists, for political and other reasons. This does not make for happy relations.

The West Indians were demanding and one of the matches nearly didn't take place. Minutes before start the top brass was still bargaining. To be expected, I suppose, but again everything was kept hush-hush for the sake of the cause!

Kim Hughes and his Australians were plagued with injury and some internal squabbles with Kepler Wessels having to become Australian again to boost the strength of the touring party. Finally, along came Mike Gatting and a huge confrontation at Pietermaritzburg, which frightened the living daylights out of Dr Ali Bacher and others. This thankfully saw the rebel tours put to bed. Granted, they had served a purpose, but a lot of what went on behind the scenes is probably best left unsaid.

Intrigue, deception and lies became the diet and while all is considered fair in love and war, and this was war, there are always casualties and consequences. Politically we were also making all sorts of statements about non-racialism and unity in cricket and there was a huge amount of window-dressing.

There had also been a mean machine in South Africa – the Transvaal cricket side. Gathered were the best cricketers in the country plus a couple of devastating imports like Sylvester Clarke and Alvin Kallicharan, and this team of internationals plundered all and sundry. Clive Rice was skipper and the side almost assumed the proportions of a cult. It helped promote player power and desecrate club cricket, but it won all the cups and trophies and for that reason was considered highly successful.

It was a power base, for sure, but the jury will always be out for me on just what good was achieved. Indeed, isolation had not been a happy time, but as a journalist there was no shortage of material to write about. At one stage, Graeme took a stand on payments when an Australian group toured the country and was told that he would never play for South Africa again. South Africa lost the first match and the selectors were back on hands and knees begging him to play.

Indeed those were hairy times in those isolation days. Sadly, so many brilliant players were to suffer. Some made their names anyway in county cricket or on the Packer circus, but the Test record books will never bear testimony to their respective skills. There would have been some outstanding Springbok teams during that period and some of the mighty West Indians who so dominated world cricket during that period still get a bit upset when it's suggested that they never beat South Africa! At least South African cricket had survived and there will always be those who contend that the end justifies the means!

One evening at a cocktail party under the tent at Kingsmead, I was chatting to my good friend David Pithey when Ali Bacher joined us. Ali had already asked me once to make myself available as a national selector, but I had turned it down. I was too busy preaching, I told him. Besides I didn't really want to get caught up with cricket and the hassles of being a selector. That evening he asked me again, this time in front of my friend. "David, tell him not to be so stubborn. We need him to serve as a selector. Speak to him," said Ali.

David started, "Do you think that God gave you talents to waste? You have an ability that can serve South African cricket. You will be honouring God by using them," was the way he cleverly followed up. In other words, don't let yourself be caught up in a church holy huddle. You need to be involved with cricket.

Initially I didn't like what he said, but as I drove home later that evening I started thinking about David's challenge. I shared the incident with Inez and she agreed with David. Ali had asked me to think about it very seriously. So a few weeks later when Vic Hohls, the secretary of Natal cricket phoned to ask whether I would allow my name to go forward as their nomination for the national panel, I agreed.

So it came to pass, my election along with Tony Pithey, Lee Irvine, Rushdie Majiet and S.K. Reddy in Peter van der Merwe's six-man panel. South African cricket was destined to return to the international fold and we were the men to select the teams. I regarded it as an honour and privilege.

I missed the historic first meeting. Suddenly a gap had opened and South Africa was invited to play a three-match one-day series in India. Decisions were made within hours, not least of them the composition of the side. There was no form to go on and Peter van der Merwe went out on a limb to explain that the side was a reward for the past season! That seemed to miss the normally sharp eyes of the controversy-seeking pundits. Clive Rice was made skipper and the team read pretty much as expected. Even I didn't question any of the decisions when I was belatedly informed! Dr Bacher was to be the manager.

A special Boeing was set aside for the trip and the UCB filled the plane with its executive, family members and well-wishers. Those who went along will never forget the welcome, the hospitality and the sheer history of it all. A South African cricket team was finally visiting India!

But there were niggles – the most notable of which were the continued strained relational difficulties between the president, Geoff Dakin and the chief executive, Dr Bacher. A meeting was even convened on tour to reprimand Ali for a press statement he had made concerning "scuffing" the ball. Dakin's frustration revolved around accountability. In the main, Geoff contended that Ali often acted without due consultation. Ali would no doubt suggest that sometimes expedience made it impossible. It wasn't the happiest of relationships. But that's the way it often goes in the top echelon of organizations, as much as it is often covered up.

South Africa lost the first two matches and were well on the way to losing the third when I received a telephone call. It was from one of the leading radio stations and they were just checking whether I would be available for comment after the game. They assumed we were going to be beaten and they warned me that the subject they wanted to address was the inept captaincy of Clive Rice. Would I be available to comment? I agreed, but the call never came. In a sensational turn around the Springboks batted like champions, the game was won and the radio station stayed silently embarrassed!

At one of our first selection meetings it was clear to me that Peter van der Merwe had some firm ideas about the forthcoming World Cup. He was keen on a new captain and was pretty determined to choose for the future. He wanted young players. He wanted to start again, build up a whole new team under a strong disciplined captain. It was a wonderful opportunity to start fresh. He had dished out a few rewards on the Indian trip, but it was now time to have some guts and some foresight as a selection panel. I liked his thinking.

The process of selection was quite involved. There were three stages. First there was a reasonably big squad, which was to be narrowed a month or so later and then finally trimmed to the touring party. We held our meeting at Kingsmead in Durban.

What a furore we caused. The convenor announced that it was possible for others to force their way in, but nobody listened to that. When Wessels was announced as captain and three stalwarts – Clive Rice, Jimmy Cook and Peter Kirsten – were left out, all hell broke loose!

The media machine went into action, aided and abetted by other interested parties.

The telephone never stopped ringing. Someone had motivated Barry Richards to phone me and question our sanity. I suggested to Barry that it was nice to know that he was still interested in South African cricket, but that living in Australia didn't exactly qualify him to be informed and objective. The only ex-player who was positive – and he was excitedly so – was Eddie Barlow. It was time to start fresh and put the oldies out to pasture was his viewpoint. I think he also admired our stand and the fact that we had the courage of our convictions. He urged us not to crack.

Edward Griffiths, then of the *Sunday Times*, led the media onslaught but I refused to get involved whatsoever, much to his chagrin and threats. I probably escaped some wrath because some newspapers got the wrong impression that the voting was 4 – 2 and that van der Merwe and his ally Pithey, had stampeded the two new and "ignorant" affirmative selectors! Those were the type of rumours and slanders doing the rounds. Lee Irvine stood alone for the old brigade. The campaign never stopped and it came from all quarters, some of them highly unexpected.

Rice and Cook got caught up in the proceedings, expressing personal anger, frustration and resentment as well as allowing themselves to be used by the media. Kirsten on the other hand, took a far healthier view. He reasoned that the best method was to make runs during the interim period and force himself into the reckoning. But president Geoff Dakin stood by his convenor and the panel, though there was a lengthy memo of no confidence from Dr Bacher!

Dr Bacher also didn't get the job as manager to the World Cup, with Alan Jordaan getting the nod. It wasn't a very happy beginning. In fact, I started to wonder what I had let myself in for. Kirsten fought his way back into the side and proved to be a greater man for it all.

World Cup 1992

So, off to the World Cup went Wessels and company, with Adrian Kuiper as understudy and a whole lot of fresh faces to world cricket. A new era had dawned, though it was a very complicated and arduous time for Peter van der Merwe and his panel of selectors!

One evening I got a phone call. It was Ken Baxter, a chicken farmer in the Piet Retief area. He was a very committed Christian. Ken simply said, "God has spoken to me. I must send you to Australia for the World Cup." Living by faith makes this type of phone call an incredible boost. "Thanks Ken, but what do you mean? How long, how much and do you mean Inez as well? What about running costs? It's expensive," was my response. "Just get the travel agency to phone me, I will fix up the lot," concluded Ken.

So off we went to the World Cup. Neil Adcock was the leader of the touring party that we joined, but we were going to miss the first four matches, the opener against Australia at Sydney and then the three games in New Zealand against Sri Lanka, West Indies and the Kiwis. Our first contact would be at Brisbane where the Proteas would be taking on the might of Imran Kahn's Pakistanis.

What a fairy-tale start. Kepler must have thought he was dreaming. Undefeated on 81, it was from his bat in the 48th over that South Africa truly announced its return to World cricket. It was a resounding win over home team Australia. I was actually ministering at a school in Estcourt, along with Trevor Goddard, when the winning run was hit. The headmaster became so excited, he sounded the bell and made the announcement over the intercom right in the middle of the period! South Africa rejoiced. What a start!

Two setbacks followed, losses against New Zealand and then lowly Sri Lanka. The latter was hard to swallow. How could these minnows beat us? The initial glory against Australia had almost been forgotten.

Meyrick Pringle had been one of those who fought his way back into contention after being left out of the original squad and he was the toast of South Africa in the early hours of March 5 1992. Batting first at Lancaster Park against the mighty West Indians, South Africa had managed a reasonable 200. But in stepped Meryck with his irresistible away-swingers. There were times when Pringle could be almost unplayable and that morning, the most likeable Eastern Province pace-man really turned on the charm – depending of course which side you are on! Four wickets were down for 19, with Lara, Richardson, Hooper and Arthurton back in the hut. That was enough. South Africa was back with a vengeance, back in the hunt.

Certainly Inez and I were most relieved because that afternoon it was time to fly to Australia. Another loss and we would have been out of the running, hardly the best news just before 14 hours economy class in a plane! Our arrival at Brisbane included the bad news that Kirsten was still injured. In the previous matches he had made 49 not out, 90, 47 and 56. The thought of being without him was too much to contemplate, hence there was much gloom and doom in our camp. I was a late arrival at the Gabba ground, having been preaching up the Gold Coast.

But that afternoon I was there to witness one of the great moments of cricket, a moment that was captured on TV and turned Jonty Rhodes into a legend. Yes, that famous run-out with Jonty diving full length to effect the dismissal. It was a turning-point in more ways than one, though nails were chewed and hearts skipped beats before finally the rain restricted calculation and outcome had the Proteas home by a mere 20 runs. Imran Kahn shaking his head in annoyance at the rain-affected result was my lasting memory of that encounter.

Canberra saw us defeat Zimbabwe and with eight points in seven games, we now only needed one win in the final two games to qualify for the semi-finals. England, to my mind, were the best team at the tournament and they handled us quite comfortably at Melbourne so all eyes were focused on Adelaide and our final match against India.

At about the same time there was a referendum at home. On the morning of the match Joe Pamensky told me that inside information suggested that a 'No' vote might triumph. Geoff Dakin as president had been urged to apply some pressure by suggesting that anything but a 'Yes' vote would see us come home right away. Maybe the spin doctors had wanted to convince the cricketers to get involved and pressurized Joe. My response was that the 'Yes' vote would walk it!

The Adelaide game was a real corker, reduced as it was by rain to a mere 30 overs apiece. Wessels won the toss and elected to field, finally needing 181 to win and with that earning a place in the semi-final. Six runs an over, in those days was a tall order in anyone's language. Peter Kirsten and Andrew Hudson were the heroes of the day.

A brilliant opening partnership of 128 ensued and South Africa scraped home with five balls to spare! It was tense stuff. I missed the last few overs. I had to go off to a preaching engagement at a big charismatic church. The result was relayed to me just prior to sharing my testimony and I have to admit I got a degree of inspiration from the news!

World Cup 1992 semi-finals

We were in the semi-finals of the World Cup at first attempt! All the controversy and ugliness would hopefully abate just a little. I had been involved in quite a few breakfast meetings, not to mention Sunday church services and the Australian media showed plenty of interest. The newspapers carried many interviews about my "finding God." I participated in a few radio interviews and even on television. My involvement with Christianity drew some interest and probably even raised some eyebrows. One interviewer asked what I did for a living. I told him that I was in the ministry.

To an Australian that somehow meant politics. When he found out I was a preacher he was quite dumbfounded, almost as if I had gone out of my mind. But for whatever reason, even if just inquisitiveness, the meetings were well attended and successful and established some excellent contacts.

I found Australia much changed in the 20 years since I had been there. If ever there was an example of the ravages of isolation it was to me the great strides that had been made in Australia. Brisbane, when we first visited it way back in 1963, was more or less an overgrown railway town with wooden houses. Now it was a thriving metropolis. Sydney impressed me markedly as did the manner of the people, the love and support they had for their country and the professionalism that oozed out of every pore when it came to their sport.

Australians don't suffer incompetence. Excellence is almost an obsession, but they do support one another. Trying to tell an Aussie that one of his kind isn't as good as one of your kind, guarantees that you will be in a heated argument pretty soon. I liked their thinking and their way of life and I was most impressed by the advances that had been made while we South Africans were beating the drums of isolation.

I once again missed the semi-final against England, being involved with ministry in Brisbane. The league table concluded with New Zealand top at 14 points, England were second with 11, South Africa third on 10 and Pakistan 9, just sneaked in by virtue of a very lucky draw with England. In fact, rain saved them from what would have been a humiliating defeat so they were very fortunate indeed to have made the big four.

Graham Hick's 83 was top score in the England innings of 252 with Alan Donald going for plenty. His ten overs cost 69 runs. South Africa's reply was bold, but never really got ahead of the rate required. With 120 balls remaining, 137 runs were required. Then it got to 47 off 31 and when rain began to fall, it was 32 off 18 with McMillan and Dave Richardson at the crease. It then got to 22 from 13 balls when play was halted.

Time was of the essence for TV and other reasons. In fact, at this great moment in a semi-final of the World Cup competition, cricket's show-piece, the greatest irony of all, was played out. As it started drizzling, a message flashed on the giant scoreboard: first 22 off 13 and then 22 off 7 balls. As South Africa watched with bated breath, out came umpires and captains.

The scoreboard spoke again! The final revised target stared bleakly at them. Believe it or not – 21 runs in one ball! That was it. South Africa was out of the World Cup. Stunned administrators and players, not to mention spectators, shook their heads. England was ecstatic, but what a sad end. It was highly unsatisfactory. Beaten by the rain was hardly a way to go. We had every reason to feel a bit cheated by the rules.

But despite the ending, it had been an unprecedented success and the South Africans had won themselves many friends as they completed a lap around the famous Sydney ground.

The final was won by Pakistan, another irony. Imran Kahn's side should never have been in the semi-finals and even in the final the game was going one-way until an incredible spell of bowling by a then unknown young left-hander Wasim Akram changed it all. The fact that England had lost, was a travesty of justice. They were in my opinion by far the best side and they had played well. But the World Cup does not seem to smile on them!

If the South Africans had felt at all swollen-headed or unduly proud of their World Cup debut, it would soon be knocked out of them. Just a few weeks later they were in the Caribbean, with Richie Richardson and company bent on revenge. What a thrashing they handed the South Africans. At Sabina Park, Kingston, it was by 107 runs, at Queens Park Oval it was first by ten wickets with 24 overs to spare and then by seven wickets with seven overs to spare. Phil Simmons brutally smashed two centuries and Brian Lara two fifties. It was devastation and humiliation and here in South Africa we didn't even want to talk about it. The only whimper I heard was, "How could the cricket authorities agree to such a trip so quickly after the World Cup?" It was like a gentle cry in the night!

South Africa in West India

There was still a Test to come. There had been much controversy in the West Indies about selections and the public demonstrated by refusing to attend the Barbados Test. This time they were not demonstrating against South Africa, but we always manage to sneak in somehow!

Nobody watched. It was quite eerie. Wessels won the toss and rather surprisingly sent the Windies in. They were all out for 262 and then South Africa, thanks to a brilliant maiden Test century by Andrew Hudson (163) had managed a first innings lead of 83. There were some smiles. At 174/7 in their second innings, the home side was less than 100 runs on and two tail-enders were left in the pavilion.

The smiles were now broad grins. But Jimmy Adams was still there. The West Indian score of 174/7 became 283 all out and a target of 200. Chasing the target, Kepler Wessels and Peter Kirsten played brilliantly and at 122/2, South Africa could not have asked for a better platform into the final day. Victory in the West Indies, at the first time of asking, would be an incredible return from 20 years of international isolation.

There was one problem however – that brilliant pair of West Indian fast bowlers Ambrose and Walsh. It was the fifth day on a deteriorating up-and-down pitch against two of the world's best.

Gary Sobers had confidently predicted a West Indies win. I am sure not even Gary expected it so easily. Only 26 runs were added that final morning as eight wickets tumbled – four each to Walsh and Ambrose. What had promised so much, ended so dismally and South Africa's first venture into the Caribbean had truly humbled all involved.

Convenor of selectors

The World Cup had silenced the critics, but now some of the knives were being sharpened again, especially those looking for the scalp of Peter van der Merwe. All sorts of rumours did the rounds, not to mention media speculation about whether the former South African captain would retain his post as chairman of selectors.

On the Friday evening, the night before the UCB annual meeting, Peter van der Merwe phoned me to ask if I had heard any inside information concerning the selectors. I had specifically kept out of it when approached by some of the executive members, but my reading of it was that the UCB would support the re-election of van der Merwe. In fact, I didn't think that they really had an option. After all the controversy I thought that in the best interest of cricket, the Board needed to stand by its servant. I advised him to stand. And he told me he would.

You can thus imagine my surprise when I heard he had changed his mind. His reading of the general atmosphere and body language the following morning prompted him not to stand. On the Sunday evening I was peacefully sitting at home watching some soccer on television when Dr Bacher phoned. "Congratulations. You are now convenor of the national selection committee." The hot seat was now mine.

I was later to find out that I was not the original choice. Apparently the Board had virtually decided on someone else when Dr Bacher intervened. He told them to reconsider and that I would be the best choice. Obviously they agreed and the job was mine. Peter phoned to wish me luck and so did many other former cricketers. In fact, I was quite overwhelmed by the origin and sincerity of the many good wishes. It was most reassuring to know that I had the support of Ali. He was undoubtedly the most powerful hand in the organization. We had gone back a long way and I know that he had always appreciated the encouragement that I gave him when he first started as a Springbok in England in 1965.

Over the years we had come to respect each other and though we did not always agree on everything, we enjoyed a good relationship. It was going to be a massive challenge. And I relished the opportunity to serve at this high level. As I had so often said, "I can never give back to cricket what it has given me, but I am going to try."

Ali Bacher's particular skill was his handling of the press. He had developed it into an art and the way he fed and used the media was often quite brilliant.

I often used to joke that when he was holding a press conference he was "merely feeding his chickens!" He was a constant source of information for the television and newspaper staffers and while often accused of over-doing it, and bending over backwards for publicity, it was his job and he did it well. Certainly he made sure that whatever story was written, it was given the right angle or slant. He was a spin doctor par excellence.

Ali was exceedingly helpful and went out of his way to get the team and me whatever we needed. Of course Ali had to be sure it was in cricket or the team's best interest, but once convinced, he would get his way. Sometimes he would deal with the matter directly, on other occasions, if it was sensitive and might arouse opposition he would cleverly circumnavigate. But it would always be organized!

At this time Geoff Dakin also moved out. His term was over, his job was done and Krish Mackerdhuj became cricket's new president. Again I must say that personally I found Krish extremely helpful and a wonderful ally. We spent many hours chatting at the various grounds and on overseas tours and I count him as a friend.

When his term finally expired a few years later, I was very sorry to see him go, for I really appreciated the support base he provided and his integrity and frankness in dealing with selection issues. It was not always easy with the outside public and political pressures, but Krish was consistent and reliable and could not be intimidated. Krish and Ali both left the cricketing matters in my hands and it was a wonderful working relationship.

I decided to give up writing a cricket column during my term as convenor because I felt that it wasn't right to fill both capacities. There were many times when I wished that I had that outlet to answer and explain some of our actions and decisions, but in the long run I believe that the original choice was the wisest. It really doesn't help to get involved in petty arguments and debates when so much in cricket is of a subjective nature.

Critics have to earn their living and with the amount of talking and writing they have to do, it is inevitable that inaccuracy, verbosity and self-justification raises its ugly head.

It's a bit of a rat race with them all competing for the limelight and acknowledgment as critics. And of course there are many private agendas. Kepler Wessels came under close scrutiny during his captaincy period and there were those who relentlessly pursued him. Some were stung by their lack of success in having him removed during those controversial pre-World Cup days, others thought him too negative and others just didn't like him.

Certainly the faxes and telephone calls abounded to the extent that I got myself an unlisted number. Some people were downright rude, others were against his Afrikaans upbringing and there were even death threats, believe it or not.

A couple of the critics were obsessive and couched their opposition to him in all sorts of intellectualism and philosophy. The United Cricket Board even agreed to allow me to travel in business class on domestic flights because the fans didn't stop pestering me.

Certainly, I can say that Kepler was the number one bone of contention during my time as a selector. Even his notable achievements were begrudgingly acknowledged. It was sad, but that's what happens when the media decide to hang you out to dry. Of course it's not right and those involved will deny it, claiming that they were only being objective and constructive. But Kepler soldiered on and for my money did exactly what we asked of him in that vital stage of South Africa's re-entry into international cricket.

India in South Africa

The first series against India produced three draws, but there was a historic victory at Port Elizabeth. Kepler won the toss and controversially sent the Indians in to bat. Who should know St George's Park better than Wessels but the typewriters were buzzing. At lunch it was a "bad mistake," "an error of judgment," but when they were finally all out for 212 there was silence, but no apologies!

Then Hansie Cronje was condemned for his painstaking maiden Test century, but when Alan Donald had the Indians 88/7 in their second innings, all was forgiven. Kapil Dev produced a scintillating rearguard with 14 fours and a six but Donald's twelve wickets in the match were to prove the winning feat. A nine-wicket victory with Wessels undefeated on 95 as the winning stroke was played, virtually clinched the series and temporarily silenced the pundits.

The one-dayers against India went 5-2 to the South Africans, but World champions Pakistan and the West Indies arrived for the Total series and not surprisingly stamped their authority. The South Africans managed two great wins over the West Indians at PE and Newlands, but the Pakistanis whitewashed Kepler and company in all three preliminary encounters to ensure that the final would be between the two visiting sides.

The Total Trophy was to end in the Caribbean display cabinet, but the Pakistanis had really started a big psychological problem for the South Africans. Fast bowlers Younis and Akram looked unplayable with their reverse swing and their batters were making merry against our attack. Their superiority and control had taken on awesome proportions and it was going to take major application and resolution to turn it around.

Brett Schultz, the fiery left-arm speedster from Port Elizabeth, was the hero and the find of the Sri Lankan tour. In the second Test match at the Singhalese Sports Club in Colombo, the thickset fair-haired tear-away, set about an errand of no mercy that truly set my heart fluttering. He dispensed pace and fear as he blasted the home side away for 168 in their first innings, after Ranatunga had chosen to bat. Wessels (92) and Cronje (122) again led the run making a massive 495 and Brett blasted them for the second time to be all out for 119.

Victory by an innings and 208 runs was significant, being the only result in the three-match series. But it was not nearly as exciting as the discovery of a new world-beater. To go to Sri Lanka and beat them for sheer pace, takes some doing. The critics were raving and the selectors were smiling. We could not wait for the Aussies, to introduce them to our new sensation!

The South Africans returned victorious and happy to have survived Sri Lanka! It's a feeling that you always get when you return from the subcontinent because any success there really has to be earned. I was proud as punch about our new menace. Natal were playing Eastern Province at Kingsmead and I decided to go and watch. When I arrived I was horrified to see EP in the field but no Brett.

"He is injured," said one of the Natal officials. My heart dropped. Was his career going to end before it had even started? His knee was troubling him. Craig Smith later informed me that he needed an operation. Mention a knee operation to me and I immediately go into negative mode. But Craig promised it wouldn't be that serious and he would be back for the Aussies.

To cut a long story short, Brett Schultz never came back. Sure he made a few raids and sorties, but the hopes and dreams following his devastation of Sri Lanka were never to be fulfilled. Gamely he battled on. Fitness test after fitness test produced frustration and anger. Desperately Brett tried to come back as he fought the odds. He was extremely brave and committed, but it was not to be. As simple as that!

The Hero Cup

Australia loomed, but on the way we had to visit India to play in the Hero Cup, Bengal cricket's diamond jubilee event. Rain halted the first game against Zimbabwe leaving it a 'no result.' We beat the West Indies quite comfortably in the second and then thrashed Sri Lanka in the third to virtually assure us of a place in the semi-finals. The game against India didn't count except to define semi-final opponents.

South Africa's loss to the home team India, ensured a re-match in the penultimate round and who will forget those TV pictures as Alan Donald came to the crease with four runs to tie and five to win. Five runs in five balls and Tendulkar was the bowler. Unbelievably, three dot balls followed. The second last ball saw a single and McMillan needed a boundary off the final delivery.

A nation held its breath. Sadly, it was just a single and India went through to the final where they thrashed the West Indians. The critics and the fans played that final over and over and over! Pipped at the post, once again and there was talk of temperamental deficiencies. Indeed I will never forget Alan Donald's eyes as he peered through his helmet. They certainly were not the eyes of a guy thrilled to be there or sensing victory! He looked absolutely petrified!

The Hero Cup had seen Hansie appointed as vice-captain. Though a tender 24 years old, it was our decision that he would take over from Wessels and we felt it was important to indicate the nature of our thinking. It would give the team prior warning regarding their future skipper and enable Hansie to be more involved in decisions along with his captain and the coach, Mike Procter.

Procter and Wessels had their moments of disagreement. Kepler had not been pleased with some comments his coach had made in Sri Lanka and that resulted in a management meeting at Kingsmead to iron out the problems and differences.

But it is never as easy as that, for there was some fundamental disagreement between the two that was not going to disappear with all the debating in the world. In a nutshell, Kepler wasn't too interested in the coach's interference with any game plans and strategies. Mike could have his say but had to accept that the captain held the casting vote. Not ideal, but not too much option!

Against the Aussies

Wessels couldn't wait for the Aussies. He had some points to prove and some scores to settle. The morning of the first Test at Melbourne saw the rain pelting down. It was Boxing Day and I was the guest speaker at the Lord's Taverners Test match breakfast. Outside it was anything but cheery. Cricket weather it wasn't.

The first day saw a mere 29 overs, the second produced just five balls more, 29.5 overs, and the third day was completely blank. It was probably just as well, for the captain was nursing a knee problem, sustained the day before the match and then to add to the problems, Andrew Hudson retired hurt. Brian McMillan had also missed the first encounter as had Peter Kirsten. Gary Kirsten had flown out from South Africa as a replacement and the touring party was now a whopping seventeen players. Sick parade was an over-crowded tour meeting! Craig Smith was having his work cut out keeping players on the field and the visitors were clearly underdogs.

The second Test was to go down in history as one of those legendary encounters, certainly if you were a South African. It all started so badly, almost as if there was a curse on the team. Kepler won the toss and at lunch we were sitting pretty with 91/2. After lunch Shane Warne struck and in 74 overs had South Africa all out for a mere 169, having collected seven wickets for 56. The pitch had turned sharply and we were in deep trouble.

The Aussies passed our first innings total with only three wickets down and a full-fledged nightmare was in the offing! Then came an incredible transformation and it came from the four bowlers Donald, De Villiers, Matthews and Symcox. The Australian lead had to be kept to the barest minimum and these four worked in tandem to make runs as scarce as ice blocks in the Sahara desert.

I sat there intrigued and very impressed by the line and length and the combined dedication of the foursome. They bowled like misers! Matthews for instance got no wickets, but he conceded only 44 runs in 28 overs. That was brilliant. Similarly Pat Symcox got two for 82 off 46 overs, in what I always regarded as his finest day in Test cricket.

The lead was restricted to 123. When the fifth wicket fell in our second innings, we had not even knocked off the deficit, but Jonty Rhodes was still there, joined by wicket-keeper Dave Richardson. Anyone suggesting a South African victory at this stage would have been committed to a lunatic asylum.

But Rhodes was brilliant, literally pouncing onto anything loose and dispatching it to the boundary. The tail-enders hung in for dear life, pushing and prodding but giving Rhodes as much strike as possible. It was a battle seemingly hopeless, but South Africans never say die. I got goose bumps watching the drama unfurl. Finally a target of 117 was set and in the executive box where we were being entertained, our Aussie hosts had every right to believe that it was a mere formality. Four sessions remained and maybe they could even claim the extra half-hour and win with a day to spare.

By close the Aussies were watching in disbelief, four wickets were down for a mere 63 and the target was starting to enlarge. Slater, Boon, May and Taylor had finished their matches and Mark Waugh and skipper Alan Border were the undefeated batters.

"We can still win this," said Mike Procter. Kepler agreed and there was a great spirit in the Protea's dressing room. "We are going to beat them," – the vibe was clear and distinct. I had said to Ray White that I had a funny feeling about that Test. Was this going to be one of those cricketing miracles?

The next morning, the guys were just as positive. If anything, even more so. "We are going to win, Boss," said big Alan Donald. That day the executive party of South Africans had been allocated to the New South Wales box where Alan Davidson, former Test legend, was presiding. We were at the top of the main stand. As the South Africans came onto the field tears came to my eyes. In ministry it's a sign to me of Holy Spirit presence, but I choked as I said to Inez, "We are going to win today. I just know we are going to win."

The second ball of the first over saw Border pad up. The ball flicked his pad and clean bowled him. Then it was Waugh and Healy and a direct hit from a Hansie throw had Warne stranded. Australia was now 75/8 and there was a hush around the ground. Craig McDermott and Damien Martyn got together and were slowly climbing back into the match.

The South Africans were starting to get worried. "Don't fret," I said "these two are going to get to within ten runs then two wickets are going to fall quickly. We are going to scrape home. Believe me." I was confident.

Martyn fell at 110 and Glen McGrath popped up a return catch to Fanie at 111 and it was all over. Tears ran down my cheeks. I could not speak. We jumped and shouted with joy. Most of our hosts had left in disgust. One of the Australian spectators came to the top of the stand to curse and castigate us. He bellowed out a few sentences of abuse and was on his way. We hoped it made him feel better, but one of the great victories of Test cricket was ours.

The scenes in the changing room were chaotic; hugging and shouting and tears of joy. Kepler had not been on the field. His knee was extremely painful and Hansie had done the honours, and done them extremely well as understudy. Obviously instructions from the dressing room were being followed. All Alan Border could say was, "We froze." The glory was ours. What a celebration!

That evening we officials were due to fly back to South Africa, but such was our elation that we probably didn't even need an airplane. We were miles off the ground, flying high. Percy Sonn, one of the executive members, had such a party that on the way back to Perth they could not even wake him up for the transit break. He literally slept from Sydney to Jan Smuts Airport! Wessels came home to have his knee fixed and the tourists turned their attention to the one-day internationals.

Brisbane and Perth lay ahead and it was going to be a tight squeeze to get into the final ahead of the New Zealanders. It turned out that in the final match against New Zealand, South Africa would have to win by at least 40 runs if they batted first or they would have to get home by three or four overs if they chased a target. Ken Rutherford won the toss, batted first and the Kiwis were igno-miniously bundled out for 150, a target that was achieved with nearly 20 overs to spare, thanks to the Kirstens, Peter and Gary. A good win in the first at Melbourne was turned around with the Aussies coming home strongly in the last two play-offs at Sydney.

Hansie had so wanted to win. Maybe they had all tensed and strained in their eagerness to succeed, but at least there was still Adelaide. One down in the series was a position that had really stirred up the Australians. The Kangaroo's tail had been well and truly tweaked. They were distinctly aggrieved and bent on revenge. There was no Kepler to steer the ship, not even from the dressing room, and though I was convenor of selectors I didn't want to interfere unduly with the understudy captain. I was a bit concerned when I heard that they were looking to go all pace instead of spinner Pat Symcox. But I didn't push. Contrary to what some pressmen suggest, decisions at this level are not taken lightly and do involve more than one voice. Anyway, "Go with what you think best. You are there, I am 6 000 miles away," was my final word.

The toss is vital at Adelaide. Border won it and capitalised hugely with 469, thanks to a massive 164 by Steve Waugh. We were just under 200 runs behind, despite being 173/2 at one stage. Then a final innings of 129 with spinners Warne and May collecting six of the dismissals, provided for a 191 run Australia triumph. There was some unhappiness about the umpiring, but we had not played well enough! A drawn series was disappointing I suppose, but realistically any other result would have been a bit tough on the Aussies.

It had not been a happy time with injuries and in the ODIs we did lose six out of ten matches. Our performances in the one-dayers were beginning to cause concern, especially as we always appeared to be chasing, rather than initiating. We were starting to think of separate teams and possibly Hansie at the helm for limited overs encounters.

The return matches in South Africa needed no advance publicity. There were going to be full houses all around. The first Test was a nightmare for me! More accurately I didn't sleep a wink for the entire duration of the contest and the cause was Brian McMillan. I took a gamble, calculated but nevertheless a risk, and the strain involved ensured that I never did anything like that again.

Ali shared my feelings and emotions for he was well aware of the medical facts and the chance I had taken. What a relief when it was all over, a huge victory for South Africa by 197 runs. Brian's knee was the problem. It had been fixed, but it all had to do with rehabilitation. Obviously we wanted him to play but the medical advice was that he needed more time. I wanted to risk going into the match at the Wanderers with just four seamers, the fourth being Brian. This of course would ensure a strong batting line-up as well.

Brian seemed tentative and Craig Smith wasn't all that confident, except he did assure me that if Brian played he would do everything possible to keep him up and running.

But was it wise for him to play? Captain Kepler wanted McMillan, but suggested that I was the only guy who could persuade him.

The final decision was obviously with the burly all-rounder. I decided to go for it, to take a gamble. I pressurised Brian, no other word for it, and he finally agreed to play.

Every move Brian made on the field, I watched with trepidation. Every phone call was a potential death-knell. I lived out each ball that he bowled. Big Mac bowled 33 overs in the match, got us four very vital wickets, including Mark Waugh and Alan Border and was a vital cog in a tremendous victory. The four-man pace attack proved to be the right call, but Ali and I, as we hugged each other after the triumph, agreed on: "Never again."

We got away with it, but who knows the damage it did in terms of stress and tension.

Personally I thanked God, but promised not to do it again! It was high risk and a big gamble. The Australians levelled matters at Newlands and highlighted for me just how dangerous the third innings of a Test match is. When the first innings scores are much of a muchness, the team batting third with the match seemingly heading for a draw, needs to be wary. Some careless application and a few quick wickets has seen many a Test lost.

At the hotel Jimmy Cook had commented, "This one is definitely a draw." I would have been happy to settle for that, but Steve Waugh with his innocuous looking seamers, believe it or not, waded in with five wickets and toppled us for a mere 164. Australia won by nine wickets. We had literally thrown this one away. It was hard to smile and shake hands. But what about the steal at Sydney? That made me feel a lot better!

The final Test at Kingsmead never got near a result, even though the South Africans enjoyed a first innings lead of 153. The pitch just got easier and easier, as it so often does in Durban. Wessels took stick for not being more positive and going for the kill, but that was frustration and personal agendas speaking, rather than good cricket sense.

Two series were drawn. Deep down I am sure Kepler was satisfied. Considering all that had happened that summer from an injury viewpoint, it was a good effort and Kepler deserved the highest praise.

He would not have been quite so happy about the one-days. In the eight-match series we led 3-1 when the itinerary broke for the three Tests. But the second half went convincingly to Australia by the same 3-1 margin, so it finished a drawn series at four-all. Border and Wessels had now become accustomed to sharing trophies. Both would far rather have won. But by the same token, both would simply have loathed losing.

A summer of regrets for both captains. Maybe. But no depression or thoughts of suicide! Australia still had not avenged the sixties and seventies. Australia was still the major enemy.

South Africa vs England

But traditionally England also appears in that picture. To beat England in England, preferably at Lord's, that's the on-going dream. Kepler's knee was painful and was clearly inconveniencing him on the field. He bravely suffered in silence, but it was catching up. He was thinking of calling it a day, a viewpoint he openly shared with me, and he wanted to finish off in England, leading South Africa to victory.

Kepler was keen to go out on top and the plan was simple. We would go to England, win the series and then Kepler would invite his vice-captain Hansie to take charge of the final two one-day Tests. It would be a wonderful gesture and would be the cherry on the top of a wonderful career for Wessels. His handing over would also indicate a smooth transition. It was time for a new skipper, especially in the one-dayers, but I was hoping that Kepler might still make himself available for Tests.

"The best laid plans of mice and men," is just asking for trouble! Something went badly wrong. I was there for the first Test at Lord's where Wessels made a brilliant century and South Africa thrashed England by a mammoth 356 runs. England was all out for 99 in the second innings and the South African pacemen were the villains in a humiliating procession of English batsmen. In the second Test at Headingly, a Peter Kirsten century gave us a highly creditable draw. At 105/5, Peter was hit on the head. Hansie was sitting next to me. "That's the turning-point. He will make a hundred," I pronounced. What motivated me to say that? It was something that Hansie often reminded me of.

Changes in the engine room

When Inez and I caught the train from Leeds as we headed back to South Africa, I was sure everything was in order. The only problem was Hansie's form. He just couldn't get any runs and it was starting to frustrate him. But for the rest, all appeared okay. That was early August.

By the end of the month there were phone calls and rumours and a whole different picture. Cronje and Procter had obviously fallen out and Wessels had tagged on to some suggestions that he was going to be booted out. "What had happened to our agreement?" was the essence of his query. The media were involved with inevitable half-truths and South Africa had lost the third Test at the Oval, thanks to an incredible nine wickets for 57 by speedster Devon

Malcolm; was beaten in Holland and also succumbed in the final two limited overs internationals. The dream finish for Kepler had not materialized, and there were some unhappy cricketers.

It was time for change. The UCB had decided it was time for a new coach and Mike chose this opportunity to slam my role in his dismissal. It ended with me being awarded a dead bouquet by one of the local newspapers for my shabby treatment of Mike. The newspaper had absolutely no idea of the facts, nor even bothered to try and find out. A couple of their staff though did phone me to profusely apologise for their newspaper, dissociating themselves completely from the award! Mike's dismissal was an UCB decision and though my opinion might have been considered, his strongest detractors came from elsewhere.

I also sat alongside Dr Bacher and Ray White in interviewing prospective candidates for the coaching position, notably Duncan Fletcher, Eddie Barlow and Bob Woolmer. Barlow subsequently suggested that it was a "put up" job and that we all had our minds made up before the interviews. Again the facts would refute that. There is no denying there were strong recommendations to the UCB from us. Bob Woolmer was the right guy in our opinion. Decision-making is the lot of those in charge. They are judged by those decisions. Unfortunately someone always loses out and the newspapers invariably spread the discontent. It makes good copy, after all!

At that time I had had an interview with Hansie. I wanted to grill him about his aspirations and ambitions, his views on South African cricket and his thoughts about captaining his country. He was heir apparent, but I wanted to sound him out on all aspects concerning the role we were about to confer upon him.

Coming up was a visit to Pakistan to take part in a three-way contest with Australia and my selectors didn't want to throw Hansie into the deep end with this rather awesome project. Couldn't we ask Kepler to do the honours? There was a new coach, Woolmer, and there were some tough opponents and some even tougher conditions. Kepler took the challenge. Statistically, it was a horrendous time for the South Africans, losing all six matches.

At Peshawer we experienced an earthquake that registered just under six on the Richter scale. The hotel shook and when we booked out there was a huge crack in the wall behind the reception desk! Journalist Iqbal Kahn asked me at a press conference whether I felt my job was on the line as convenor.

On a day-off we toured the Khyber Pass and as I marvelled at the rugged terrain and the rugged lives of the local inhabitants, I managed to console myself about the tough times we were negotiating in cricketing terms. I felt rather like a visitor to the paraplegic ward complaining about my headache! But those many hours of enforced solitude on my first visit to Pakistan enabled much thinking and soul-searching. I knew it was time to move ahead with Hansie and Bob and leave the past behind.

169

Saluting skipper Kepler

It was something like ten defeats in a row. We needed to relook the one-day game and who better to help than Woolmer. In Tests we had done okay. Except for the one off visit to the West Indies we had not been beaten in a series, something Kepler was rather proud of. A platform had been laid and it was a good one.

The Pakistan trip was best forgotten, but a few incidents will always remain with me. The first was at a cocktail party in Rawalpindi. I was very friendly with Bobby Simpson and he was then the much-vaunted coach of the Australians. Chatting to him, I confessed that I was very impressed by one of his young bowlers, Glen McGrath. I liked his fine high action and his endeavour to maintain line and length, rather than look for speed.

"I think he has a big future," I told Bobby. "Won't you tell him?" he asked. I was suddenly embarrassed. He called young McGrath and I gave him my few words of encouragement. I had always been very impressed by Curtley Ambrose, for exactly the same reasons that I commended the Aussie. It was later to become the same advice that I gave my son Shaun! McGrath has certainly lived out that prophecy!

While we were in Lahore, the captain interrupted my lonely breakfast session. Kepler had a startling revelation. The previous evening he had been partying with the Australians, most of whom he knew pretty well, and they admitted that they had been approached to "throw" a match, obviously for a considerable sum. I was shattered, as was the head-shaking Wessels. Years later it emerged officially that Warne and Mark Waugh had been implicated in passing on information for financial gain.

The final was between Australia and Pakistan and was played at Lahore. The team could not wait to get home, but president Krish felt he had to attend and invited me to stay on with him. What an experience. First no transport arrived to collect us, so we took a cab. He didn't know what entrance to utilize. There were no tickets and we were just on the point of going home when a pressman recognized us and got us in. The executive accommodation was sparse, to say the least, and the catering was virtually non-existent. For lunch we got a box with some sandwiches, bananas and a hot coke. Nobody spoke to us and by the time the match finished, with Pakistan losing comfortably, there was nobody left in the executive suite.

We had to find our own way home, but counted our lucky stars that we lived in South Africa. Krish, who was known to fly off the handle now and then, jokingly promised never again to complain back home.

Finally, on the last morning, there was time to kill before departure and Bob Woolmer decided that he was going to have a team meeting and let all the players speak their minds! It was dangerous, but he felt he would be able to control the discussions. He invited me along, but I didn't think it would be a good idea.

A few hours later I came down to book out and there was captain Kepler, prowling like a caged lion. "How did the meeting go?" I asked. Obviously not well by the look on his face. "Hansie got out of his box," he commented. Kepler inferred that his vice-captain had obviously said some things that he felt were out of place. Wessels was not happy.

I asked Bob about the meeting and while he did concede that some severe things were said, he didn't feel that it had got out of hand. But he had no idea how Wessels had perceived it all! That meeting was to become a major stumbling block in the strained relationship between the two players. But still with us as we boarded our flight home, was this psychological barrier concerning Pakistan. Three more defeats and this ogre was getting too realistic for my liking!

I have a great respect and admiration for Kepler and my next task was to see that the transition to a new captain was effected smoothly and with due credit all round. It was not just because it was the right thing to do, but because I felt very strongly about the magnificent job that Wessels had done. I spoke to the left-hander a few times and even asked him to consider being available to play in the Tests against New Zealand. I asked him how he wanted to exit and left the decision in his hands.

He took some time and then contacted me to say that he was going to make a clean break of it. He felt that would be the best way. Personally and selfishly I wanted him as a banker in our batting, but he was adamant about quitting the Test arena. It was never a case of firing him. It was more specifically about a new phase and future planning. There was no question that new thinking and direction was required in the limited overs game. We needed to become innovators and pioneers, rather than followers and Bob and Hansie had that vision.

Life's experiences contribute to the baggage that we carry. This luggage is not easily discarded. With Kepler and the criticism he endured came much of the frustration and the agonies of a game swept up by the ravages of man's inhumanity to his fellow man. Spilling over into the sport were all sorts of unique influences that merely underlined the enormity of the challenge that faced South Africa.

As we said goodbye to Kepler and thanked him for having done his very best, I could not help but be saddened that so much of the disapproval and criticism had gone so deep.

12

REINSTATEMENT

Captain Hansie

Hansie Cronje's first summer as captain of South Africa promised much. New Zealand would be playing three Tests, there would be a one-off Test against Pakistan and the Mandela Trophy would have Pakistan, Sri Lanka, South Africa and New Zealand in limited overs combat. Dr Bacher as usual, had been busy lining up the matches. Finally there would be a trip to New Zealand, just for good measure. Then the players could rest!

I was on the international committee and I supposed we all should have been consulted when invitations were accepted. Usually the first we knew was the release of an itinerary! But nobody complained, Doc was doing his usual efficient job! Principle issues always concerned me more than the dotting of i's and the crossing of t's!

I like people who get things done, even if they sometimes annoy the finicky or those who love to get embroiled in red tape, and endless debates. Ali thankfully wasn't in the latter category.

Bob Woolmer's start as coach was anything but auspicious. Six losses in Pakistan were followed by a defeat in the very first Test. Allan Donald was injured, there was no more Wessels and Cronje lost the toss. That had been the end of the world, but his bowlers soon changed that.

In one of the worst displays since readmission, our quickies bowled like millionaires. Bouncers and long hops abounded and there was no attempt at line, length and direction. From the moment that Ken Rutherford's men put 411 on the board, it was an up-hill struggle on a wicket that became quite difficult towards the end. One ball bowled by Simon Doull hit a crack just short of a length outside the off-stump only to fly head-high far above the wicket-keeper's outstretched arms down the leg-side. I had never seen a delivery like that, nor ever hope too again! It had everyone in hysterics.

A comfortable loss by 137 runs now had Hansie behind the proverbial eight ball. The prophets of doom were lining up the statistics about how unlikely it was for a team to come back and win a three-match series after losing the first encounter. But Cronje was adamant at the press conference. "We are going to come back and win. We have no option."

True to his promise, the captain delivered with an eight wicket victory at Kingsmead and then a seven wicket triumph at Newlands, where he personally threw in a century for good measure, ably supported by a three-figure contribution from Man of the Match, wicket-keeper, Dave Richardson.

A couple of weeks later saw the historic first-ever Test against Pakistan at the Wanderers and what a resounding win for Hansie. South Africa gained a first innings advantage of 230 but didn't enforce the follow-on. Cronje preferred to grind the opposition, the ultimate winning margin a massive 324 runs! Fanie De Villiers had statistically played his greatest Test, bagging a ten-wicket haul with the ball, not to mention an undefeated innings of 66 with his flaying bat.

The fans and the critics were smiling. The greatest pleasure had come though in the Mandela Trophy with six wins out of eight matches, but most importantly three successes in four outings against the "hoodoo" team, Pakistan.

The final was the best of three, but only needed two games as we walloped Pakistan. So started a complete reversal in the fortunes between these two countries. Many years later it was the Pakistan players who began asking themselves, "How do you beat these South Africans?" There seemed to be a new method and urgency and a plan was starting to come together. There was that knowing smile on Bob's face while Hansie's general appearance, demeanour and body language was heralding the arrival of the 'Green machine' – Hansie and the boys! I liked what I was seeing! So did the public and the sponsors!

The Centenary Test at Eden Park in Auckland also turned out to be another feather in Cronje's cap. A sporting declaration, that had us all worried at one stage, confirmed that fortune does favour the brave. The Proteas had not only won the handsome trophy, but more enthusiasts and critics were joining the Hansie Cronje fan club. More importantly, I was not getting so many of those lousy, anonymous phone calls.

There was one exception, however, and it was that same guy who kept badgering us about Kepler's Afrikaner background. He was unrelenting in his attack on their culture and school. Grey College in Bloemfontein is in my opinion, one of the greatest institutions in this country and I mention this criticism only to convey the type of obsession and thinking that does exist.

What I was exposed to in my eight years as a national selector, really did open my eyes. In the main, I just watched and listened as a silent witness to what was often a rather disturbing parade of human nature. On many occasions, and my wife Inez will confirm it, I seriously questioned why I had ever become involved.

Shaun – a star was born

England and the World Cup lay ahead – after the short break! A short trip to Zimbabwe had been arranged to help warm up the troops and this had the desired affect. We had some crushing victories and confirmation that Alan Donald was back at his best. Eleven wickets in the match confirmed he was over his nagging injury and operation.

I had developed an interest in the Hong Kong sixes event. Simply, when I was first asked to pick a team to travel to this annual competition, I told Ali that as selectors we're not into social stuff. Unless it was our intention to win the event, count us out. That's how we felt. Ali was as keen to win as ever, so we went for it, planning and doing our specific selection homework.

We enjoyed some success, but never won. This time there was a snag at the last minute. Alan Donald didn't want to go, so belatedly we included my son Shaun. His face literally beamed when told he was off to Hong Kong. South Africa triumphed and Shaun was one of the stars. Dermot Reeve, the England captain couldn't praise Shaun enough suggesting that "a star had been born."

Then while Cronje and company were in Harare plundering the opposition, Shaun was doing his own demolition job of the Zimbabwean B-side, both with bat and ball. Shaun had been making his way steadily on the first-class scene for Natal. In a brave moment though he once told me, "I am going to play at the World Cup." I liked his determination and vision, but at the time it seemed just a little precocious.

Shaun had always been a top sportsman. In junior school he played for Natal at the annual interprovincial tournament. His cousin Anthony was in the Transvaal side and their clash was virtually a "Test," won that time by Natal. His soccer skill with Virginia United saw him belting in goal after goal as a hungry forward in the junior leagues and then later he excelled at hockey. But cricket was his first love, from the days he and his elder brother Gavin hotly contested their drive-way tests.

Shaun was going to play for South Africa. Poor Gavin always had to be the opposition. Physically Shaun was a late developer so his fast bowling had to wait. He was mainly a batsman, always elegant and stylish. In his second last year at school, he was chosen to captain the Kingsmead Mynahs, a combined schoolboy side. This honour was to prove a great fillip at this vital stage of his cricket career. In fact, it was one of the most significant decisions of his life, as I look back, for not only did he do a great job with the Mynahs, and was widely

174

acclaimed for it, but it set the path right at his school, Northwood.

Leadership was his destiny, but somehow circumstances had contrived otherwise.

He was head boy and cricket captain at his junior school, but at high school he broke his service at Northwood to go to Michaelhouse for a short spell. He didn't enjoy it there and was soon back. But in the short term it cost him in terms of continuity and perceived disloyalty. Anyway, he captained Durban schools in his final year and dreamed of the double – he wanted to play for South African Schools at cricket and hockey. Nothing shy or backward about Shaun!

He had to be satisfied with provincial hockey colours, a mere second best, but he made his cricket target along with cousin Anthony. That opened the door for a Natal contract and this was established by Natal's sponsorship of his B Com degree at the Durban University.

Shaun and I had an agreement about getting this degree. He wanted to make cricket his life, but we both accepted that to make a decent living from the game you had to be a Test player. Anything less was a struggle. Just in case he didn't "make the cut" as it were, we agreed on a degree as a back up. I will never forget when he finally passed. He was so determined. He passed without any hitches then declared, "Here is my degree, Dad. Now I am off to play for South Africa."

Stage one had been completed with maximum speed and minimum fuss. He had toured Sri Lanka with the National under 24 side with average success. There had been great schoolboy rivalry between Shaun, Dale Benkenstein who was at Michaelhouse, Mark Bruyns at Maritzburg College and Sven Koenig, son of famous tennis player Gaeton. Sven was at Hilton College. They all played in the same Natal schools side and became good friends. Rivalry is healthy, as long as it does not become obsessive and they were good for each other.

Shaun was not one who needed to be told to do his homework, to learn or to practise. He was always a pretty good self-starter and did listen when advice was offered. I found this a most endearing quality. He had his own mind and clear-cut goals, but would always be open to consider options. Fiercely competitive, a family trait, he nevertheless has this ability to couch disappointment with a smile or shrug of the shoulders. That does not mean he is happy about losing. He hates losing. But it's the bitter taste of defeat that makes you want to avoid it and stay a winner.

Shaun's career at the beginning of the 1995 summer was heading in the right direction to the extent that I spoke to both president Krish and Ali about Shaun's possible selection for South Africa. I needed to know how they felt because I didn't want a situation of having to recluse myself when my son's claims were being discussed. As the chairman of selectors it was simply not acceptable, in my opinion, that you would have to leave the meeting. What if Shaun's inclusion revolved around other key team selection issues? I would either have to participate fully or not be there at all!

The UCB response was that they backed my integrity and then Ali added with a smile, "And don't make it harder for your son." That I would have to guard against, but I did feel it was different when selections involved a whole company of opinions.

Granted, the convenor wields power, but I was not going to be able to select Shaun if my colleagues didn't agree. I must admit I had a lot of peace about this issue throughout my selecting days. Often a pressman would ask me about how tough it was having this father and son problem! Thanks to my co-selectors and the UCB, and of course Shaun's good form, I can honestly say there was never a hitch or even a hint of embarrassment.

His original selection, for instance, just saw a massive gap open up and very little discussion because he was the obvious candidate.

The incumbent Fanie De Villiers was injured and out of contention and some of the other candidates were battling as the selectors gathered at Kingsmead to pick the side for the first Test at Centurion against Mike Atherton's Englishmen. Shaun was having a good run of form and even as we met, he was rolling over the Gauteng batsmen before our very eyes. Talk about first-hand evidence! You could not have written the script better! He was nominated, discussed and selected. It was as simple as that.

After the meeting I was writing out the team for the announcement when a hand touched my shoulder. I looked up it was Bob Woolmer, who had been involved in the discussions. "Well done, Dad," he said. For the first time it really struck me. All before had been business. Now it was time for family. Yes, Shaun was my son.

I didn't have to announce the team. I am pleased because I was totally overwhelmed by the massive response to Shaun's inclusion. Admittedly it was his home ground and he was amongst his team-mates, but that moment was supreme. Even as I am typing, tears tug the emotional chords. "Well done, boy," was all I could say as I thought back to my dad acknowledging me in similar circumstances some 34 years back.

The Centurion Test was a wash out! I recall seeing a long-range weather forecast and was perturbed about the prediction of three days of rain. "Never at this time of the year," was Ali's adamant response. Well rain it did, for days and days! I didn't dare remind Ali of his call. England's innings of 381/9 was the sum total of the action over five days. But at least I had the satisfaction of seeing Shaun's career successfully launched. Graham Thorpe was his first Test victim and he followed up with Mike Atherton and Graham Hick. Certainly you can't start much better than that.

At this time another youngster was hitting the headlines – Paul Adams. The eighteen year-old had made a spectacular debut both for Western Province and the South African A-side in their victory over the tourists. His action was unusual to say the least and he was mesmerizing some top batsmen. They would study videos and work him out in time, but there was no doubt he had a definite wicket-taking potential, even at international level. Thrown into the media hype was the coloured issue and this drew wide interest.

I was determined though to use him wisely. He would need to be introduced in spinner friendly conditions, not that there are many of those in South Africa. He would also have to be treated as a fifth bowler. In other words, he needed to be a wicket-taker who could be whipped in and out of an attack. Certainly he should not have to carry any load in terms of any donkey-work bowling. He was too young and inexperienced for that. We could kill him for life by throwing him to the wolves. I regarded him as a great find, a potential match-winner, but I was going to protect him at all costs.

Those looking for political mileage and expedience banged at my door and pestered me with phone calls and messages. The media jumped in with the usual innuendos. At a press conference after the Pretoria wash-out, I was asked a question relating to the Adams issue. I don't recall its context, but it was a very stupid question. Normally though, you answer queries, no matter how inane or ignorant.

But I chose to take him on. "That is a very stupid question," I stated firmly as I looked at him. There was a moment of silence. He looked rather sheepishly at me and then replied, "Yes, it is, isn't it!" He brought the house down. The laughs, guffaws and sniggers suggested we were at a comedy revue rather than a press conference. "It must be all this rain that's dampened our minds," was an apt conclusion.

The second Test at the Wanderers was 'The great escape', set to make nearly 500 to win. England at best could hope for a draw. But even that would require a mammoth feat. Mike Atherton was the Houdini. For a staggering 644 minutes he occupied the crease and kept South Africa at bay. His undefeated 185 was off 485 deliveries and represented one of the greatest rescue acts in cricket history.

Every other performance over the five days paled into insignificance by comparison and even the thwarted Proteas had to admire, respect and acknowledge the achievement. Maybe to the ignorant it was boring and unproductive; maybe to sponsors and prophets of doom it's what is sinking Test cricket as a spectacle, but to me it was a brilliant performance.

It was a very wet summer. But it's always risky coming to Kingsmead before the New Year. True to form, the ground resembled a lake on one of the days. Only one and a half innings were completed. On the first morning there was a little drama involving Shaun. His ankle was painful and he had owned up to the injury. Dad's policy on injury was rather straightforward. I had broken the rules with Brian McMillan and I was not going to do that again. Aches and pains were part of being a fast bowler. Blood in the socks was just a token of a hard day at the office!

If it was more than that, then it was better not to play. He would not break down, assured Craig Smith. "I want him to play," said Hansie. And the youngster went off, satisfied that a burden had been lifted from his shoulders. He didn't break down because you can't sit in a changing room watching the rain! So, it was off to St George's Park for Christmas.

This was to be the momentous occasion for Gogga Adams, his Test debut. Thorpe was also his first scalp, much to the delight of a packed gallery. He then added Atherton and finally Peter Martin for a great start. The Test followed much the same pattern as the Wanderers game. England batted out the last day to a tame draw on a pitch that just got easier and easier. I saw Geoff Boycott in a pavilion corridor and with a huge smile he delivered this worrying thought, "You guys have made the running all series. You have dominated the whole series. What a tragedy that you are going to be pipped at the post in Cape Town." I really didn't want to hear that!

The Newlands match didn't last three days, but its outcome was not as Boycott had mooted. Winning the toss at Cape Town is normally cause for celebration. It might have been initially for Atherton as he confidently decided to bat. But just under 70 overs later there would be cause for reflection – 153 all out. Allan Donald and Shaun did the damage. Things were not looking much rosier for South Africa when they were 171/9 in reply, but Adams strode out to join Dave Richardson who seemed to have a penchant for performing great things at Newlands.

They put on 73 runs and did it quickly. Shaun's first five-wicket haul followed in the England second innings. Only 70 runs were needed for victory and in a mere 16 overs Hudson and Kirsten clinched the series. What a relief.

What Boycott had said, worried me. I had this nagging feeling that injustice was going to be done! And to make it all the more pleasurable for me, Shaun's first fiver was safely tucked away in the record books. Dad was a proud man, to be even prouder less than a week later at this very same venue.

The first one-day international had a packed Newlands' hushed in shock and disbelief as Shaun came to the crease about mid-afternoon. On debut he was taking guard with South Africa 107/6. Awaiting him was another debutante Jacques Kallis. Between these two and Craig Matthews, the home team finally totalled 211, Shaun's contribution being an undefeated 66.

When England were 155/3 in reply, some of the Newlands faithful even started heading home, deserting the apparent lost cause. But if Shaun was to earn his Man of the Match award, he needed more than just a good innings!

Four wickets, and clean bowling Darren Gough with the last ball of the match, did the trick.

Victory was South Africa's by six runs in a sensational turn-around. As my heart thumped I wondered just how many more of these would put me in the grave! The one-day series went 6-1 to South Africa and Shaun was presented the Man of the Series award in Port Elizabeth by none other than our esteemed President Nelson Mandela.

During that final day I was honoured to spend about 20 minutes sitting next to the great man. He was surprised to hear that I was a preacher. I in turn had the temerity to ask him whether he was a Christian, to which he replied that he was a "devout Methodist."

I asked him if the rumours were correct that he had given his life to Jesus after listening to a Billy Graham Crusade while on Robben Island. The President just smiled without an answer. He told me that religion was a problem because of "the regime," as he always termed them. They had manipulated the Scriptures for their own purposes and this had left a bad taste for the Christians. He also added that some of the other faiths had done more than the Christians to help change South Africa.

I asked him what his favourite sport was. "Boxing," came the almost guarded reply. "But don't tell anyone," he joked. It was a short time, but a great privilege to have enjoyed his company and attention.

World Cup 1996

Now the World Cup was beckoning. Dave Richardson was out with injury, Steve Palframan replacing him, and Paul Adams had made it. Suggestions that he might not make it had roused the activists and the media. Those were the main news items regarding the team. Shaun went to see a foot specialist in Pretoria for some precautionary advice and to ensure that he would not break down on the subcontinent.

Port Elizabeth gave Hansie and the boys a rousing send-off, again thanks to Ali's orchestration. A week later I was winging my way to Calcutta with Krish and Ali. We had a seven-hour stop-over in Bombay and there were some problems because Air India had torn out the wrong ticket coupons at Durban Airport and the Doc's best organizational skills were severely put to the test for the next leg to Calcutta. Ali's bookmaker friend looked after our seven hour sojourn as we experienced just a little of the plusher side of Bombay.

Then it was Calcutta for the opening ceremony where I was to join the team and become an official member of the touring party. It was quite a big group because Ali was leaving no stones unturned in quest of the World Cup. The team was based in Rawalpindi in Pakistan but distances and times are great on the subcontinent so it involves much herding and organisation to move around a huge touring party!

The opening ceremony was particularly poor. But worse was the return. We had to go via Dehli, with a five-hour stop-over, then Lahore, with three hours to wait and finally Islamabad, which is right next door to Rawalpindi.

The opening match against the United Arab Emirates had to be postponed with a day because of a wet water-logged outfield. We learnt early on that the TV moguls were controlling the show when we had to wait upon their decision about the restart.

Gary Kirsten's undefeated 188 was the highlight of a massive 169 run win over the lowly Emirates, but four days later South Africa were even more impressive in shutting out the New Zealanders by five wickets with nearly 13 overs to spare. Chasing a meagre 177, Hansie decided that it wasn't time to mess around and he was particularly severe on Larsen and Harris whose 'diddley-dobblers' had often caused us frustration and anguish.

England was next to feel the bite of the Proteas. We had thrashed them 6-1 in South Africa and with that lay a huge psychological advantage. But the other side of the coin was, unfortunately, you just can't keep winning one-day games. It only needs one good individual performance by an opposition player to swing the fortunes of a game. The element of luck is a real factor in the limited overs game! England went down by 78 runs, bowled out for a mere 152.

Beating the home side Pakistan, before their highly partisan crowd at a packed National Stadium in Karachi, is a tall order. Sohail's century delighted the fans, but the raucous cheers soon became silent as the Protea's machine moved into awesome top gear. The target of 242 was negotiated with five wickets in hand and nearly six overs to spare.

The critics unanimously proclaimed that South Africa was the team to beat for the World Cup. They were certainly looking fearsome. Holland was swept away in the final encounter, this time with Andrew Hudson notching a massive 161. Without any doubt, Hansie's boys were the hot favourites after clean-sweeping the preliminary rounds.

The quarter-finals had us drawn against the West Indies at Karachi. We were quite pleased about it. The match got some unwanted advance publicity with Brian Lara making some ill-chosen remarks after their sensational loss to Kenya. The media turned it political and were looking to fan the flames of controversy when the West Indians arrived at the Pearl Continental Hotel in Karachi.

We were already there and I will never forget the carnival atmosphere as the camels, jockeys firmly saddled, and bands led the procession ahead of the West Indian contingent. They had done the same for us as part of the drummed up ceremony. Within half an hour I received a telephone call from the front desk. It was friend and fellow Christian Wesley Hall. "Lara has made a mess. We need to fix it," he stated. "Contact Ali," I suggested. "No, let's sort it out, you and me, the Christian way" – whatever that meant. I went down to their team room and there was Richardson, the skipper, Walsh, Lara and Hall. "What do you think?" asked Wes.

"I think it was a stupid statement and Brian should realize that he is high profile and needs to be careful when he speaks. But it's Brian's problem. Whatever he says he needs to fix up personally at the press conference." Our participation would be unwise. "We need to treat it with the disinterest and contempt it deserves," was my view. They all agreed and that's the way it was played. It died a natural death.

But I was having my problems. Radio stations and pressmen were hounding me about Paul Adams. Why hasn't he played? He is just window-dressing! The public was outraged. Most of it was sadly gross media exaggeration. They were more interested in Paul and their political angles than the important semi-final and the huge threat that Brian Lara always posed. Hansie, Bob and manager Cassim Docrat were getting the same pressure.

President Mandela phoned to wish us luck. The selection committee had met and Adams was now an issue. Naturally nobody would have conceded any outside pressure, but a valid case was being made for his inclusion at the expense of Allan Donald.

And the reasons were pretty solid from a pure cricketing perspective. Donald had been expensive in the Pakistan game with 50 runs from his eight overs. The Karachi pitch did spin a little and Adams, besides being new to the West Indians, was a wrist-spinner. The Caribbean batsmen are notoriously disinterested in trying to read these bowlers so it might be worth a try. That was the majority view. Yes, there had been pressure and pestering, but the selectors picked Adams on cricketing grounds.

On the way to the ground, I happened to be sitting across the aisle from Tim Noakes, the sports scientist who was part of the back-up entourage. I happened to ask how well he thought our boys were prepared, mentally and psychologically. He could not have been more confident, adding that he felt that President Mandela's phone call had been an added boost.

Imagine thus my surprise when months later I was to read an article by Tim suggesting that South Africa's loss to the West Indies should have been anticipated because of some syndrome or the other that had to do with being away from home for an extended period!

Brian Lara, as he is wont to do from time to time, almost single-handedly sent us packing. His 111 and his onslaught on Pat Symcox, who conceded 64 runs in his 10 overs was the executioner's block. Chasing 264 was always going to be an up-hill task and I think that finally we did extremely well to finish 19 short.

Certainly the Proteas didn't give up until the final ball was bowled. But the Cup campaign was over. Silence and disappointment ruled supreme and it was time to go home. "As quickly as possible, please Cassim," was the final plea to the manager. There was no time for post-mortems or ifs and buts. In fact at times like these, the least said the better. There was huge disappointment all around. As a vote of confidence the team went en bloc to Sharjah, with wives and girlfriends along for the ride.

India and Pakistan were the opponents. The score-line tells it all. Five matches were played, five victories were achieved and South Africa stood supreme. The victory margins in the five games were 143 runs, 80 runs, eight wickets, five wickets and 38 runs in the final against India. But Sri Lanka had won the 1996 World Cup. In many ways it had been highly unsatisfactory because of Australia and the West Indies refusing to visit the island in the preliminary stages. It would be foolhardy to suggest that Ranatunga and company were the best in the world. Simply they had won a tournament in their own backyard. In context, it was meritorious, but World Cups should never be overstated by a sports hungry world.

Five years had elapsed since our return from isolation. Colin Bryden, editor of the *South African Cricket Annual* asked me to comment. This was the nub of my review that summer of 1996:

It is essential to have vision, a plan and an objective. In a world of science, seminars and meetings theories abound, yet so often fail to crystallize into practical action. We are obsessively inclined towards success and achievement, but sometimes rather vague about what we are really aiming at. South African cricket must have a vision and it is imperative that it is a collective vision with collective responsibility and collective commitment.

Our vision needs to be threefold, as I once told a UCB seminar at San Lameer on the Natal South Coast. We should desire to be the best cricket side in the world, to become a highly successful and professionally administered sport and be a major role model, catalyst and contributor to the new South Africa. That should always be the big picture. It would always be a great challenge. Glibly it was suggested that five years should be the time frame.

More important to me was the process. It needed to be genuine, honest and self-embracing. Political expedience and short cuts had to be averted. I felt that we had come a long way in a short time. Eighteen wins out of 20 matches was a massive turn about in our one-day performances while the bogey of the sub-continent had also been laid to rest. I emphasized again the key role played by Kepler Wessels in terms of discipline, dedication and commitment and the new spirit released by Cronje and Woolmer. I suggested that in future, top teams would be judged on their away performances, because winning at home was becoming the rule.

South Africa needed to become innovators. The South African stable had pushed all reverse sweeping and pinch-hitting. World champions are leaders not followers. All the right rhetoric can abound, all the right thinking can be theoretically in place, but we needed clear-cut vision and some clear-cut fruit in terms of success. To define achievement around a very specific goal is both dangerous and obsessive.

The ministry was getting busier, but after the World Cup I discussed the future with Ali and agreed that my job was not finished. He expressed relief when I confirmed that I would continue. It had worried him that I was travelling to the United States and England for ministry, noting that my time was being squeezed.

But I knew that my part in the task was not over. I was happy with what I saw, but we needed to win more consistently, triumph in more finals and collect some more trophies for the UCB office! And the Board was quite happy with the Pollock father and son set-up. I had to clear that!

Shaun had accepted a contract to play for Warwickshire and he started in sensational manner, claiming four wickets in four balls in his very first limited overs outing against Leicester. This even got him into the Guinness Book of Records. A couple of first-class centuries confirmed his genuine all-rounder status but the ankle was needling him.

Finally it was wisely decided to take the bull by the horns and have it fixed by Dr Ferreira in Pretoria. This meant being released from his county a month early and also meant that he would miss the Centenary tournament in Nairobi as well as the tour to India. But there was no point in trying to avoid it. Initially it was even suggested that he might recover quickly enough to join the tour party for the second Test at Calcutta. But when I suggested that to Craig Smith, he just shook his head in disapproval. "When will these administrators stop pushing recovery and rehabilitation," he must have thought to himself.

Kenya saw another trophy with a massive win over Pakistan in a one-sided final. Kirsten, Rhodes and Cullinan all made centuries during the short tournament that also involved Sri Lanka and of course the home side Kenya.

India

Visiting India is a massive challenge and all the positive talk in the world can't hide the awesome task that revolves in the main around unfamiliar playing and living conditions. It's a whole new ball game. A few one-dayers is one thing, a fully-fledged three-Test series, plus a whole lot of limited overs games, is another!

First there was the Titan Cup involving the home side and Australia. Six preliminary matches, three against each saw us with a clean sheet. India scrambled into the final at Mumbai and there, thanks to a shocking wicket, which was underprepared to say the least, the toss was going to decide the match. Tendulkar called right and the Titan Cup was his. The Proteas were seething and justifiably livid but thankfully managed to keep their cool.

It became that much harder when Tony Greig suggested that the South Africans didn't have big match temperament and "had frozen" in the finals! I travelled with Inez to watch the first Test and on the same flight brought Paul Adams. He had recovered from injury and would be an asset in the Tests. All sorts of delays and hiccoughs convinced us that this was the normal run of things as we arrived first at Bombay and then moved on to Ahmedabad, a huge industrial city.

When Geoff Boycott first heard our itinerary and where the first Test was, he was scathing in his assessment. "I can't believe it," – and he should know. Sadly he was not exaggerating. The hotel accommodation and the pitch were in the same category – awful! Brown and dusty – it had not seen water for days, the toss would take the match and it did.

A typical last-ditch fighting innings of 67 from Fanie De Villiers gave us a 21 run first innings lead, but by the time we came to chase a modest 170 for victory, the top crust had come off the pitch.

Fast bowler Srinath made merry in the unplayable conditions and took six wickets for 21 in just about 12 overs as we tumbled out for a miserable 105. At times like that, you truly feel a long, long way from home. Taking my mind and temper off the whole experience was helped by the desperate need to be positive and cheery with the team.

Tough as it was, in a situation like this, a pity party would have been lethal. But I was very angry. Our fans had expectations. They were disappointed – we were all out for 105. But they will never know what the Proteas had to contend with because it will all just sound like sour grapes.

Everyone who comes to India has to put up with this. It doesn't make it right, though! At least we were off to Calcutta and we knew that Eden Gardens is a lovely ground. An opening partnership of 236 between Andrew Hudson and Gary Kirsten got the Calcutta Test off to a magnificent start and it just went from strength to strength. Having lost seven tosses in a row, Hansie was beginning to wonder about Indian rope tricks, but this time his call started an avalanche of great individual performances.

Two centuries from Kirsten secured him a place in the record books alongside Alan Melville and Bruce Mitchell, while Hudson and Cullinan also joined in the run-making spree with three-figure contributions.

But the hero of the 329 run victory was undoubtedly Lance Klusener.

Controversially we had included him instead of Fanie De Villiers and his body language suggested he was not very pleased about that. Fanie probably headed the line of those who knowingly smiled at the apparent selection botch-up when Klusener's 14 overs in the first innings had cost a massive 75 runs.

The Test debutante had been unceremoniously slaughtered. But a great last laugh was when Lance literally picked himself up from the canvas like a punch-drunk boxer and rallied with a spectacular knock out punch. His answer was eight wickets for 64 in about 22 overs!

At last there was something to celebrate in India and we did that afternoon around the pool of our plush hotel. Our first Test win in India was a moment to be savoured. I must admit though we were happy to leave for home after that memorable game, for the thought of a decider at Kanpur only spoilt the taste of the champagne! There would also be no Alan Donald. He had bruised a heel and was travelling back to South Africa on the same plane as us. We had brought Adams and were taking home Donald. He was going to be sorely missed. Tony Greig once observed, "We bring spinners to India but still win the matches with our fast bowlers. Ironic, isn't it?"

And we had just proven his point. Only three wickets had gone to Adams and Symcox at Calcutta, the rest to the quickies and three run-outs!

Fanie De Villiers did have a highlight at Calcutta. Always one for a bit of fun and publicity, Fanie climbed up one of the floodlights. He had to be ordered down by the management, but it was, for sure, a highlight! Kanpur and a loss by 280 runs had nothing to commend it from a South African viewpoint, except that Adams collected his first fiver, in fact six wickets for 55.

A grassless pitch that puffed dust at each delivery from the first day presented a rather hopeless situation from the moment Hansie once again lost the toss. The guys couldn't wait to get home and get revenge on their own bouncy wickets.

There was one final match – the Pepsi Challenge. This had become a bone of contention. It was a benefit game for Mohinder Amarnath and had been agreed to by Ali Bacher. The management and players were steamed up about it. As it was later to emerge, it was at this time that a few team meetings were held about a financial offer to throw the game. They were in a very vulnerable frame of mind but the offer was turned down and seemingly swept under the carpet. I never heard anything about it, except if anyone had said to me that they were offered money in the subcontinent I would not have been surprised after what Kepler Wessels had confided.

Revenge was sweet back home. On lively wickets at Kingsmead and Newlands Alan and Shaun, now recovered from his ankle operation, brutally turned the tables. The first Test was won by 328 runs and the second by 282 and you would not have thought Tendulkar and company to be the same fellows who had looked so good in their own backyard. These disparities do confuse the ignorant and uninitiated rather the same way as tennis fans don't comprehend why Pete Sampras and other big hitters can't win the French Open on those clay courts.

It is the same sort of story with the subcontinent. The final Test at the Wanderers should also have been one-way traffic because that pitch is usually bouncy and lively. But the curator produced a feather-bed and with it a draw.

There was a great moment for Shaun. In our first innings he made an excellent 79. As he notched his 76th run, he waved his bat at me sitting in the change room. He had passed his dad's personal best, the 75 not out I had made against the Australians. Needless to say, the wide-awake TV crews picked up this memorable moment and made it all that more special.

The Standard Bank one-day series had Zimbabwe added, but South Africa won all seven of their matches to make a total and clean sweep of the event. There were a couple of anxious moments, especially in the final at Kingsmead with Tendulkar, Dravid and Azharuddin firing on all cylinders. Another trophy was in the UCB cupboard and another final had been won.

Australia

Australia was next, at home, and expectations were high. Too high perhaps because that's the way we were becoming with this foe. It's good to be fired up and motivated. But when that eagerness changes into obsession, the pressure tends to become counter-productive. You can recognize the signs, but unfortunately there is not a lot that can be done. It seems almost incongruous to talk of winning and relaxing at the same time. That tends to have more to do with individual personality and temperament and unquestionably is acquired, not taught!

Batting first and 198/8 was a poor start, later rectified to some extent by Dave Richardson and the tail. A total of 302 was just about okay and looked even better when the Aussies had replied with 174/4. At this point Greg Blewett joined Steve Waugh. It was going to be just over eight hours before the stand was broken.

Just about everything fell, from records to reputations as 385 runs were compiled from 769 balls. On the third day, a Sunday – it sounds biblical – I had to preach at an evening service. Not a single wicket fell that whole day. I don't recall the subject of my sermon, but that day Hansie and the Proteas had certainly spent in the wilderness. It was devastating. Our spirits were crushed and victory by an innings and 196 runs became a mere formality. In fact, it was a relief to get away from the Wanderers and lick the heavy wounds. It was utterly demoralizing. The pitch once again needed to be bouncy and lively, but the request had fallen on deaf ears. Before the match Ray White had suggested to me that the Wanderers' surface could be a death sentence for our attack.

Blewitt's double century and Waugh's 160 had assumed nightmarish proportions. How come elsewhere in the world teams get pitches prepared for their own strengths, but here in South Africa we have become so visitor friendly? Our thoughts turned to St George's Park, the pitch for the second Test. "Leave it to me," Doc Bacher assured us.

The first morning in PE was a shock for most. The pitch looked under prepared and there was an unusual amount of grass, but South Africa had to bat first. At 70/5 and 95/7 Ali and I were avoiding each other's glances. It was too sporting! Richardson and McMillan restored some sanity at 209 all out. Australia feared the worse. Shaun knocked over Hayden and Taylor in quick succession then strained his hamstring, never to bowl again in the match. Manager Colin Egar was pacing all over to control his anger as the Aussies were shot out for 108. According to him the pitch was disgusting. A first innings lead of 101 and then 98/1 in our second innings at the end of the second day was a very strong position.

It was Sunday and preaching time for me. Off I went to Uitenhage to the Assemblies fellowship, preached my sermon, ministered an altar call then came back to the ground.

That 98/1 and supremacy, was slipping away fast. All out for 168 and a target of 270 to win promised an exciting finish. Unfortunately Shaun wasn't playing and Brian McMillan was also struggling physically. A few catches were dropped.

Later it was revealed that an edge from Mark Waugh didn't even get an appeal. But Australia sneaked home by two wickets and with it they won the series. The pitch was forgotten, to Ali's great relief, but this time it was his turn to say to me, "Never again!" He didn't sleep much at that time.

Clearly you need to be an expert to prepare pitches. It's done worldwide, but we accepted that our own expertise, or lack of it, made it extremely dangerous to look for anything but the normal pitch. How often had this point been proven and I recall that debacle at Kingsmead in 1964. Not a lot had changed. Centurion Park had Schultz recalled for Shaun and the pitch was conducive to the speedsters. Donald took eight wickets, Schultz six and Hansie's boys got some sort of consolation in an eight-wicket victory margin.

There was to be no solace in the one-days. It was two-all after four encounters, but the fifth at the Wanderers, a thriller involving a 73 run seventh wicket partnership in 83 balls between Hansie and Shaun just failed to clinch it for South Africa. With the skipper still at the crease the home side finished eight runs short.

The next game at Centurion Park seemed all settled for South Africa with a target of 284, but Bevan and Steve Waugh set another record, this time with 189 from 171 balls and the series was decided in favour of Australia, with an over to spare! A big wining margin – 109 runs – for South Africa in the seventh and final game at Bloemfontein, had to be the consolation prize this time.

It had been very close. You could not deny that there was very little to choose between the respective combinations. This was becoming a problem especially as media and fans kept reminding the modern players about how that great team of the late sixties had pounded the baggy caps from Down Under. In my book they were just getting a little of their own back, but I would strictly have to keep that to myself! You are not allowed to get too philosophical or mature in the modern world of sports motivation and obsession. The fans after all only want us to win! That's the ultimate marketing tool – it beats whatever is second by miles!

Years and years of intense physical activity was taking its toll on my frame. As fitness fanatic, I needed to sweat and strain for any sort of satisfaction. My hip was starting to give trouble. It started with an ache, then a limp and then pain that affected sleeping. It was time to do something about it. I tried all sorts of other methods, but all I was doing was delaying the inevitable hip replacement procedure.

Finally I plucked up the courage to visit Dr Weber at the Sandton Clinic. A date was set, some six months in advance, but as the time grew nearer I got decidedly nervous and agitated. I did not dare to read the material I had been given to explain it all, and the very thought of donating my own blood for the transfusion that would be necessary, was positively repugnant! The final days saw a very different, very silent me. When I booked in I was horrified to see all the artificial devices that lined the wall. They looked menacing. Then the physician told me that the chance of a blood clot was about 60 percent. I had consoled myself with a figure of 5 percent. I don't know where I had got that. Ali didn't enjoy hospitals. Nor did I. I was given a sedative, but was anything but calm when going into theatre. I felt like running away.

There was one great truth. I could take nothing with me into the operation except Jesus. That for me was a profound moment of truth because it is the whole profound truth of life.

Yes, as I went under that anaesthetic I had only God. Who better, but what a great moment of revelation! The operation was a success. The first day or two slipped by, but as I started to regain myself I happened to suggest to the nurse, "I feel as if I have been through a mangle." She just smiled. "Have you been involved in this type of operation?" I asked her. "Many times," was her reply. "Tell me then what did they do to me?" I asked. "You really don't want to know," was her immediate response. And indeed we left it at that!

Blood clots usually form due to much tension. But none materialized. Eight weeks later I had dispensed with the crutches and rehabilitation was well under way. I had planned to go to Pakistan for the second and third Tests –just three months after the operation. But at the last minute – in fact, the day before I was due to depart – I phoned Ali to cancel. I would never manage it. Besides, it would be a risk to be so far away so soon.

I had set aside my ministry during the recuperation period, so thanks to television, I was able to watch every ball bowled in that three-match series with Pakistan. The first at Rawalpindi was a yawn and the second at Sheikhupura produced three days of rain. This was perhaps fortunate because the ground was clearly not up to international standard and the weather saved any embarrassment or ill feeling. But the decider made up for all the other frustration. Played at Faisalabad, it was quite an amazing contest. South Africa, at one stage at 98/7, scrambled to an incredible 239.

Pat Symcox was the man of the hour with 81, to aid Gary Kirsten's unbeaten 100. The left-hander had batted through the whole initial disaster.

Pakistan got 308 and was beginning to take a grip on the match. South Africa's second innings stood at 140 when the seventh wicket fell. It was tickets, for sure.

In strode Symcox, again another half-century, some help from Lance Klusener and definitely with some divine intervention, we scrambled to 214 – 146 left for Pakistan to score. Symcox, so the television confirmed, was actually bowled, but incredibly the ball slipped between the stumps and didn't dislodge the bail. How often does that happen in Test cricket?

With victory imminent, a local holiday was declared and the ground was packed in anticipation of Pakistan glory. Sixteen runs came from the first three overs and there was a dropped catch into the bargain. Things looked extremely bleak. Then came one of the most incredible bowling spells in Test cricket.

Four wickets in seven balls was Shaun's brilliant effort and Pakistan had suddenly dived to 31/5. The crowd was silent in utter disbelief. At home I was leaping around the lounge –hip replacement and all! Even dreams are not as good as this. Three wickets from Simmo to cap his great all-round performance and South Africa had won the series.

Series wins in Pakistan are about as rare as airborne ostriches. The impossible had been achieved. Just like at Sydney against Australia, we had seen a miraculous turn of events. Two in a lifetime! Who should be so lucky?

The Golden Jubilee Quadrangular event followed. Sri Lanka, the West Indies, South Africa and home team Pakistan were the invitees. Three preliminary games and a final was the format. South Africa won all four, inflicting a second defeat on Sri Lanka in the final. Another trophy for the display cabinet and another final win. Who said anything about big match temperament or the lack of it? Come Australia!

Proteas Down Under

Christmas Eve heralded my arrival, along with Inez, for the first Test at Melbourne. The massive Anglican cathedral was venue of the message of goodwill, something we were not expecting the next day from Mark Taylor and company. At one stage on the first day with Australia at 77/4, we looked healthy. From then on, we just got deeper into trouble. A brilliant century on the final day by Jacques Kallis, and a defiant 70 from the captain Cronje saw us eke out a draw.

The fact that we had survived the whole final day against Warne was a feather in the cap, something that had not happened often against the world-class leg-spinner.

It was a nerve-wracking day. I walked around the ground a couple of times that day. The final hour or so became so unbearable that I walked back to the hotel and didn't even dare to turn the TV on until I was sure it was all over. The relief was short-lived. The Sydney pitch had spin written all over it as Hansie won the toss. Despite the skipper's own 88, Australia's Warne soon settled in. Eleven wickets for 109 earned him the Man of the Match award as the tourists were defeated by an innings and 21 runs.

To think that we actually felt guilty at Port Elizabeth! Why had South Africa, with its renowned pace attack never been accorded a Test at Perth? We did know, however, that no tampering is allowed at Adelaide. The groundsman runs the show and he is more interested in a good Test wicket than in manipulating an Australian success! "Shane Warne hates the Adelaide ground," confirmed Tony Greig. "But you must win the toss," he added.

We did. Nobody scored a century, but five – Bacher (64), Kirsten (77), Cronje (73), McMilan (87 not out) and Symcox (54) – passed the half-century. Such a consolidated, concerted effort materialized in 517 to which Australia replied with 350.

Shaun was the spearhead with a best-ever Test performance of seven wickets for 87 from 41 overs. A great effort of line, length and stamina, but no wonder they did not enforce the follow-on. Kirsten weighed in with an undefeated century as the Proteas set a formidable target of 361 in 107 overs. Controversy, dropped catches and a few lucky escapes highlighted a frustrating final day as the home side held out and secured the series.

Mark Waugh was the object of the controversy. Hit by a Pollock bouncer, he stumbled away, shook his arm, with the bat hitting the stumps. The television umpire ruled not out as controversy reigned for several days and weeks. South Africa was to return empty handed again because the Carlton and United Series had seen them edged out narrowly in a best of three, final. The separating margins in two of the finals were 6 runs and 14 runs.

After Pakistan and Australia, a rest might be in order! You would think. But not when Dr Bacher is organizing the schedule. Still to come were three Tests against Pakistan and two against Sri Lanka and, naturally enough, the inevitable Standard Bank one-day matches.

The Pakistan trip was controversial. Two players claimed to be mugged outside their hotel. It was world news and didn't exactly enhance South Africa's reputation as a destination for holiday-makers and tourists. Later it emerged that there had been a cover-up. Political expedience finally swept it all under the carpet and even postponed the first match by one day. The UCB's generosity was misguided. As truth emerged, it left a sour taste as well as some embarrassed officials and politicians.

Dave Richardson had retired and we opted for Mark Boucher, much to the disgust of many. And they told me so in no uncertain terms. Denis Lindsay was one of the few encouragers. "That's the right choice. He is going to do great." Many did have to eat their words. Even from the start he seemed destined to be a record-breaker.

At 166/8, the first Test was off to a shocking start for South Africa under the leadership of Gary Kirsten. Cronje was recovering from a small knee operation and would be back for the second Test at Durban. But Boucher (78) and Pat Symcox (108) set a world record for the ninth wicket – a massive 195 runs. Rain and plenty of bad light mercifully condemned this Wanderers outing to a draw.

For Durban, a decent grassy, bouncy pitch was expected. It even looked that way when Hansie sent Pakistan in to bat, having omitted spinner Symcox for swinger Fanie De Villiers.

From the first over we could see there was no pace. Alan Donald's body language was not good either, but once Shaun had fired through, Donald picked up his attitude and five wickets! Mahmood's daring and extremely chancy century proved the key in a total of 259, to which the Proteas disappointed with a 231 reply. Shaun claimed six in the second innings and a target of 255 didn't seem too much.

Leg-spinner Mushtaq Ahmed turned the match on its head, literally and figuratively. At 133/8, the home fans were bleating and the media were moaning about the non-selection of a spinner. But Boucher and De Villiers made the critics wait nearly a 100 runs before they could write their obituaries!

We desperately needed a win in the final game at Port Elizabeth. It was to be Fanie's swansong. He took six for 23 in the first innings and two for 25 in the second as Hansie and the boys stormed home by 259 runs. Phew! We were pleased to have sneaked home, satisfied that we had emerged 2-1 in the aggregate home and away series with Pakistan.

The selection panel had decided that Sri Lanka was going to be an experiment with Makhaya Ntini, the Dale College and Border fast bowler.

He had been to Australia and done well in a one-day outing against New Zealand at Perth. We felt he had definite potential but needed to be exposed at Test level. The Sri Lankans we felt, were just weak enough to allow us some latitude. We most certainly were not going to take victory for granted, but it was vital to expose both Ntini and Adams to front-line roles as bowlers.

It was not political, but Ali was very pleased with the news, so much so that he excitedly suggested that two non-whites would probably be included against Sri Lanka. Some members of the media and public wrongly interpreted this as political pressure and were a little antagonistic.

Both encounters were probably a little tighter than anticipated. Shaun, with 92 runs and six wickets was Man of the Match at Newlands in the 70 run victory, while Donald with eight wickets took the award at Centurion. The Pretoria Test was probably a lot closer than a six-wicket margin suggests. The visitors enjoyed a 103 run first innings lead, but were bundled out for 122 in the second.

Chasing 226, Hansie hit eight fours and six sixes in ensuring that Muralitharan didn't take advantage of a wearing pitch. I have always had a problem with his action. Irrespective of the wording of the law or the findings of toothless committees, I just think it's a pity that one day the leading wicket-taker in Test cricket is going to be someone with such a dubious action. Anyway it's not my problem. But that Centurion Park game could so easily have gone wrong.

A captain's innings it was in every essence of the literal and figurative meaning of the description. As for Ntini and Adams as front-line bowlers, many were still unconvinced. The jury was still out. Personally I was very pleased with the venture, but happy that we had won the series. I gestured as much to Ali in a crowded room at the aftermatch cocktails. There had been pressure! Winning sadly is the only answer in sport management.

The Standard Bank series saw Pakistan qualify for the final on a count-out with Sri Lanka. Both had four points from six games in the round robin preliminaries. South Africa headed the table with a massive ten points and confirmed their dominance by obliterating Pakistan in the final at Newlands. Bowled out for a meagre 114, Pakistan could not get off the field quickly enough as Kirsten and Kallis knocked off the runs with 23 overs to spare.

The display cabinet was filling fast. Adjectives like "dynamic" and "awesome" were starting to emerge amongst the opinion setters while Woolmer's coaching and tactical appreciation and Cronje's leadership were also starting to occupy column inches. Of this I was reliably being kept informed via photocopies from the UCB offices. Nobody could argue. We were now fully reinstated as a cricket power and a cricket voice.

13

FAREWELL

The decision

*T*he ten year itch was an interesting and challenging publication that I once read. It dealt with leadership and the problems of dictatorship. In the United States a president can serve a maximum of eight years. That's it! No more than two four-year terms. It's highly beneficial, as the author points out, because it prevents leaders from becoming tyrants, out-staying their welcome and finally doing a whole heap of damage. The illustrations were highly illuminating, featuring De Gaulle, Thatcher, Mitterand, Helmut Kohl, Konrad Adenauer, Stalin, Hitler, Saddam Hussein, Idi Amin and countless others. It emphasizes that leaders have to be restricted and held accountable otherwise they run amok – at all levels.

How do things go wrong? It starts with political palsy then moves to delusions of grandeur, followed by an aversion to criticism and opposition. Soon there is boredom with mundane politics and the normal channels, arguing that they slow the process down. Short cuts are taken, red tape is condemned, even side-stepped and that is when these leaders start placing themselves above accountability and politics. They even start playing God.

Obsessed by their own wisdom, they believe that only they have true vision and they become concerned about how their integrity is portrayed and how history will accord and acknowledge them. They are involved in media manipulation, always ensuring that their own perceptions and visions are regularly aired. They firmly believe that they are God's answer to everything.

The conclusion? Simply this – much anguish, bloodshed and heartache would have been avoided if their leadership life-spans had been restricted.

In my small way I was going to make sure that eight years was enough. Only seven of the years were as convenor of the national selectors, but to me seven was again highly biblical! I discussed this with friends, advisors and my family and they all agreed. Shaun too felt it was time for Dad to move on. He too needed some space of his own.

As chairman you hold a strong hand in terms of dictating policy and establishing long term strategies. It's also the chairman who constantly liaises with the captain and coach. Hansie had expressed thoughts about possible retirement in the not too distant future, while Bob Woolmer's contract had a year to run. I had enjoyed a wonderful relationship with these two as well as with the respective presidents Krish Mackerdhuj and Ray White.

The 1999 World Cup in England seemed the right and proper finishing point. I prayed about it as well and once I was absolutely sure of the wisdom and timing of it all, I conveyed my decision and the promise to abide by it to those closest to me. Winning or losing the World Cup, pressures or not, it was time to call it a day.

The Proteas were in England at the time when I officially moved into the final term of office and they were doing extremely well. I was in London preaching a mission in the Square Mile when they first arrived and I came back in June to watch them brilliantly thrash England in the second Test at Lord's. The weather had not been particularly kind, but Hansie and company became the first team in six series to win the Texaco Trophy.

Two tight matches were played at the Oval and Old Trafford had seen South Africa's all-round superiority clinch it, but they relaxed somewhat in the third outing at Headingly and were unmercifully thrashed. Though the series had been won, it was still hard for Hansie to accept the final beating, by seven wickets and with 15 overs to spare. Other international teams had maybe learnt to throw away the odd off day and defeat, but not the South Africans. Every game was a new challenge to Hansie.

This does tend to keep up the pressure. Naturally this can be both good and bad, especially if it's out of balance. The first Test at Edgbaston saw the captain win the toss and sent England in to bat. Donald, Shaun and the others, seamed and swung the ball all over the place to justify the captain's choice, but it never materialized into dismissals. I don't think I have ever seen the ball beat the bat so regularly with so little reward. England's first innings was a massive 462, headed by an Atherton century and contributions from just about everyone else. Jonty Rhodes led the reply, missing his century by five runs. Prior to the England tour a very interesting selection decision was taken when picking the original touring party.

It was simply decided that Rhodes would not only be an A-category player, but that he would bat at number six in all the Test matches and be told that in advance of the tour. We felt that he had been messed around too much. What a difference it made to him on that tour. The results speak for themselves.

Rhodes is a born again Christian and often testifies powerfully about his faith. He and Andrew Hudson, another player who speaks at breakfast meetings and schools, had been in and out of the South African teams over the years. Their detractors would often suggest that their selection had revolved around the fact that they shared the same Christian views as the convenor.

Jonty's answer will come quick as a flash, "Just look at the records. If anything, it would suggest the complete opposite! I think it was tougher for us because we are Christians!"

A drunkard one evening called me after one of our defeats and, slurring and slobbering, suggested that I should pick Ray McCauley, Archbishop Tutu, Reinhard Bonnke and a few others. I was quite impressed that he knew so many preachers. In England the tabloids were constantly on the lookout for any misdemeanours or verbal slip-ups. With bated breath they were waiting for one of the Proteas to suggest that we were doing well "because God is on our side." For starters, that wasn't my doctrine and though I was always very careful not to intrude, I often counselled those involved to be careful saying things that could be misconstrued and manipulated. The wolves were just waiting!

Anyway, back to Edgbaston, where Rhodes, ably supported by Kallis, Cullinan and Klusener, all with half centuries, totalled 343. England had 170/8 in the second innings and a great finish was in prospect. But rain, as it so often does in England, won hands down. The players didn't even get on the field on day five.

Alec Stewart returned the compliment by winning the toss at Lord's, inviting the visitors to bat. Initially he had better results. 46/4 was good work on the first morning. Jonty and Hansie changed it all around with the fifth wicket finally falling on 230. Cronje's 81 and a century from Rhodes, plus tail-end support saw 360 posted. Donald and Pollock blasted England out for a mere 110 in 46 overs and then invited them to try again.

Following on is a decision that any enforcing captain needs to consider carefully in Test cricket, especially if time isn't a factor. To expect fast bowlers to do it all over again is a tall order, one that many critics and commentators don't appreciate. Cronje must have had his doubts when in reply it was 222/3. In stepped Jacques Kallis with a spell of four wickets for four runs in eight overs, five of which were maidens. England lost six wickets for 11 runs. We were still having lunch in the MCC President's Box while this collapse was stunning the huge crowd to silence. It spoilt the lunch and even Colin Ingleby and McKenzie's humour couldn't restore the pre-lunch sparkle. It was Sunday and I had to travel quite a distance to preach that evening.

That meant I was not there to watch us knock off the 15 runs needed for the ten-wicket victory. The church I preached at had a South African pastor, and quite a few members of his congregation had emigrated from the Republic.

Needless to say, cricket did intrude on the gospel!

Inez had travelled with me for the Lord's Test and we flew home very happy with the way the tour was progressing. But I was to return a month later for the final two encounters at Trent Bridge and Leeds and there was a distinct change in the atmosphere. It had been a long tour, but there were some niggling gripes and groans.

Essentially it had little to do with the cricket, but rather with some of the hassles and inconveniences involving wives, girlfriends and kids. I understood the pressures of modern cricket and its affect on marriages and families, but I had seen far too much that was negative to be of any other opinion than that on tours this very sensitive issue needs to be strictly disciplined and controlled. It never is one big happy family. Wives and girlfriends have different agendas, motives and jealousies, and quite frankly nobody can speak honestly for fear of retribution. It is a problem. There are no quick solutions, but when, like me, your concern is team efficiency and performance, it's frustrating to say the least. It takes rules and regulations and strong management to keep the players and their families happy.

Matters had not been helped by the Old Trafford Test, the third of the series. It started so brilliantly. Shaun had strained a thigh – that was the bad news – but a double century from Gary Kirsten and a century from Kallis enabled 552/5 wickets to be posted. Then England was all out for 183 and victory seemed a mere formality.

It turned out to be a nightmare. First Lance was injured and went home. Then it was Alec Stewart and Mike Atherton. A third wicket partnership of 226 was the granite core of the huge stumbling block that England cast in the way of the rampant Proteas. Finally, it was just one wicket away for the South Africans. Robert Croft had seen out 125 balls for his undefeated 37, but Darren Gough at number ten stayed for 76 balls and last man Angus Fraser stood firmly for just over two whole overs!

We had had our chances but couldn't clinch it. The draw was as good as a victory for England and by looking at the way they celebrated, you would have thought they had won the World Cup.

As the Proteas trooped off the field, I was left with that raw feeling in my stomach. We had only ourselves to blame. But worse, I just had this funny feeling that it was going to represent a very significant change of fortunes. I said as much to Inez. "This is going to cost us big," I grumbled, little knowing the prophetic truth of my utterance of discontent. All the excuses in the world wouldn't suffice. We had let it slip, thrown away a 2-0 lead in the series. Just one ball would have sealed the series. That sometimes is the ridiculously small margin between success and failure.

England were rejuvenated, the South Africans were frustrated and bothered.

Adam Bacher had now joined the long injury list which had also claimed Ntini and Steve Elworthy, who won his first Test cap. South Africa did reasonably well at 374. Cronje had gone to three figures and it seemed a pretty safe tally when England replied 38 short.

But then came that vital third innings, that time of the match that is so dangerous. I actually reminded the skipper of it, but it didn't help. Helped by two shocking decisions from umpire Mervyn Kitchen, we were suddenly 21 for three and had our backs firmly to the wall. Despite another bold bid from Cronje, a total of 208 was just not enough!

Victory by eight wickets and the series square was the bad news as we stared out at the huge crowd that had gathered to salute the English players. It's at times like this that packing a bag, throwing it over your shoulder and walking through the crowded throng to your tour bus outside the main gate, is an experience akin to hell.

Trent Bridge, a ground that so often smiled generously on South African cricket teams, had not granted any favours this time. Umpire Mervyn Kitchen, by his own admission, had a shocker. He was going to retire. "Pity he didn't do that before the match," grumbled someone on the bus!

But if we thought Kitchen was bad, there was a bigger shock for us. At Leeds, Javed Akhtar of Pakistan was the neutral official. Alan Donald had been fined after the Trent Bridge match because he wrote in his column, "I think that Merv Kitchen realises he made a few shockers which swung the result. If you lose concentration out there you are playing with players' careers. One decision can swing a game – and if you are not up to it, then get out of the game rather than cause yourself more damage."

Tough words, obviously ghost-written for Donald, but it earned him a hefty fine. Players, captains and managers are dealt with pretty quickly and often officiously by some of the match referees. Pity they are not so diligent when it comes to marking down poor decisions.

Aktar's umpiring was downright atrocious by comparison. Subsequently Ali Bacher landed in hot water for his accusations and allegations about Pakistan's performance.

Ali also acted rather impetuously and rashly in deciding in the heat of the after-match emotions, that the Proteas "had been robbed!" The UCB, he announced, would consequently pay the players the R500 000 that they had offered them for winning the series, even though they lost! Ali was fuming. He was absolutely livid and with every justification. Even the English critics admitted that the match had been tarnished severely by the umpiring blunders and that these had weighed heavily against the South Africans.

But finally history recorded a 23 run victory for England. It had been a fast bowler's pitch. Darren Gough got nine in the match while Fraser, Donald and

Shaun all got eight. Mark Butcher was Man of the Match for his century. Ironically the TV cameras showed him to benefit from a shocking decision early on. Symbolically, it probably reflected the tide of the match. It was the innings that swung the game and it was conceived out of an umpiring error!

And what could we, as officials, do about the debacle? Absolutely nothing. The losers' complaints are seen as sour grapes, the winners say it's tough, but all part of the game and the umpires plead that they are, after all, only human. Finally the administrators leave well enough alone, lest anyone takes too much offence.

That's why nothing can be achieved with such major problems as "chucking." There is simply too much at stake and it causes too much political intrigue and expediency. Ruffling feathers for the truth and gaining unpopularity is avoided like the plague. It's a lot easier just to smile, turn a blind eye and continue travelling around the world.

Ali Bacher had made a special effort to attend the Leeds match. One of my contacts in the UCB office told me he was coming, but I did not tell the team. They really appreciated his gesture. The one afternoon we gave the brass a miss and even sat amongst the plebs on the popular stand just to soak in the atmosphere and enjoy Ntini taking four quick wickets, his best Test performance at that stage. As we shared a taxi back to the hotel after play the one evening, we were agreed about the general laxity and passivity in cricket administration. But hands were tied.

That's the way it is in international matters, a sort of synthetic unity at all costs. It's best to leave problems on the back burner!

After the Leeds Test, with all its controversy and disappointments, at least Ali and I could go home. For the players another ten days had to be negotiated, including a couple of one-days.

At Trent Bridge the Sri Lankans beat us comfortably by 57 runs. This margin was big enough to ensure that even if we then beat England, but not by too much, we could avoid the final at Lord's and get home. Beating England though was essential, especially after the Leeds fiasco. The guys were fired up for that. It would at least be some small consolation!

A half-century, then two for 36 earned Pat Symcox Man of the Match as England went down by a mere 14 runs, a result that ensured a Sri Lankan-England finale. Fortunately the Proteas caught the first available flight home!

Some administrators don't seem to get the message about the preponderance of limited overs cricket. It's not possible to stay motivated when you are playing so many games against the same people day in and day out. Maybe the heavy one-day scheduling is even asking for trouble, dare I suggest! The South Africans didn't throw any match, but by the same token it was hard to get motivated.

One of the most memorable incidents of the whole tour involved Mark

Boucher. From the moment I first saw him in an A-side match against Sri Lanka at Pietermaritzburg, I knew he was going to be Dave Richardson's replacement. I also did some homework on his background and was even more convinced that greatness was his destiny as a wicket-keeper. But if I ever needed to be convinced, Trent Bridge provided it in an embarrassing moment for him.

Alan Donald had fired in a short-pitched delivery that Mike Atherton so very obviously gloved, but Kiwi umpire Steve Dunne would not stick up his finger. Tempers flared, bouncers flew and then Nasser Hussein got to the striker's end and edged another fiery Donald delivery into Mark's gloves. The young South African unbelievably grassed the opportunity. At that stage it could have made all the difference and fired up the Proteas. The dropped chance had the opposite demotivating affect.

About half an hour after close I went into the shower area to get myself a cold drink. Lying in a full bath was Mark. He was sobbing. It embarrassed him that I had caught him in this weak moment, but it touched me deeply. No excuses. No frivolous bravado. That catch was his job. He had fluffed it and owned his mistake. I just thought to myself, "With a youngster like that, and an attitude like that, we can take on the world."

The self-motivators like Boucher are priceless commodities! You can't drag or push people to the highest levels of sport. Self-starting comes from within. It can be fired up and ignited by careful management, but it can't be manufactured if it's not inherently there. Surely any programme can be designed or implemented to make people better than they are, but a silk purse doesn't come from sow's ears.

Those who want to make big money out of conning the ignorant and naive into false promises of success will obviously disagree, but it's the Boucher type that makes top-class sportsmen and top-class teams.

Gold at the Commonwealth Games

The Commonwealth Games at Kuala Lumpur was the next commitment, but the senior players had managed to get released, so a largely young and inexperienced side, led by Shaun made the trip. Australia, New Zealand and Zimbabwe sent their best available combinations and Steve Waugh's squad made no bones about the desire to win the gold medal. "That's what we are here for," declared the confident captain. For Shaun, official understudy to Hansie, it was a wonderful leadership opportunity.

Lance Klusener and Adam Bacher had to withdraw from the original squad, but they basically had nothing to lose and a lot to gain. Shaun declared that they were going to get a medal, "the colour of my hair." Was that bronze or gold? He didn't define, but either way a medal was the first goal. In the preliminary games Northern Ireland, Bangladesh and Barbados succumbed to the South Africans.

The nail-biting semi-final against Sri Lanka was enacted on a rather awkward pitch. The Sri Lankans scratched together 130, but at 96/9, it looked a winning score. Nicky Boje and Alan Dawson batted for an excruciating 55 minutes against spinners of the class of Chandana and Arnold. Snicks, byes and leg-byes all counted in one of the most exciting finishes I have *not* watched! The tension was so unbearable, that I left home and went for a long walk.

"We've won!" was the shout that welcomed me home. "We are destined to win the final as well," was my comment. And sure enough it happened that way.

Shaun shook the critics by sending in Steve Waugh's side. It worked. They were all out for 183. Openers Rindel (67) and Hudson (36) then put on 73 for the first wicket. Kallis (44) joined the party and at 172/3 – eleven runs short – I decided to come out of hiding. I was ministering in Johannesburg and I had decided I was not going to watch at all. At 172/3 Inez said "Come watch your boys win the gold medal." I promptly watched three wickets fall, including Shaun's as he went for glory with a big hit. But I stayed to see the finish. One of the first callers was Ali to say it was well done. But I was too emotional to speak. He understood.

A gold medal, five wins in five matches, and Shaun had made his mark as a captain. There will always be those traditionalists who argue that mainline bowlers shouldn't be captains – like that schoolmaster who had ruined it for me – but I knew that Shaun could do it. I had not doubted the wisdom of Shaun's appointment as Hansie's understudy. In fact, when Shaun was chosen to take the side to the Games, Hansie was convinced that he would do well. The captain would often say to me, "Shaun has come a long way. Believe me."

Even as he talked about retiring, he was confident that he was not going to leave the country in the lurch from a leadership point of view. "Shaun's ready. Believe me," emphasized Hansie. "It's always tough at the start as the players and media get used to a new style," he added.

There will always be one or two knockers who will just never stop – the way Kepler Wessels did with Cronje. Anyway, Shaun had survived his first major Test. "It was tough," he admitted. "I am happy to give the job back to Hansie," he joked.

Some suggested he was a reluctant skipper. What else could Shaun have said? That he wanted to retain the captaincy! It's often horrendous what ignorant media men and women read into situations or chance remarks. They then write about their misguided perception and then the moment it is in print, they believe that it automatically becomes the truth.

Aiming for the World Cup

Early in October 1998, Bob Woolmer, Hansie, Ali and I met in Johannesburg to focus on the West Indian visit and the World Cup. It was agreed that we should have a meeting with all the contracted players and management and that Ray White, Ali and I should speak straight and firm in terms of our expectations for the next nine months. No punches were pulled. The talk was straight and challenging and the goal was simple. We needed to turn our skill into impressive and even ruthless results.

There was a stunned silence. Management had never laid it down so clearly and firmly. These were the expectations. We didn't need to hear talk about heavy programmes or any other negative suggestions. Hansie and the boys needed to go out there and stamp their authority. They needed to believe in themselves and produce the results.

Off they went to the ICC tournament at Dhaka in Bangladesh. In the first outing against England a formidable total of 281 looked imposing enough. But with 20 balls left and six wickets in hand, South Africa firmly declared their intentions. The semi-final was against Sri Lanka. Kallis posted a century as we managed 240 and then in a mere 24 overs, Sri Lanka were knocked over for a mere 132 runs. It was very impressive indeed. It was the ruthless stuff we had talked about at that goal-defining meeting and the captain was smiling.

The final was against the West Indies. This time we triumphed by four wickets and three overs to spare. The mini World Cup was ours and Jacques Kallis stood head and shoulders above everyone else as the Man of the Series. The blond all-rounder took five wickets for 30 and made 37 in the final against Brian Lara's men, after 113 not out in the semi-final against the men from Colombo.

But the great win had its undercurrent back home. In all three matches they were all-white sides. Makhaya Ntini was there, but as his form was highly problematic, the selectors could not chance him. Apparently Ntini wasn't happy and told Dr Bacher so on the team's return. The Doc suggested he should take a rest, even from Border. He simply wasn't bowling well. Furthermore, mentally and psychologically he was in bad shape. A rest was probably the best advice.

The West Indies tour got off to a highly controversial start. Problems obviously ran deep in West Indies cricket. There was a farcical situation with some players having already arrived in South Africa and others were stuck at a hotel in London, refusing to budge until their Board of Control met certain demands.

Dr Bacher entered the fray waving a letter from Nelson Mandela. Brian Lara and Carl Hooper had been sacked, but were reinstated and then finally Jimmy Adams reportedly sliced through a finger tendon while cutting a bread-roll on the flight to Johannesburg. It was quite bizarre. But the tour got under way.

With the first Test looming, the biggest problem facing the national selectors was the form, or lack of it, of Makhaya Ntini and Paul Adams. There was no way that they could be included in the vital first encounter at the Wanderers. I passed this on to Ali so that he could prepare himself for any possible political reaction. Forewarned is forearmed, they say.

The following week I received a disturbing phone call from Ali. He bluntly told me that if Ntini wasn't picked "you will put South African cricket back five years." I asked if this was an instruction from the UCB! It wasn't, but though appreciating his bad form, Ali was concerned about the politicians and their reactions. Shortly after that, I got a call from the late Khaya Majola who told me that he had just spoken to Ntini and given him a motivational talk. He assured me that the young fast bowler would rise to the occasion and would be a credit to his country.

I had to pinch myself. As selectors we represented the judicial system in respect of the ambitions and aspirations of our young cricketers. It was our task to pick the best team for South Africa. We were much aware of the political pressures and keen to acknowledge talent from the previously disadvantaged groups. But the candidates had to be good enough.

We could not risk Ntini. Worse, we would not be able to justify his inclusion. Adams too was really struggling and desperately needed help. Our predicament had been conveyed to the hierarchy.

We met on the Sunday morning of November 22 at Kingsmead and we considered all the options and all the pressures that had been applied. The six selectors, plus Hansie and Bob had given their input and Ntini didn't make it. All except one out of eight dissented on the decision and David Terbrugge replaced Ntini. We decided to include Adams as stand-by, so that coach Bob could work on him during the first couple of Tests. We actually indicated this when Ray White first announced the line-up.

Well, it certainly got the media and politicians going. This was run-in time for an upcoming election and time to make statements and score points. To increase the tension, the West Indian board president Pat Rousseau was held up and robbed while visiting the Soweto cricket oval.

Ali Bacher had apparently made a statement that there would be no more all-white cricket teams. A general, blanket statement like that was bound to rebound and it did.

The focus moved away from the cricket and our great victory seemed of little importance as the political drums drowned out Hansie and the boys.

Shaun was Man of the Match in an enthralling encounter. His nine wickets in the match just shaded Jacques Kallis' two valuable half-centuries as South Africa successfully chased 164 to win. Though the final margin was four wickets, it was more comfortable than that, because two wickets fell right at the death as first Rhodes, then Shaun went for the glory hit.

There was much celebration for selectors, players and fans, but the UCB boardroom seemed otherwise engaged. David Terbrugge had done an excellent job as third seamer and more than justified his selection, but some response from the UCB was obviously necessary for the politicians and media. A selection policy document was formulated that decreed that all national teams "should" include a player or players of colour. A get-out clause gave the selectors the right, for reasons of form or injury, to pick an all-white side only if approved by a four-man monitoring committee.

For the second Test at Port Elizabeth I had reason to test the waters with this monitoring quartet. Herschelle Gibbs was the instant answer to our problems, but there was a little doubt about Terbrugge's fitness. I phoned Dr Bacher who, after calling his panel, responded that Ntini would have to be the replacement despite his form. Theoretically we already had one non-white so I didn't have to consult them! But I was interested in testing the waters.

St George's Park turned out to be a massive triumph for the home side, by a huge 178 runs. Innings totals of 121 and 141 by the West Indians showed that they could not handle Donald, Pollock and Terbrugge.

The dose was repeated at Kingsmead, this time the wining margin being nine wickets. Two half centuries by Brian Lara ensured a little more resistance to the South African fast bowlers, but it was all over in four days.

The Newlands Test went into the fifth day – only just – but again the winning margin was a pretty conclusive 149 runs. Darryl Cullinan made a magnificent 168, but Kallis with a century in the first innings and an undefeated 88 in the second, was the star of the Proteas' performance. He also took seven wickets to confirm his status as one of the best all-rounders in the world.

Hansie was now looking for a 5 – 0 whitewash.

If anyone thought there would be strong West Indian resistance, they were wrong. Victory was by 351 runs. Three South Africans notched centuries; Kirsten, Boucher and Rhodes, with the jaunty Natalian setting a new South African record for the fastest century – a mere 95 balls.

South Africa's cricket was awesome, ruthless and ominous. But it all managed to get hidden behind political rhetoric and the critics slamming West Indian incompetence. It was a historic feat that was seemingly sidelined even by our own administrators. This fuelled some discontent with Hansie and the players. Cricketing priorities and that confrontational October meeting appeared to have been replaced by political expedience.

It had not been easy for the selectors, though the action was mainly media based. I didn't have to attend any meetings, listen to any lectures or face the Board. Sir Clyde Walcott was very supportive of "picking the best team" as was West Indian fast bowler Wesley Hall. The support base encouraging the selectors was massive and totally transcended political or racial lines.

203

I had strongly opposed politicians interfering with cricket way back in the 70s and there was no need to change that philosophy. Whether their faces are white or black, motives and agendas tend to stay pretty much the same.

Hansie had been a bit difficult with me in Durban when we decided to bring Paul Adams in at the expense of Pat Symcox. I recall Bob Woolmer rushing up to me to tell me that the captain was furious and didn't want to accept it.

I had to deal with that tantrum. But clearly Hansie was on the warpath. The UCB had erred in their rather disinterested and somewhat passive response to the brilliant whitewash. Certainly Hansie saw it that way.

Then came the one-days. Ali had consulted with me and asked that we should enlarge the squad to accommodate a sort of disguised affirmative action. He was sure we could fit the players in with a game or two once the series was decided. I didn't have too much of a problem, nor did the selectors. We would always try to accommodate as long as selections were not dictated by the UCB.

Hansie hit the roof. I sat with him and Bob in the dressing room at Centurion Park and talked it through. He thought 17 players unwieldy, too many for a changing room. He mentioned all sorts of snags, but I asked him just to cool it. We would negotiate it all with minimum fuss and try not to overly affect performance.

That's when he said, "You expect me to win everything, but shoot me in the foot by not giving me the best players." Top cricket was about runs and wickets and winning, not playing politics. He reminded me of how it had been his decision, and his alone, to include Ntini in a one-day Test against New Zealand at Perth, but how he was hounded and slandered when he left him out.

Politics, and politicians, care little for those they use or hurt. Anyway, the following morning Ali had a meeting with the side and without my knowledge he was going to deal with selections and the need to accommodate affirmatively!

Ali was heading into the lion's den. Hansie walked out on him, vowing not to return to the team. Some of the senior players also had their say. Then I got a phone-call from a distraught Ali. Hansie has walked out on the team and publically snubbed the CEO.

I could not believe that Bacher had chosen to tread such sensitive ground. He had not even consulted us. My suggestion was that he should just stay away.

I immediately phoned Ray McCauley, of the Rhema church in Randburg. Hansie respected and often consulted Ray and I was sure he would help rectify matters. He did, phoning me back to confirm that the captain would be returning to the team and to the one-day action. He added though that there needed to be a meeting with Ali to sort out some of their differences. There was much relief all round and the series started at the Wanderers. Ray McCauley had been invited as a special guest, obviously to acknowledge his efforts at reconciliation.

Lance Klusener starred in a thriller with South Africa winning in the last over, but the biggest surprise for me was to learn from president Ray White that he knew nothing about what had happened during the week. All the drama had escaped his ears. "The South African captain goes walk-about and I as president am not even informed," was his startled response. Even more amazing for me was that the press never knew about this.

While understanding the background and extenuating circumstances, Cronje's outburst and walkout was ill-chosen and ill-timed. But clearly there were wounds that needed healing especially between him and Ali. Ray offered to help.

The series was as one-sided as the Test rubber, finishing 6 – 1 in South Africa's favour. Most of the wins were by big margins as the Proteas ruthlessly exposed their dominance. Sadly too, the thrashing had not helped to inspire black interest for there were certainly no black heroes!

The Proteas in New Zealand before the World Cup

New Zealand was a rush job. Even the players didn't know what had hit them. Jet lag and acclimatisation were obviously not even taken into account as the weary, bleary-eyed Proteas found themselves way down south at Dunedin for the first one-day international. A Kallis century was the only redeeming feature of a three-wicket defeat, but in the second match at Christchurch the tables were turned rather conclusively thanks to Kirsten (81 not out) and Cronje (74 not out). Celebrations however were muffled because the tour management had erred. Another all-white team had participated in the victory.

I assumed that there had been injury problems and didn't bother to follow up. I hated interfering from 8 000 miles away. I was going to join the team shortly, but reckoned that there would be a valid explanation.

Three days later I was due to speak at a breakfast in Dalton, up the Natal north Coast. I had not bothered to switch on the TV. I had woken up late and had to rush to my speaking engagement an hour or so away. On arrival I asked the score and established which South African batsmen were out.

When the name Gibbs was mentioned I rested easily. Forget the score as long as it's not all white! It was becoming like tinnitus, ringing in the ears! They say ignorance is bliss. Well it was, until after the breakfast when I found out that my earlier informant had erred. Gibbs was not playing. It was another all-white team! Heaven forbid. What's more, we lost and were now 2-1 down in the series.

That day there was a UCB meeting. I got a phone call from Ray White in the evening. All hell had broken loose. They wanted Hansie flown home to explain why. That was after they had found out that I was preaching at Stanger, was still in South Africa, and couldn't be directly blamed. Dr Bacher, I am told, managed to restore some sanity to the proceedings. I told Ray White I would be happy to meet with the Board, but that I would not pull any punches. I was not called in, but Ray McCauley had to come to the rescue again to calm down the skipper. This was really becoming a bit of a circus and again the media just guessed and surmised mostly inaccurately!

The first Test was played on a glued pitch. There had been some problems and the curator opted to apply wood glue to the surface. It stuck and the pitch was a bowler's nightmare. South Africa lost only five wickets in amassing 621 with Darryl Cullinan breaking brother Graeme's all-time Test record of 274. The South Africans did well to get New Zealand out for 352 without conceding any centuries, but bowling them out twice was just not a possibility. It was the first time I had heard about glue.

I flew into Christchurch for the second Test and I arrived in rain. For five days it was cold, wet and uncharitable. We started magnificently thanks to the great Donald-Pollock duet.

Gibbs then cracked a double century and Kallis, an undefeated 148 in an unbroken second wicket partnership that started at 127 and was still going at 442 when Hansie declared. But the match wasn't going anywhere as the Jade Stadium produced weather that was more appropriate for the Canterbury Crusaders rugby side.

My final Test as convenor was played at the Basin Reserve, scene of my 50th Test wicket way back in 1964. Much had changed, but not the wind! I dearly wanted to go out with a victory. In 1964 I had captured six wickets in the home side's first innings. Shaun produced five for 33 to gladden his dad's heart. Gibbs and Cullinan were the century makers as the Proteas made 498/8. The Black Caps improved slightly on their first innings 222 with 291, but with only 16 to win, the series was ours.

Hansie said some kind things as he bid me an official Test farewell.

But there was still the small matter of the one-day series. Napier saw a thriller. The first attempt had been washed out with no result. There seemed little chance of a restart the next day, but incredibly the sky opened up, the sun came through and a 40-over match took place. Shaun reached the milestone of 100 wickets and 1 000 runs – in the fastest time ever – but this went by unnoticed in all the excitement and drama. A six from the very last ball of the game from Lance Klusener clinched it. Even I ended up running onto the field at the end to acclaim Lance!

Enough said. Auckland was murder. Kallis and Cullinan were the executioners in 290/5 from 50 overs and the Kiwis just crumbled, losing by 143 runs.

We were ahead in the series, there was no tension as rain frustrated efforts to play at Wellington and when the game was finally abandoned, we literally dashed away to catch an earlier flight back home.

I held a very important meeting with Ray White, Hansie and Bob at which I told them that Ali had approached me to specifically include Ntini in the side for the World Cup. He was up on a rape charge, but Doc was sure he would get off.

I had often said at selection meetings that we had to treat the discussions as if we were live on TV. In other words; no secrets, no deals and the understanding that whatever is said will get out anyway! We always needed to operate transparently and the Ntini request was to be treated the same way. There were problems, there was no form, but we had been asked to consider the wider implications.

At Wellington and later back in South Africa for the final meeting to select the World Cup squad, the issue was clear-cut. It was a political request. We acceded. Interestingly enough we also picked Dawson as a stand-by just in case the Ntini verdict went awry. Ali got the case moved forward because he didn't want the youngster to still have this rape accusation hanging over him at the World Cup. He reckoned there would be undue interest from the media. The initial verdict was guilty. Ntini had to withdraw and in came Dawson.

What annoyed me most about it all, was the way he had been kicked around like a football. At that time he was one of a kind, politically speaking. He was black, not coloured, and little thought was given to his plight. Political expedience was the operative word. For him personally and for other black cricketers, it was essential that recognition was earned, not handed out. The Tests he had played and no doubt will play in the future, were because he was good enough. That was the least we could do for him – treat him as an equal!

Cricket is a tough taskmaster. It's about hard work and discipline. Success and reputations are earned and history records the deeds and accomplishments of those who have made the grade. Cricket is not about handouts. It's about earning your laurels. It's a game that will outlive those who attempt to manipulate it for their own causes. It's a game worth defending, if only for its high ideals. Ntini, I hope and believe, will rise far above those who had used him so blatantly and prove that he is worth his own salt. It's a vision far bigger than any political expedience and it's my earnest prayer for him.

World Cup 1999

So the stage was set for the World Cup 1999 and my farewell. During the New Zealand tour a small problem arose between Daryll Cullinan and Shaun. With all the rain and its consequent frustrations at Christchurch, Shaun misbehaved with a temper tantrum. He vented his anger on Darryl who was quite affronted and justifiably took the matter to the tour committee. They had invited me to attend the disciplinary hearing before I even knew the circumstances and was involved. Imagine my surprise to learn that Shaun was in the dock!

I listened to the evidence, with Shaun clearly out of order. You just don't vent your frustration or anger on any team-mate. I said as much before excusing myself on the grounds that I really wasn't part of the tour committee and leaving them to come to a verdict and a penalty.

But as I walked out of the room it was confirmation to me that it was time to get out, time to call it quits. Shaun, as vice-captain, sat in on some of the selection discussions and again I felt that Dad now needed to move out to give him his space. I had become increasingly aware of my presence being just a little unwieldy and much as Shaun would not have confronted it head-on, I knew that he was looking forward to my retirement. Indeed the timing was perfect.

It had always been my ambition as convenor to take South Africa back to the top of the world rankings. Way back in 1970 our claim as the best in the world was unchallenged but mythical. By 1999 there was a far more acceptable basis of ranking. In the May edition of the much respected *Cricketer Magazine*, South Africa was number one in the world, both in Tests and one-days. In Tests we had 69 points, with Australia second at 63 and Pakistan third at 51. The lead in the one-days was more substantial with 78 points against Australia's 68 and Pakistan's 59. The April edition also reflected the same dominance as did July and even October, despite our defeat in the World Cup semi-final.

Simply, rankings need to express and acknowledge consistency rather than just a one-off triumph and as prestigious as the World Cup is, the *Cricketer's* ratings were reflecting a more accurate and acceptable basis of comparison. The cricket world acknowledged South Africa as number one in Tests and one-days as Hansie and his boys gathered in London for the World Cup. There is no question or argument about that, and even the bookmakers would have confirmed this.

The dream had been achieved by a healthy margin. Now we just needed the cherry on the top! The South African contingent had worked hard and planned wisely. Psychologically and physically we had done our homework and we believed that we were going to win the Cup.

The warm-up match at Hove was washed out, but Mark Boucher made merry with the bat against Kent and Middlesex, confirming himself as a form batsmen for any upfront pinch-hitting. I joined the team the day before the opening match against India at Hove. It was a comfortable though controversial start because Bob Woolmer got himself into hot water for using an earpiece to communicate with his captain.

The ICC obviously had its nose put out of joint because it had not been informed. They immediately banned the earpiece and put out a statement, "The World Cup is not the time to experiment with new ideas without first seeking permission." Interesting! Did that mean that if you had decided to reverse-sweep for the first time in one-day cricket, you could not do it at the World Cup unless you had first asked permission! Ridiculous. But the real problem was that Woolmer and Cronje were ahead of the field. Innovators and pioneers tend to spark reaction from those lagging behind.

The golden rule is: don't ever embarrass the powers that be! Some 14 balls were left when South Africa struck the winning run, but the next game at Northampton produced a lot of anxious moments. Sent in by the Sri Lankans, we were 69/5 at one stage and later 122/8. The pitch was lively and would suit our attack, but we needed more than 150 to defend.

The World Cup was to be Lance Klusener's event. Single-handedly he strode supreme, winning the Man of the Series award by miles. The 122 became 199 /9, after Klusener's demolition in the final overs. His undefeated 52 with two sixes and five fours had us all very relieved, but he wasn't finished. Three wickets for 21 runs with the ball helped blast out the timid Sri Lankans for a mere 110.

In the next match, England was dispatched with almost indecent haste. Sent in again, the Proteas had the Nelson 111 before the openers Kirsten and Gibbs were separated. Then despite a small middle-order collapse, the target was 225. Donald and company blasted them out for 103 and the despondent home supporters trudged home from the Oval, not very buoyant in spirit.

Amsterdam was the venue for another comfortable win over Kenya and a spot in the next stage – the Super Six – was assured. A hiccough was to follow. The arrival of the wives and girlfriends coincided with our return from Amsterdam, resulting in delays and inconveniences that severely hampered preparations for the final preliminary game against Zimbabwe at Chelmsford.

I had been assured that the break between the preliminary round and the second stage – just under a week – would be the period allotted to the wives. But somehow this period got extended to include the last game of the first section and the first game of the second. But it was too late to say anything. I would not dare to suggest that their arrival was the major cause of below standard performance against Zimbabwe – a loss by 48 runs. But it certainly contributed to a loss of focus. My plea to the UCB and the players for the World Cup was simply, "Give us six weeks of your lives to focus on winning the World Cup."

Anyway the loss is history, our first against lowly Zimbabwe and who knows what a difference it might have made to the whole campaign. I had a deep feeling that it might have cost us more than we imagined. You get that feeling sometimes, a sense of destiny!

The Super Six started brilliantly with another triumph over Pakistan. With 220 on the board and South Africa at 58/5 and then 135/6, Pakistan skipper Wasim Akram must have believed that the hoodoo was finally over. Klusener with three sixes and three fours did the impossible, with a whole over to spare and three wickets in hand!

New Zealand was next to feel the brunt of the South African machine, mangled by a massive 74 runs at Edgbaston. A semi-final spot was now secure and all that remained was to establish our opponents. The Proteas were marching triumphantly. Already some South Africans were talking about arrangements for the final!

So near and yet so far

Australia was our last Super Six opponent but the game's only significance revolved around whether Australia would make it to the semi-finals. As the coin was spun, Australia had to beat us otherwise they would be catching the next plane home. Naturally we wanted them out the way and hoped to oblige at Leeds. When we had made 271 from our 50 overs, thanks to a fine century from Gibbs we felt more than halfway there.

When the Aussies were 48/3 in reply, a couple of the spectators carried an ominous banner saying goodbye to the Aussies and wishing them a safe trip home! "I don't like that," I said to Bob Woolmer. It was tempting fate or God's law!

Steve Waugh turned it around. Good fortune sailed with him and Ricky Ponting to the extent that Gibbs, a brilliant fielder, dropped the simplest of catches. In fact, he looked as if he had pocketed the catch, but in his keenness to throw it over his shoulder in triumph, he lost control.

"You have just dropped the World Cup," the Aussie skipper must have uttered. If so, it was prophetic, for indeed that catch cost us that match, thrillingly won with two balls to spare.

This loss for us meant a rematch in the semi-finals against Australia, this time at Edgbaston. New Zealand were meeting Pakistan in the other. To all intents and purposes the World Cup was to be decided in Birmingham on June 17, 1999.

It was one of the greatest games you could ever hope to see. You could not have written a better script. It competes with the famous match at Brisbane in the early sixties between Australia and the West Indies as the most famous tie of all time. It was a game that had millions all over the world glued to their TV sets. It was a privilege just to be there to witness it live. And tragically, almost ironically it was a game that was never won or lost. But it was the game that decided the World Cup 1999!

Sent in to bat, the Aussies made 213 – not a great total but competitive, considering the nature and tension of the contest. At 48/0 the game was South Africa's. Three wickets in rapid succession, including a run-out and a bad decision involving Hansie and the tables had turned. The afternoon progressed intriguingly as Kallis, Rhodes and Shaun kept up the South African challenge. Thirty nine were needed from 31 balls as Lance Klusener joined Shaun. The tension was unbearable. Then it was 16 runs off eight balls, with the last man Donald at the crease. It needed a miracle. I was sitting alongside Hansie. Intensely we peered through the dressing room window.

A six and two fours and the miracle was happening. Finally the scores were level, Klusener on strike and three balls to go. Klusener drove Fleming to mid-off and set off for the winning run. Donald failed to respond and chaos ensued. Alan, who had dropped his bat, was run out even though the ball was first thrown to Fleming the bowler who had the presence of mind to lob it to Gilchrist.

As Klusener completed his run, Hansie and I hugged each other because we thought we had won. Lance had safely negotiated the danger end and we were ecstatic. But Donald was stranded. We had not been watching him. Suddenly the Aussies were jumping around and hugging each other.

We just couldn't believe our eyes. I will never ever forget the scenes in the changing room that hour after the match. Silence, tears, sobs! It wasn't a time to speak. It was just too emotional, too disappointing. How near can you get and be so far? One of the most incredible moments of my life was to be so totally part of this devastating disappointment. It defies words and descriptions.

It was the cruellest disappointment ever. Yes, you could not have written a crueller script. For me it was the culmination of eight years of hard work. We were the favourites. We were the best in the world. We had tied – but it was a loss. Surely at the semi-final level of the World Cup, a tie should ensure a replay not a count-out!

There was a spare day, after all. But the Super Six loss to the Aussies at Leeds was to come back and haunt the South Africans. I just sat there and watched. In my heart I even asked God why it had happened this way. It was in that changing room, as I sought answers, that one of the great truths hit me: The greatest challenge in life is not how you win, but how you handle losing!

"God is Australian," was one of the headlines that greeted our exit. Indeed it was cruel and heart-rending, but why blame God?

It is often the case when it involves Christian combatants, that attempts are made to draw conclusions regarding God's favours. There are those who believe that fame and success are somehow linked to some sort of Christian invincibility and that it is a reward for one's merit as a righteous believer.

Biblical principles do work and you do tend to reap as you sow. Gifts and talents are from God to be used to best advantage. But it's the attitude that counts. How you handle fame, success and failure and your perspective is what glorifies God, not the trophies, prizes and acclaim.

True glory

The success of the SA team in my book went far beyond just reaching the last four. Statistically it was all down in the book, and in the *Cricketer's International Ratings*. But coping with this disappointment was going to be the major challenge.

In a world of obsession it's hard to understand that the final victory, even for a cricketer, is not the World Cup! Easy to say it, but not so easy to live it!

As we were clearing up and the time had arrived for someone to say something, I made two points, "Bad luck fellows, but nobody can argue. We gave it our very best shot. I am proud of you. We lost this game together. It was nobody's fault. It's over and finished and please, I don't want to hear anybody ever blame anyone else. We gave it our best. We lost. And we must move on."

My eight years were over. And that was my parting speech. What a privilege and honour to have been involved. We were the best in the world, but without the Cup. I couldn't help but think back to Sydney and our exit from the semi-finals at the first World Cup – 22 runs in one ball! Now a tie and out!

As I had suggested to the players, I too refused to get involved with any witch-hunts. How wonderful it would have been to bring the Cup home, a sort of reward for all our endeavours. We probably felt we deserved it. But that's the way it goes, the way the cookie crumbles as they say. Cowboys don't cry – they also say – but they cried in the changing room at Edgbaston because there it was: life in all its reality, not a fairy-tale romance!

Afterwards I heard one of our leading administrators suggest that he was pleased we didn't win because "it would have set the transformation process back five years."

I had heard that phrase before. Any set of circumstances, however traumatic or tragic, always pleases someone! I remembered how once at Newlands, before a capacity crowd, the UCB had shown a video on its unity only to be meeting within hours in an attempt to either remove or censure its president, Ray White, because he had the audacity to tell the politicians to get out of cricket. Great isn't it, that cricket eventually rises above unwanted bedfellows, sooner or later!

The Australians thrashed Pakistan in the final at Lord's in a match that was a huge anti-climax. I was already home, exhausted and disappointed, but knowing that my time was over and that my job was done. I was tired but relieved and thankful to have been given the opportunity to serve. I could never give back to cricket what it has given me, but it was a small attempt, as I said to the UCB executive when they presented me with an expensive pen and pencil set as a token of their appreciation.

I had travelled the world, I had met many interesting people, lived through many incredible experiences and cricket had been a wonderful vehicle and platform to share the gospel. That had always been my number one priority.

The truth of cricket being my transporter and the many other revelations that were opened up to me during the eight years that I served cricket, only helped to convince me that God isn't just for church meetings, prayer meeting and cell groups. He is God of everything and needs to be represented all around. It also made it easy to hear "Over up" for God's fast bowler!

The match fixing

You can't just switch off. I watched with interest as Hansie and the boys won again in Nairobi and then beat England, both in the Tests and one-days. I was horrified when Hansie made that sporting declaration at Centurion Park and gave away the match. And nothing thrilled me more than their triumph over India, in India. What was particularly reassuring was to see someone like Nicky Bojé finally make the grade. I am not often caught for words, or too emotional to be able to respond, but during the Test against England at Kingsmead, Hansie had invited me into the changing room after play on the third day.

I had not suspected anything, but they made a presentation to Bob Woolmer and me to thank us for the past five years. The watches were fancy and very expensive and it was emphasised that the presentation was from the players and had absolutely nothing to do with the UCB. It was their money and from their hearts. I was deeply moved, so much so that I could not even reply properly. I had to phone Hansie later to say thanks more coherently.

During that same Test I spent some time chatting to Ray McCauley at Terry Rosenberg's box and Ray told me that he was a little perturbed about the team spirit and the relationship between Wessels and Cronje. I had once spoken at Grey College in Bloemfontein and the headmaster had also talked about the animosity between two of his school's greatest sons.

Later I felt prompted to phone Kepler. I had heard that he still resented the way things had been done when he retired. He denied that and also suggested that he had no problems with Hansie except that as a critic he was entitled to write what he felt.

Then one day, as I was driving to Dundee for a preaching mission, my cell-phone rang. It was Shaun. "Hear the latest," he said, "Hansie is being accused of match fixing." He had to be joking! That was the Friday.

On Monday morning I got a message from my great friend Trevor Goddard to say that he had been in touch with Hansie's brother Frans, and wondered whether I could go and see Hansie. He was in a bad state. The team was in Durban for the first of the three limited overs Tests against Australia. I phoned and asked if he would like me to come.

He broke down in tears. I said I would get there right away. He was meeting with Goolam Rajah and Graham Ford when I arrived at his room, but they left immediately. Hansie seemed composed, but as they left the room he burst into tears. I did my best to console him for the best part of 90 minutes. I asked him why anyone should be gunning for him! He protested his innocence. In conclusion, we had a short time of prayer during which I asked very specifically that the truth should prevail.

The next morning early the phone woke us up. It was Ray McCauley, "Peter, he did it all. He has come clean." He had phoned the Rhema pastor in the early hours of that morning, confessed everything, as he had done to Ali Bacher.

I was shattered to the core. I would have given any odds against it. But what do we really know. To me, coming clean was the only option. Legal advice was to deny, shut up and let them prove it. But Hansie chose to tell all, except that he was going to try and protect some of the young cricketers who had inadvertently been swept into the mess.

The whole unsavoury episode dominated world headlines and its repercussions were widespread. What Hansie had done was not acceptable, especially because he was the South African captain. The damage he caused his family, his friends and cricket was massive. It was a big mistake, major error in judgment and no amount of rationalizing, justifying or excusing makes it any more acceptable or explainable.

But, accepting all that, I was nevertheless quite shocked and even amazed at the ferocity and intensity of the anti-Cronje onslaught. It was ruthless, to say the least, and the media treated him as if he was the worst criminal ever. Anyway, I knew that my role would need to be helping him get his life back on track. God is in the restoration business. He always has been, irrespective of the severity of the crime.

Shaun

But now South Africa needed a new captain. Shaun had been groomed, as well as you can prepare a vice-captain, but certainly not for a moment and for circumstances as dramatic as these. The World Champions under Steve Waugh were here and South Africa had been well and truly devastated by the Cronje revelations. My first response, interesting enough, was that in the short term the Proteas might well surprise everyone. They had absolutely nothing to lose as they took the field at Kingsmead and a mixture of anger, resentment or whatever you could throw into the cauldron, might just upset predictions.

Well, they won handsomely, as well as clinching the third match at the Wanderers to take the series in sensational manner. There appeared to be an aftershock at Newlands, with a rather large defeat in the middle match. The prophets of doom were ready to pounce. But thankfully they recovered magnificently in fairy-tale fashion.

Shaun was an overnight hero. Sure, he had been forced in the back door. Sure, there were not too many other candidates. But does that mean he is less of a leader? He was essentially a bowling all-rounder and tradition says bowlers should not be captains. I don't really know why. So many brilliant batsmen have been such terrible leaders, but they somehow are automatically given the job!

If they did a little homework about the number of bowling all-rounders who became top-rate international captains, maybe some pundits would change their views. One critic, an ex-player who I know was upset at my handling of him, came out strongly against Shaun, as I expected. The sins of the father were visited upon the son! It is a pity when personal agendas so obviously cloud the issue for top commentators.

Once Shaun had recovered from the initial shock of the circumstances that saw him thrust into leadership, the honour and responsibility of his new role became a reality. In politics they talk of the big difference between governing a country and being the opposition. It's a massive step from vice-captain to skipper. Shaun had been given the reins in Sharjah for a game against Pakistan, little knowing that it would become reality pretty soon. I can still see Hansie, caught by the TV camera, sitting pensively watching Shaun leading the side at Sharjah. I still wonder what he was thinking.

In my mind's eye, I saw a young determined red-headed boy. Who would ever have thought that I would be blessed by watching him grow up to be in the lead, making important decisions ...

Shaun gave his life to Jesus at the age of nine. He virtually "shanghaied" his mother as she tells, "I had been born again for about five weeks and during that time the three older children, Gavin, Anthea and Nicola had attended the youth meetings at the Church of the Good Shepherd. They had all responded to altar calls and gone forward to commit their lives to Jesus. There was much excitement in the family and we often would discuss Christian things. We spoke of the joy of having a relationship with the Lord and the assurance of eternity in heaven. Those were key issues. Shaun had been an interested listener at most of those discussions."

"One night Shaun came to me. 'I want to give my life to Jesus,' he insisted. I had never led anyone to Jesus. I thought it involved a very spiritual prayer and could only be done by experienced counselors. I was feeling very vulnerable and embarrassed. I answered by fobbing him off. 'Wait until we see Auntie May again and I will ask her to pray with you,' I said. May had led me to my commitment.

Shaun was absolutely devastated and burst into tears. 'What's the matter,' I responded. 'What if I die tonight and don't go to heaven!' he exclaimed.

"I felt so upset and challenged. I had to do it. I prayed. I don't even remember what I said or if it was any good doctrinally! But God saw my heart and undertook Shaun. He went to bed happy that night and so began his strong relationship with Jesus," concludes Inez.

Typical of his young and vibrant faith, he came to me one day a few years later. "Dad, I have got a problem," he confessed. His face reflected frustration and anguish. It had to do with sport, which was his life. He was playing soccer for Virginia United and thoroughly enjoying it, as well as excelling with regular goal harvests. He was a goal-hungry bustling young centre-forward.

But now there was a clash of interests. He was due to play in a vital soccer match, but at the same time was required for a schools athletics meeting. The soccer was an extra-mural activity and he knew full well our feelings – the school always came first! "But Dad, I really want to play soccer," he pleaded. "It's not even a debate," was my firm reply. He knew that was the rule, but he was nevertheless an unhappy little redhead as we set off to school the next morning.

Suddenly I had a thought. "Why don't you pray about it?" It was almost a throw away line! It was advice given almost flippantly, but young Shaun heeded those words. Later that day Inez received a phone call from the callbox at school. "Mom, God does answer prayer," he declared excitedly. "Remember my problem with the soccer and the athletics? Well the athletic meeting has been postponed."

When Inez phoned me at the office to tell me about Shaun's call and the news of the "divine intervention," I was touched to the very core. He believed, he prayed and the problem was solved. Certainly one of those precious family moments! Shaun's faith and conviction level has stayed high ever since.

What challenged Shaun to become a Christian? "It was basically through my parents who became Christians," he once said in an "In Profile" interview for the *Today* magazine. "The change in them really influenced me. I saw a greater love coming from them and realized that was what I wanted for my life. I became a Christian when I was very young, but my personal turning-point was when I went to boarding school for five weeks. I really struggled through that. I spent a lot of time reading the Bible and depending upon God for advice. Those five weeks were definitely a big turning-point for me and greatly increased my dependence on God."

Christian sportsmen somehow come under the magnifying glass. There is added pressure on them from the media and even from other Christians. But they are, after all, merely saved sinners, not professing to be more righteous than others. Christianity is about accepting your faults and weaknesses and allowing God to change you. Sport at the top isn't easy. It's about tough times. It's about blood, sweat and tears and hard work.

Shaun explains, "As a sportsman you are often faced with injury or a slump in form. It's natural to ask why. I believe it is all there for a reason, all part of life's learning curve. If you didn't have the low points you couldn't enjoy the high points. The low points build character. God isn't there to make things cushy for you, but He's there to build your character. Tough times definitely build character. For example, when I came back from Warwickshire I had to undergo an operation that put me out of action for quite a while. It was frustrating to sit on the sidelines. How much more did I appreciate being out there when finally the drought was over!"

"When we lose it's definitely not God's fault. You usually lose when the opposition plays better! God is not in the winning of matches. But he helps you to get winning and losing into the right perspective. The only prayer I pray on the cricket field is that God will help me perform to the best of my ability. That's where you have to leave it," adds Shaun.

Shaun's favourite biblical character is John the Baptist, though he would quickly point out that he is not like the longhaired locust-eating prophet.

Shaun's pet illustration is the one about the footprints in the sand. It's where a person looks back on his life and sees two sets of footprints. But strangely at the times when he was really struggling, there was only one set of prints in the sand. So he turns to God and says, "What happened there? Why did you leave me on my own in the hardest parts of my life?" God answers, "There was only one set of footprints because I was carrying you."

And Shaun's favourite Scripture? " ... *with God all things are possible.*" (Matt. 19:26).

I believe that it was Shaun's faith that sustained him in the days when he was in the tough position of taking over from Hansie. That day in his hotel room prior to confession, Hansie told me that he was thinking of retiring anyway and that, whether I believed it or not, Shaun was ready to take over. It was reassuring, but didn't make it any easier when D-day finally arrived.

Hansie had found it tough. You can't just walk in and take over. You have to earn the respect, admiration and loyalty of your team-mates and it does not come overnight. I spent years getting Hansie to be more assertive in his decisions and conviction. You couldn't just step in after a colossus like Kepler Wessels. The same applied to Shaun. You could not just walk in after Hansie, irrespective of how much of the way had been prepared.

Leadership is individual, not always definable but highly recognizable! Now there were new pressures in my life. I was managing to watch the South African games without getting too agitated or involved, but now that Shaun was captain it was a whole new ball game. I was now living every ball, watching every move and analyzing every decision.

That first Test against Sri Lanka, especially the first two days when we fielded to a massive home total, could have ended in a heart attack for me. Eventually

I had to switch off. It was a poor start. Even Dad thought so. But Shaun has always been a good listener and he accepts advice readily as long as the source is legitimate.

The Sri Lankan Test series was turned around after the humiliating opening defeat. And that is no mean achievement in the subcontinent. Under prepared pitches that have not been watered for days and spin like a top from day one, present a mammoth challenge to a young team with an even younger captain. It was off to Australia for the second half of the one-day series, indoors and under lights in Melbourne.

A huge beating in the first game had jaws on the ground in South Africa, but back came the Proteas with a tie – the second in a rather short time – and a victory in the final game, to share the trophy or, as our critics preferred, a 3-2 win in the over-all home and away series!

More good was to come with a one-day title in Singapore, again Pakistan were the losers. The ICC mini World Cup in Nairobi saw us beat up England before losing to India in the semi-finals, but the South African summer was to be magnificent one-way traffic for the Proteas.

The Test series against New Zealand went 2-0, after a whitewash one-day bout of contests 5-0. Sri Lanka arrived as the number one rated limited overs side in the world to be downed 5-1 and then 2-0 in the Test series, both victories, by an innings.

"Bring the Aussies," yelled the fans.

A milestone for Shaun

History and statistics combine to acknowledge and acclaim, and yet life, and cricket for that matter, goes far deeper than those books and statistics. It was the third Test against Sri Lanka at Centurion Park.

Just before tea on the first day I turned on the television. I was just in time to see new boy Justin Kemp run out and South Africa slump to 206/7. The players went in for tea and I switched channels to watch some tennis from the Australian open. I rejoined the cricket for the resumption after the break and watched the first ball faced by Shaun. What was to come, would take its place amongst the most treasured moments of nearly 40 years of Test cricket involvement.

Two hours later I had not moved from the chair. I didn't dare to! But I was sitting there, tears running down my cheeks and too overcome to answer the streams of telephone calls that had inundated us. I was sobbing like a baby. And I was not ashamed to admit it.

Shaun had just scored the fastest century in South African cricket history – sharing the mark at 95 balls with Jonty Rhodes. For 51 Test matches Shaun had battled for the three-figure mark. Most of his team-mates had got there. Even

Pat Symcox had got there! He was playfully teased while some critics suggested that it was now an obsession or had even become a mental block. He was too good a player not to have scored a Test century.

At Kingsmead against the Sri Lankans Shaun had passed the 200 mark in Test wickets and a special presentation on the field of play had both Graeme and me in attendance.

That evening we had a family supper at his flat in Durban North and there Graeme and I had playfully jested, "Now for the century." We had advised that he should stop fiddling around and get back to hitting the ball aggressively as he did at the start of his Test career. We suggested that he should attack the bowlers rather like Ian Botham, for he had the ability to emulate this Englishman's impact as a batsman.

Botham would have been proud of him! Boundary after boundary had the packed ground in rapture as he totally dominated a 150 run partnership with young Neil McKenzie.

In the eighties I received a phone call from friend Carol Rosenberg, "I hope he is going to make it." "He is," I replied firmly. "I know he is going to make it today." In the nineties, my eldest son Gavin phoned just to find out if I was awake and wasn't missing this great moment. "I have watched every ball," I assured him.

He reached the mark with a two into the mid-wicket area and thunderous applause greeted his return to the crease. His team-mates rose as he lifted his helmet and raised his bat and hands. I noted tinges of emotion but that was to come later. For the next ball the camera focused up close as the bowler ran in. His sight was blurred for sure. Tears were flowing, but he played the ball.

I knew that that was a special moment for him with the Lord! I asked him later that evening. He confirmed it. My daughter summarized it well, "He has had to wait a long time. But when God finally grants it, He sure does it royally."

Final flash-backs

That air crash that I had with Ted Dexter came to mind again. I had cried out to God, but after surviving the crash never took a moment out to thank Him or even acknowledge that He might have answered a prayer or might even have granted a miracle.

But after that crash I became a neurotic in airplanes, something that was only remedied many years later when I had given my life to Jesus.

The night my life had changed, the profound aspect of my visit down to the bottom end of the garden, was that I changed knowing about God to actually knowing Him. As eyes open and perspectives change, it is this spiritual relationship and dimension that sharply reshapes value systems and wonderfully enhances those precious moments of life.

Through those eyes, I look back and I marvel. I wonder what I did to deserve a life like that. If I were asked to live again, I would ask, "The same again, please Lord."

Nothing was wasted in life's education process. The school of hard knocks is still the best learning institution, but it's the final realization that is the greatest prize of all.

It's what the richest, wisest king ever, King Solomon, found when he declared as he looked back at his life, that it's all meaningless and a chasing after the wind if you have not found God.

The Western world is all about success. You have to be successful. Of course all sportsmen strive for glory and winning trophies, but we should never forget what Paul says in 1 Cor. 9:25: *"Everyone who competes in the games goes into strict training. They do it to get a crown that will not last; but we do it to get a crown that will last forever."*

Soli Deo Gloria

Think successful, act successful and you will be successful. It's mind over matter. That's what the positive thinking gurus tell us. There is merit in being positive. It's certainly better than being negative. But the real answer isn't as glib or as instant as these psychological salesmen try to indicate.

Goals and ambitions are vital, says the Bible. We need to run the race to win. But obsession is dangerous. Unfortunately, that is what is demanded these days.

Single-mindedness to the exclusion of all else is what sport and business are about. We are judged by the ability to succeed or top the rankings. But there is no happiness. The effort to succeed narrows the mind and hardens the heart and success may in fact become a soul-destroyer.

The winner is seldom happy for long. He is eaten by fear of failure, a drop in the ratings or the latest pretender to the crown. The drive to succeed at all costs is a good thing gone wrong, ambition perverted into obsession. Sports fans can also be caught up in this succeed-at-all-costs-syndrome.

A famous movie star once confessed that fame was "a puff of smoke, a mirage in the desert." He explained that you aim, achieve and there are some moments of pure exhilaration. Then the dust settles, the mirage clears and emptiness remains.

Beating England in England was my dream. Achieving it at Trent Bridge, was the ultimate, so I thought. We celebrated. But the next morning as we drove from Nottingham to London there was still a nagging emptiness. It was the same even amidst a heroes' welcome at Jan Smuts Airport.

In a nutshell, gifts and talents come from God. He deserves all the glory.

They are ours to use or abuse as we seek to win in life's race. But ironically the final victory is never the World Cup or any other trophy. Nor does it lie with fame and fortune.

As a youngster, Grantland Rice's famous quote often haunted me especially in times of tough combat. It underlined that more important than winning or losing, was how you played the game. It didn't suit my philosophy or ambition. Maybe, I didn't like the idea of a Great Scorer or more particularly, the suggestion that in life's race there are winners and losers! There was always that nagging doubt, that restlessness and a most definite lack of peace and fulfilment.

Somehow, it never did really matter what success had been achieved, it was as if someone always moved the goalposts! The pot of gold at the end of the rainbow is never quite there. But the frenetic chase for glory just never abates.

By 30 June 1999, my exit date as chairman of selectors, South Africa sat top of the world ratings in limited overs cricket. *Wisden's*, the cricketer's bible, records a victory percentage of 63, 69 which ousted second placed West Indies (62, 29) and Australia (56, 39). Level with Australia in win-loss statistics but clearly dominant over every other contender, there would be reason for satisfaction, even maybe a little self-congratulation!

It had been a rather miraculous return from isolation. An intriguing campaign, for sure!

Mighty King Solomon said that all man's anxious striving or toiling is meaningless – a chasing after the wind. I agree. True fulfilment can only be found in the Lord.

The greatest moment of all my 60 years was the decision to become a fast bowler in God's side. It is the ultimate winning team. I am striving to get a crown that will last forever, while giving all the glory for all my achievements to God.

ADDENDUM

Peter Pollock's Test Appearances

NEW ZEALAND IN SOUTH AFRICA 1961 – '62
1st Test at Durban
South Africa 292
(McGlew 127, McLean 63,Waite 25; Alabaster 4/59,Cameron 3/60, Motz 2/64)
New Zealand 245
(Harris 74, Barton 54, Bartlett 40, Walter 4/63, Pollock 3/61, Lawrence 3/63)
South Africa 149
(Waite 63, Bland 30; Cameron 3/32, Alabaster 3/36, Motz 3/51)
New Zealand 166
(McGregor 55; Pollock 6/38, Bromfield 3/37)
South Africa won by 30 runs

2nd Test at Johannesburg
South Africa 322
(Waite 101, Elgie 56, Barlow 47, P. Pollock 37; Cameron 5/83)
New Zealand 223
(Dowling 74, Reid 39; Lawrence 8/53)
South Africa 178/6 declared
(McGlew 47, Barlow 45, McLean 45; Motz 4/68)
New Zealand 165/4
(Reid 75 not out, Dowling 58; Pollock 2/18)
Match drawn

5th Test at Port Elizabeth

New Zealand 275

(Barton 109, Dick 46; Adcock 3/60, Pollock 3/63, Lawrence 2/71)

South Africa 190

(Lawrence 43, McGlew 28 not out; Motz 3/33, Bartlett 2/10)

New Zealand 228

(Dowling 78, Reid 69; Lawrence 4/85, Pollock 3/70)

South Africa 273

(Barlow 59, P.Pollock 54 not out; Reid 4/44)

New Zealand won by 40 runs

SOUTH AFRICA IN AUSTRALIA 1963 – '64

1st Test at Brisbane

Australia 435

(Booth 169, O'Neill 82, Lawry 43, Benaud 43; Pollock 6/95, Goddard 2/52)

South Africa 346

(Barlow 114, Waite 66, Goddard 52; Benaud 5/62)

Australia 114/1 declared

(Lawry 87 not out)

South Africa 13/1

Match drawn

2nd Test at Melbourne

South Africa 274

(Barlow 109, Bland 50, McKenzie 4/82)

Australia 447

(Lawry 157, Redpath 97, Shepherd 96; Partridge 4/108, Pollock 3/98)

South Africa 306

(Waite 77, A Pithey 76, Barlow 54; Hawke 3/53)

Australia 136/2

(Simpson 55 not out)

Australia won by eight wickets

3rd Test at Sydney

Australia 260

(Booth 75, Simpson 58, Benaud 43; Pollock 5/83, Partridge 4/88)

South Africa 302

(G.Pollock 122, Goddard 80, Bland 51; Benaud 3/55, McKenzie 3/70)

Australia 450/9 declared

(Benaud 90, Lawry 89, O'Neill 88, McKenzie 76; Partridge 5/123, Pollock 2/129)

South Africa 326/5

(Bland 85, Goddard 84, A. Pithey 53 not out,G.Pollock 42)
Match drawn

4th Test at Adelaide
Australia 345
(Burge 91, Simpson 78, Shepherd 70, Booth 58; Goddard 5/60, Pollock 3/96)
South Africa 595
(Barlow 201, G.Pollock 175, Lindsay 41; Hawke 6/139)
Australia 331
(Shepherd 78,O'Neill 66; Barlow 3/6, Halse 3/60, Pollock 2/73)
South Africa 2nd innings: 82/0
South Africa won by ten wickets

5th Test at Sydney
Australia 311
(Booth 102 not out, Burge 56; Partridge 7/91)
South Africa 411
(Bland 126, Goddard 93, Lindsay 65; Benaud 4/118, McKenzie 3/110)
Australia 270
(Booth 87, Veivers 39; Pollock 3/35, Seymour 3/80)
South Africa 76/0
Match drawn

SOUTH AFRICA IN NEW ZEALAND 1964
1st Test at Wellington
South Africa 302
(van der Merwe 44, Bland 40; Cameron 3/58, Blair 3/86)
New Zealand 253
(Chapple 59, Sparling 49; Pollock 6/47, Partridge 2/50)
South Africa 218/2 declared
(Barlow 92, Bland 46 not out)
New Zealand 138/6
(Gedye 52, Bland 2/16, Pollock 2/31)
Match drawn

2nd Test at Dunedin
New Zealand 149
(Sinclair 52; Partridge 4/51, Pollock 3/53)
South Africa 223
(Goddard 63, Barlow 49; Reid 6/60)
New Zealand 138

(D. Pithey 6/58)
South Africa 42/3
Match drawn

3rd Test at Auckland
South Africa 371
(Bland 83, Goddard 73, Barlow 61; Blair 4/85, Reid 3/77, Cameron 3/107)
New Zealand 263
(Sinclair 138, McGregor 62; Partridge 6/86, Pollock 2/60)
South Africa 200/5 declared
(Barlow 58, Waite 41; Blair 3/57)
New Zealand 191/8
(Gedye 55; Goddard 4/18, D. Pithey 3/40)
Match drawn

ENGLAND IN SOUTH AFRICA 1964 – '65
1st Test at Durban
England 485/5 declared
(Barrington 148 not out, Parks 108 not out, Barber 74, Boycott 73; Partridge 3/85)
South Africa 155
(Lindsay 38, McLean 30; Allen 5/41)
South Africa followed on 226
(Bland 68, A. Pithey 43, Titmus 5/66)
England won by an innings and 104 runs

2nd Test at Johannesburg
England 531
(Dexter 192, Barrington 121, Barber 97; Pollock 5/129)
South Africa 317
(A. Pithey 85, Barlow 71,Titmus 4/73)
South Africa followed on 336/6
(Bland 144 not out, G. Pollock 55; Allen 4/87)
Match drawn

3rd Test at Cape Town
South Africa 501/7 declared
(A. Pithey 154, Barlow 138, Bland 78)
England 442
(Smith 121, Dexter 61; Bromfield 5/88, Pollock 2/89)
South Africa 346
(Barlow 78, G. Pollock 73, Bland 64)

England 15/0
Match drawn

4th Test at Johannesburg
South Africa 390/6 declared
(Barlow 96, Pithey 95, Waite 64)
England 384
(Parfitt 122 not out, Barrington 93; McKinnon 4/128, Pollock 2/42)
South Africa 307/3 declared
(Goddard 112, G.Pollock 65 not out)
England 153/6
(Boycott 76 not out, McKinnon 3/44, Pollock 2/27)
Match drawn

5th Test at Port Elizabeth
South Africa 502
(G.Pollock 137, Barlow 69; Allen 3/80)
England 435
(Boycott 117, Barrington 72; Barlow 3/55)
South Africa 177/4 declared
(G.Pollock 77 not out, Barlow 47)
England 29/1
Match drawn

SOUTH AFRICA IN ENGLAND 1965
1st Test in London (Lord's)
South Africa 280
(G. Pollock 56, Lindsay 40, P. Pollock 34, Brown 3/44)
England 338
(Barrington 91, Titmus 59, Dumbrill 3/31)
South Africa 248
(Bland 70, Barlow 52; Brown 3/30)
England 145/7
(Cowdrey 37, Boycott 28; Dumbrill 4/30, Pollock 2/52)
Match drawn

2nd Test at Nottingham
South Africa 269
(G. Pollock 125, van der Merwe 38; Cartwright 6/94)
England 240
(Cowdrey 105, Barber 41; Pollock 5/53, Botten 2/60)

South Africa 289

(Barlow 76, Bacher 67, G. Pollock 59; Larter 5/68, Snow 3/83)

England 224

(Parfitt 86, Parks 44 not out; Pollock 5/34, McKinnon 3/50)

South Africa won by 94 runs

3rd Test at London (Oval)

South Africa 208

(Lance 69; Statham 5/40, Higgs 4/47)

England 202

(Cowdrey 58; Pollock 5/43, McKinnon 3/50)

South Africa 392

(Bland 127, Bacher 70, Lance 53; Higgs 4/96)

England 308/4

(Cowdrey 78 not out, Barrington 73, Russell 70; Pollock 2/93)

Match drawn

AUSTRALIA IN SOUTH AFRICA 1966 – '67

1st Test at Johannesburg

South Africa 199

(Lindsay 69, Lance 44, McKenzie 5/46)

Australia 325

(Lawry 98, Simpson 65; Barlow 3/39)

South Africa 620

(Lindsay 182, G. Pollock 90, van der Merwe 76, Lance 70; Cowper 2/66)

Australia 261

(Veviers 55; Goddard 6/53)

South Africa won by 233 runs

2nd Test at Cape Town

Australia 542

(Simpson 153, Stackpole 134; Barlow 5/85, Pollock 2/84)

South Africa 353

(G. Pollock 209, van der Merwe 50, P. Pollock 41, McKenzie 5/65)

South Africa (followed on) 367

(Lindsay 81, P. Pollock 75 not out, D. Pithey 55; Renneberg 3/63)

Australia 180/4

(Redpath 69 not out)

Australia won by six wickets

3rd Test at Durban

South Africa 300
(Lindsay 137, Bacher 47)
Australia 147
(Lawry 44; Barlow 3/18, Procter 3/27)
Australia (followed on) 334
(Simpson 94, Redpath 80; Procter 4/71)
South Africa 185/2
(G. Pollock 67 not out, Bacher 60 not out)
South Africa won by eight wickets

4th Test at Johannesburg

Australia 143
(Procter 4/32, Goddard 3/36)
South Africa 332/9 declared
(Lindsay 131, Goddard 47, P. Pollock 34 not out; Renneberg 5/97)
Australia 148/8
(Redpath 46; Goddard 3/23)
Match drawn

5th Test at Port Elizabeth

Australia 173
(Cowper 60; Goddard 3/13, Pollock 2/57)
South Africa 276
(G. Pollock 105, Goddard 74; McKenzie 5/65)
Australia 278
(Cowper 54; Trimborn 3/12, Goddard 3/63, Pollock 2/42)
South Africa 179/3
(Goddard 59, G. Pollock 33 not out)
South Africa won by seven wickets

AUSTRALIA IN SOUTH AFRICA 1970
1st Test at Cape Town

South Africa 382
(Barlow 127, Bacher 57; Mallett 5/126)
Australia 164
(Walters 73; Pollock 4/20, Procter 2/30)
South Africa 232
(G. Pollock 50, Procter 48; Connolly 5/47, Gleeson 4/70)
Australia 280
(Lawry 83, Procter 4/47)

South Africa won by 170 runs

2nd Test at Durban
South Africa 622/9 declared.
(G. Pollock 274, Richards 140, Lance 61; Gleeson 3/160)
Australia 157
(Sheahan 62; Barlow 3/24, Pollock 2/31, Procter 2/39)
Australia (followed on) 336
(Walters 74, Redpath 74, Stackpole 71, Procter 3/62)
South Africa won by an innings and 129 runs

3rd Test at Johannesburg
South Africa 279
(Irvine 79, Richards 65, G. Pollock 52; Gleeson 3/61)
Australia 202
(Walters 64, Pollock 5/39, Procter 3/48)
South Africa 408
(Barlow 110, G. Pollock 87, Irvine 73; Gleeson 5/125)
Australia 178
(Redpath 66; Procter 3/24, Goddard 3/27)
South Africa won by 307 runs

4th Test at Port Elizabeth
South Africa 311
(Richards 81, Barlow 73; Connolly 6/47)
Australia 212
(Sheahan 67; Procter 3/30, Pollock 3/46)
South Africa 470/8 declared
(Richards 126, Irvine 102, Bacher 73)
Australia 246
(Sheahan 46; Procter 6/73)
South Africa won by 323 runs

CAREER TEST RECORD
Played: 28 Tests; won 1O, drew 14, lost 4.

Half his Test career was against Australia – 14 Tests matches of which eight were won, four drawn and only two lost.

In 1972 Peter Pollock played in two Tests for the World XI against Australia, the one in Melbourne and the other in Adelaide. Both Tests were won, enabling Gary Sobers' World side to triumph 2-1 in that "unofficial" series.

Pollock's first-class career:
1958 – '59 to 1971 – '72:
MATCHES: 127.
BATTING: Runs: 3028. Average: 22.76.
Highest score: 79.
BOWLING: 485 wickets at 21.89.
Best bowling: 7/19.
Catches: 54.

Test career:
1961 – '62 to 1969 – '70:
MATCHES: 28.
BATTING: Runs: 607. Average: 21.67.
Highest score: 75 not out.
BOWLING: 116 wickets at 24.18.
Best bowling: 6/38.
Catches 9.

A COMPARISON WITH HIS CONTEMPORARIES
(All those who played either with him or against him during 1961 – 1970. The qualification is 25 Tests or 100 Test wickets)

	Matches	Wickets	Average	Strike-rate	5-wkts	wks-pr-Test
P. Pollock (SA)	28	116	24.18	55	9	4.14
J. Snow (Eng)	49	202	26.66	59	8	4.12
G. McKenzie (Aus)	60	246	29.78	71	16	4.10
W. Hall (WI)	48	192	26.38	54	9	4.00
N. Adcock (SA)	26	104	21.10	61	5	4.00
B. Statham (Eng)	70	252	24.84	63	9	3.60
A. Connolly (Aus)	29	102	29.22	76	4	3.51
R. Motz (NZ)	32	100	31.48	70	5	3.31

Pollock never played against Freddie Trueman or Wesley Hall in a Test. But Trueman's career largely preceded Pollock though it did sporadically extend into the first half of the 1960s.

The Englishman played 67 Tests, with 307 wickets at an average of 21.57. He had a strike rate of 49 balls per wicket, took five wickets seventeen times and had a career record of 4.58 wickets per Test.

Pollock reached his 50th Test wicket in his ninth Test – interesting when compared to Mike Procter whose short and illustrious career only involved seven Tests – with 42 wickets at that stage!